MAKE IT A PLACE OF SPRINGS

Promoting a Culture of Life in Traditional, Classical, and University-Model® Christian School Communities

MICHAEL CHRASTA

Printed in the United States of America

Library of Congress Cataloging-in-Publication Data is on file at the Library of Congress, Washington, DC.

ISBN-10: 1537377787
ISBN-13: 978-1537377780

DEDICATION

To Rose M. Chrasta (1926-2015),
a woman of strength, endurance, kindness, and faith,
who believed in us.

TABLE OF CONTENTS

ACKNOWLEDGEMENTS

I am grateful to all the parents, teachers, deans, and leaders in the Christian school communities where I have served in various capacities for the past decade. I want to thank a faithful women's prayer team at Lucas Christian Academy, and to Lucy, Bill, and Julie whose friendship sparked many of the ideas in this book. My sincerest thanks and appreciation to Brenda and her leadership team at Wylie Preparatory Academy, to Ellen Schuknecht at Veritas Academy, and to Barbara Freeman and John Turner at University Model® Schools International (formerly NAUMS). Blessings to all those saints at Meleah and in the many small groups who have prayed for me in the past years and to friends Jerry, Ellis, and Alan. I am most grateful for my wife Kathy who read the entire manuscript and was encouraging at several points along the way. Finally, I want to thank Paula McDougall (inspiration), Melani Bromfield (editing), Julianne Fowler (cover design) and Laurie Sibley (formatting, editing), for without their assistance at crucial times in the process, this book would not have been completed.

INTRODUCTION

The title of my book, *Make it a Place of Springs*, comes from Psalm 84:6, which describes the believer's journey and purpose in this world. Filled with the life of God and trusting in His grace, the believing pilgrim transforms every valley of trouble into refreshing, life-giving springs and pools. I have quoted a portion of verse 6 so as to turn the phrase into a command: we are to make it a place of springs, to be intentional about building a Colossians 2:2 culture wherever we go.

When a group of believers is "encouraged in heart" and "united in love," Jesus will be revealed in their midst. Consequently, they should then have access through Him to all the treasures of wisdom and knowledge (Colossians 2:2) for everything they do. Putting it another way, they will be in a position to receive Kingdom templates for every type of work in their Christian schools. They will discover, for example, Kingdom ways to conduct a sports program, set up a business office and manage finances, assemble curricula, minister to parents, oversee the spiritual formation of students, and lead the school itself. In each of these areas, God longs to reveal His ways to us just as He did when Solomon set out to build his kingdom. Because Solomon was filled with the wisdom of God, his kingdom became the head and not the tail among the nations of the world. Dignitaries came from faraway places to hear his wisdom and to see what he had done.

A Christian school community ought to be the head and not the tail when it comes to educational ideas, practices, and policies in any given locality. As believers, we have been given the Truth. We have God's power. God is actually, really present with us today through the

Holy Spirit. We can freely ask for His wisdom and we are tremendously disposed to receive His ongoing revelation. Educators should be coming to us from across the globe to observe and marvel at the wisdom God has given to us.

I hope that, in some way, *Make it a Place of Springs* will make Christian school communities the places where the greatest wisdom, the best practices, and the greatest success can be found anywhere in the sphere of education—public or private, elementary or junior high, high school or college. My focus is on culture-building, and the book's sections ("Foundations of Culture," "Prayer Culture," "Parent Culture," and so on) reflect that emphasis. As such, all stakeholders in our school communities will find value in it. Students, parents, and teachers have separate sections devoted to them. Leaders will benefit from the sections on foundations, prayer, protecting culture, and curriculum. The book should be read selectively by the different audiences who should choose the titles and topics most appropriate to their group. I see the book as a collection of templates for all who are culture-builders in their community. That would be everyone.

Finally, in order to circumvent any possible confusion with my subtitle, I want to say a word about the three kinds of communities I have listed. My use of the terms "traditional" and "classical" refers to curricula. Some Christian schools offer the traditional subjects (English, history, science) much like their public school counterparts do. Other Christian schools offer a curriculum based upon the Trivium (Grammar, Logic, Rhetoric) with an emphasis on orienting the soul toward the good, the true, and the beautiful. The newcomer to Christian education, the University-Model®, refers to a particular *model* of education, a model where students attend school two or three days a week (as in a university) and continue their studies on the other "satellite" days at home under the tutelage of a parent co-teacher. These University-Model® schools can offer either a traditional course of studies or a classical one.

Regardless of one's preferred form of schooling, any students, parents, or leaders interested in promoting a culture of life in their schools or in building cutting-edge Christian school communities will find useful ideas in the variety of short, informal essays that comprise this book.

Michael J. Chrasta
January 6, 2017

FOUNDATIONS OF CULTURE

INTRODUCING THE CHRISTIAN SCHOOL COMMUNITY

Those of us involved with Christian education understand that our work takes place in several contexts. We realize we are workers in a ministry—making disciples—but we do not see ourselves as a church. We are convinced that parents are vital to the educational process but sometimes we do not know how to bridge the distance between home and school, let alone get home and school operating from the same cultural, academic, and spiritual playbook. We know we are educating students—through traditional courses, chapels, and extra-curricular programs—but we also know we are doing much more: we are modeling a way of life as well. To understand the wide range of interconnected contexts in which Christian education actually takes place, our understanding of "schooling" must change, the belief that Christian education takes place in a "school."

We are not merely building schools. As Christians, we know that when "two or more" are gathered together, the presence and power of God is in our midst. And we know that with God in our midst, our focus on Him binds us to one another in whatever project we share. We become a fellowship, a community. In our case, we become a fellowship of believers doing school together.

Whether we are building traditional, classical, or University-Model® schools, whether students attend school five days a week or three, educational leaders and parents are a group of Christians who, whether they know it or not, are building Christian school *communities*.

Thinking of our schools this way has enormous implications for how we are to proceed—how we should think, what we should value, what we must practice and learn to protect.

Identifying ourselves as a community means that our *relationships* with one another are vital. Since we are in partnership, with parents and school working together to disciple and train our children, we must change our mindsets about "school" in several ways. First, we need to make efforts to really get to know one another by bringing parents, teachers, and school leaders together more often. Second, we must be vigilant about how we treat one another, especially when we face conflict or when trust breaks down. And third, we must get very good at dealing with conflict and reconciling those members whose relationships have been damaged.

All stakeholders have a duty to guard the five vital relationships in any Christian school community. These are the relationships between: 1) the board and the chief administrator; 2) the administrator and his or her leadership team; 3) the administration and the teachers/staff; 4) the parents and teachers; and, 5) the teachers and the students. We know we have an enemy who is constantly working to disrupt and divide these vital relationships. An unresolved conflict in any area can invite oppression, conflict, and dissension and ruin a community.

Members of any Christian school community will face significant obstacles to their unity. Obstacle #1 is the brokenness each of us has inherited from our own family dynamics and our past. Obstacle #2 is the sin nature we struggle with every day. Obstacle #3 is the toxic influence of contemporary culture, which constantly exerts pressure on us to compromise and conform to its standards. Obstacle #4 is the active and incessant work of the Accuser of our souls, who is looking for a platform in broken, sinful people to destroy the community.[1]

Large numbers of people with different kinds of baggage, different kinds of sins and degrees of cultural influence means conflicts with one another are bound to occur. Therefore, we must get very good at facing and resolving conflict if our partnership is to succeed. And this is an area where we all can use some improvement.

---

[1] Margie McComb, "Family Education: Guarding the Heart of our Schools." National Association of University-Model® Schools National Conference (Now University-Model® Schools International, UMSI), *Maintaining the Vision.* Southwestern Theological Seminary, Fort Worth, TX. 21 July, 2006. Breakout Session.

Because our relationships are so important, we do not run from conflict, we run to it. We know every conflict presents two possible outcomes: the people in dispute will achieve either depth or distance. Running away and finding excuses to not confront one another creates distance; addressing the conflict with the tools God has given to us, especially the call to think the best of one another and speak the truth in love (Ephesians 4:15), can create depth. This depth comes about, first of all, when leaders establish a common understanding of the problem; then when they help offenders work through repentance and forgiveness; and, finally, when the leaders press for reconciliation and the restoration of the relationship. Sadly, many conflicts never reach this final stage. Many of those in conflict never even reach the first stage of simply establishing a common understanding of the problem! That is because most people prefer to avoid the issue, hoping it will go away by itself, or else they will minimize the issue by rationalizing that it is not that important in the first place. We all know what happens when people think this way: the problem gets worse because the issue festers.

School communities that depend on relationships require a people who are virtuous. That is to say, we all need to grow in the fruit of the Spirit, the love, joy, peace, patience, kindness, goodness, faithfulness, gentleness, and self-control that the Holy Spirit freely gives to us (Galatians 5:22-23). Combined with the manifestations of "the wisdom that comes from heaven" in James 3:17—wisdom that is "first of all pure; then peace-loving, considerate, submissive, full of mercy and good fruit, impartial and sincere"—we have a good place to begin.

We can no longer think that a Christian school is simply a dressed-up public school run by nice people. We are finished with the dry sterility of secular educational thinking, the fragmented science-hallowed curriculums, the learning divorced from wisdom and virtue, the godless social engineering, and the belief that parents are to surrender their children every week to state-appointed "experts" who merely fill the mind with trivia, facts disconnected from their true contexts, leftist political philosophies, and outrageously false worldviews.

We are building instead unified Christian school communities centered on the presence and power of God in our midst and dependent on the virtues God provides. Understanding this will encourage us to more highly value our relationships with one another and resolve to grow in our ability to get along, keeping the "unity of the Spirit through the bond of peace" (Ephesians 4:3b). The result will be a powerful interactive partnership built on mutual respect and trust and success in our common mission.

WHAT KIND OF CHRISTIAN CULTURE?

Students and visitors to our campuses are very good at distinguishing between what we **say** about ourselves and what we actually **do**. They know that our actual behaviors and practices very often reveal more about what we really believe than what we profess to believe in our policies or statements of faith.

We should make sure our school culture not only reflects what we truly believe but also reveals exactly what we say it is. Any school that contains the word "Christian" in its name or statement of beliefs, but whose culture exhibits control and domination, rigidity and law, punishment and condemnation, is hypocritical and antithetical to the gospel. Although its leaders may claim to know God, it is clear that by their actions they deny Him (Titus 1:16). The fruit of such a culture will be disillusioned young people turning away from the faith in droves and an embarrassing witness for Christ in the community.

Our behaviors, attitudes, and practices should winsomely reflect the "good news" of our faith. Dull, boring Christianity or harsh, judgmental Christianity are contradictions in terms. We believed good news, we are good news, and good news is what we share with the world. Do our school environments reflect this? How do our academic programs or various student activities express good news? What about our athletics, our spiritual formation programs, or our approaches to discipline—do they derive from this good news? Are we building a "good news" culture? Do our teachers exhibit this good news?

Traditional, classical, or University-Model® schools will more likely express the good news of the gospel when their culture takes shape from a focused mission statement based on an agreed-upon set of core values. The following broad cultural proclamations reflect some of the common core values we might embrace. Singly or together, they can serve as standards for reorienting any school so that everything it does expresses the good news of our faith.

We Are a Festive People. This statement should define our general culture—our families and our community overall—how we wish to live and work together. We are a covenant people, the Church, doing school together and serving a benevolent and loving God by faith. We, therefore, want to live our lives in a state of joyful celebration. As a festive, joyful people we celebrate the goodness of life and the pleasures of knowing God through our rituals of worship, prayer, student activities, and community gatherings. That is, we heartily live out 1 Thessalonians 5:16-18: "Rejoice always, pray continually, give thanks in all circumstances; for this is God's will for you in Christ Jesus."

We Are a Positive, Optimistic, and Hopeful People. This statement also defines the general culture in our schools and homes, and expresses the goal of all student training—to produce overcomers and difference-makers. It is a statement about what we want our students to be. "Positive" means our students are clear, precise, categorical, and unwavering about what they know and believe. "Optimistic" means they look for the good and strive to see the best in every situation. "Hopeful" expresses their stalwart confidence and faith that, in spite of difficult circumstances, good will come in the end.

We Are a Bold, Courageous, and Inventive People with Great Initiative. This statement defines what we desire students to be from the standpoint of will and action. Because we are made in the image of God (natural artists who are inventive; rulers who rule) and because the Truth is our sole possession as the Church, we are bold and courageous in calling heaven down into our world, bringing God's answers and divine templates for all we are to do. In this way, we bring new ideas, new pathways, and redemptive new solutions to a world that has lost its way. Complementing the attitudinal virtues of optimism and hope, these are the strong virtues of the human will that dynamically inform the heart and soul of every difference-maker and overcomer.

We "Make It a Place of Springs." From Psalm 84, this statement captures our essential purpose or mission, what we want our students to do with the virtues and truth they possess, which is to bring life to the dark and despairing valleys of trouble in our world: "As they [pilgrims] pass through the valley of Baka [trouble] they make it a place of springs; the autumn rains also cover it with pools. They go from strength to strength, till each appears before God in Zion" (Psalm 84:6-7). As the people of God on pilgrimage, we (and our students) carry the indestructible life of the resurrected Christ wherever we go. This means we are preparing our students to go into the most difficult of places, from the slums of the inner city to the boardrooms of corporate America, to transform the dead wastelands of our world into life-giving, hope-filled springs of living water.

Have Fun, Do Your Best, and Be a Blessing. A standard against monotonous and boring drudgery, hyper-perfectionism and the soul-wasting disease of introspection, this statement expresses the good news of our academic programs. Learning, by nature, is exciting, and the revelation of truth is liberating. "For wisdom will enter your heart, and knowledge will be pleasant to your soul" (Proverbs 2:10). On the whole, learning should be fun and pleasurable, sometimes even thrilling. As for effort, the best one can do under the circumstances is all one can expect; perfectionism is unnatural because only one man is perfect and that is Jesus. Finally, being a blessing is a Kingdom mindset that produces joy in the believer while also reminding him that intellectual and spiritual gifts are intended for the benefit of others.

Make Your Faith Your Own. This is the one consistent message we want our students to hear, especially at the secondary level, because it expresses the good news of our spiritual formation programs. God is not a theory, concept, or doctrine; He is alive and personal, a God whom we can know through repeated encounters with Him and infillings of His Spirit. Always pointing to Christ, we want to make God famous and attractive to our students, stressing a relationship with Him over religious practices and encouraging them to love and encounter Him for themselves.

You Are Not in Trouble; You Are in Training. This is a statement that governs our approach to discipline. Discipline philosophy and practices reflect what we really believe more than anything else. Some schools present God as harsh, condemning, and unforgiving and students as bad, sinful, and always about to fail. This kind of program usually values punishment more than correction. Other schools run discipline programs based on the reality that God is gracious, loving, and merciful along with the idea that students are works in progress. These programs value correction more than punishment. "You are not in trouble; you are in training" captures the good news of who we are to God. We are on pilgrimage; we are all in training. These facts should create a positive atmosphere of encouragement, perseverance, and hope when we are called to correct students who have made poor choices.

WHO CARRIES THE PASTORAL MANTLE FOR YOUR SCHOOL COMMUNITY?

If we are building Christian school communities, implying that our relationships with one another are vital, then logically, someone in the community needs to manage this interface. Someone needs to be responsible for keeping this community together. Someone needs to help referee conflict. Someone needs to keep parents "confident, competent, encouraged and involved"[2] to bring them more closely into the natural partnership they have with the school. In other words, someone needs to carry the pastoral mantle for the most important stakeholders in the community—the parents.

In the University-Model® community, that person is the Dean of Family Ministry. Traditional and classical Christian school leaders would do well to take a page from their playbook. In the University-Model®, the community is built around a leadership team of at least four people—the Head of School, the Dean of Academics, the Dean of Student Life, and the Dean of Family Ministry. Together they function as the core leadership team of the school.[3]

---

[2] John William Turner, Jr., Character Driven College Preparation: Parents and Teachers in Partnership Through University-Model® Schooling (Fort Worth: Magnolia Media Group and GPA Ministries Inc., 2001), 32.

[3] This leadership structure varies, of course, with the size, type, grade-level, and stage of the school. In younger schools or those having only the elementary grades, these positions may be combined, while in more well-developed schools the positions

Because it runs a university-type schedule (three days at school, two at home under the supervision of the parent co-teacher), family ministry in the University-Model® school has both home and school dimensions. Ministry to the home involves strengthening relationships with parents, training them, and helping them to move through conflicts. Family Ministry in the school consists of school-wide culture-building based on the community's core values, student spiritual development (oversight for chapels, retreats, Bible studies, or community outreaches), and sometimes the administration of student discipline.[4] These home and school duties make it clear that the Dean of Family Ministry is a cultural architect who carries the pastoral mantle for the school.

While the dean's school functions can vary according to the gift mix of the leadership team and the specific needs of the school at different stages of its development, this leader's ministry to the home is fairly clear. Parents' biblically mandated roles, to be responsible for the academic, moral, and spiritual education of their children according to Deuteronomy 6:6-7, call for a tight partnership between home and school. Gone are the days when parents cede all their authority to the public or Christian school by dropping their children off at the doors of the school and then remaining largely uninvolved the rest of the week. Christian education requires strong, protected relationships of mutual respect and trust between home and school. It requires that parents be significantly more involved with the school than what most parents have known. It is not easy; American individualism and our hyper-narcissistic culture do not promote the virtues needed for this kind of relationship to work. Parents' natural tendencies are to surrender their authority to the school and stay away. Unfortunately, they have stayed away far too long, and so are lacking the wisdom and skills they need to be optimally successful in their natural roles.

The Dean of Family Ministry has the very difficult job of coaxing parents back into the process, bringing home and school closer together, and then supplying the education and training parents need

---

might be separate. Classical Christian schools might have a different leadership core altogether, and so on.

[4] Generally, the leader overseeing student discipline should not be the same person who manages the spiritual and character development programs. The disciplinarian often has a difficult time earning the trust of students, while trust is the very basis for spiritual formation. Two separate leaders are best.

to be successful. He (or she) does this in three ways. He gives **pastoral direction,** provides for **co-teacher training**, and develops **parenting skills**. Pastoral direction could include private meetings to help parents and teachers resolve conflict, occasional special seminars to exhort them to protect their marriages, and school-wide parent nights encouraging them to continue growing in the Lord. Co-teacher guidance might involve scheduling annual fall workshops that train parents to work with the school's elementary reading and writing programs or a certain curriculum, show them how to mentor their children in specific subject areas like worldview or writing the research paper, and help them to exhort their children to love the Lord and grow in the virtues. Finally, parenting skills training might include putting on monthly coffee shop gatherings or scheduling special parent training evenings to show parents how to talk to their children about sexual issues, teach them how to work with the learning style of their child, or show them how to honor and affirm their child's unique God-given design.

The Dean of Family Ministry flings open the doors of the school and invites the parents in as true partners in the education of their children. He ensures that the parents are edified, empowered, and encouraged to continue with the difficult, self-sacrificing work of training up their children in the ways they should go, providing them with the academic, moral, and spiritual training their children need to become difference-makers and overcomers in the difficult days ahead.

THE CORNERSTONE OF TRUTH[5]

We live in a world of opposites, paradoxes, mysteries, and "sides." Good and evil, reality or illusion, the known and the unknown, the right side or the wrong side. Trying to navigate this world, we make hundreds of choices every day and millions of choices in a lifetime. These choices do indeed have consequences. In this life, our choices will lead to freedom or bondage, happiness or misery; in the next life, they will lead to heaven or hell. What we choose to believe and do here on earth right now really matters because our choices have eternal consequences.

Choices informed by truth generally lead to happiness. Unfortunately, on this earth, truth is on trial (John 18:37-38).[6] It is difficult to discern and challenging to follow. The kingdom of darkness has obscured it. Sin has suppressed it. Evil deeds have replaced the truth with deception and confusion. Truth is on trial because the Accuser—a murderer, a liar, and the father of lies (John 8:44)—has "blinded the minds of unbelievers, so that they cannot see the light of the gospel that displays the glory of Christ" (2 Corinthians 4:4b). That is why the enemy's kingdom is called the kingdom of darkness.

---

[5] The cornerstone of Truth and the three cornerstones that follow in this section (Virtue, Family, and Purpose) are adaptations of the core values originally defined by Wylie Preparatory Academy in Wylie, Texas.

[6] That there are "sides," that truth is on trial, and that Jesus came to testify to the truth are insights from Del Tackett's "Veritology: What is Truth?" Lesson 1 of Focus on the Family's *Truth Project*, 2006. The *Truth Project* is a good introductory worldview video series for parents, teachers, and students in Christian schools.

Jesus, the light of the world, came to the earth to make the truth plain and clear. His purpose was to testify to the truth; He said that everyone on the side of truth listens to Him (John 18:37). He broke into this present evil age to proclaim the truth, pointing the way to freedom and eternal life. That is why "Jesus answered, 'I am the way and the truth and the life. No one comes to the Father except through me'" (John 14:6).

Truth characterizes all three persons of the Godhead. Jesus described the Father as the only true God (John 17:3), who sanctifies us by the truth of His word (John 17:17). One of the several names for the Holy Spirit is the Spirit of Truth (John 14:17), who goes out from the Father (John 15:26), and who convicts the world of sin (14:26; 15:26; 16:8). As our Advocate, the Spirit supplies the truth that we need to make the choices that will shape the rest of our lives.

As believers, we live in various stages of truth and deception. We sometimes forget we are all in the *process* of renewing our minds. Much of our thinking—assumptions about ourselves, our culture, even Christian education itself—contains error that blocks us from freedom and revelation. And our students, who find it nearly impossible to resist the attractions of this culture of death and for all practical purposes are being parented electronically, are most in need of formation in the truth.

We counter destructive cultural influences, deceit, lies, and false presuppositions by remembering three direct and very practical applications of truth. First, truth is a guide. As Psalm 1 reminds us, we are not to walk in step with the wicked. We don't take our view of the world from those who frame it falsely. Delighting in God's law and meditating on it day and night will set us in the right direction and bring prosperity (Psalm 1:1-3). Joshua heard the same counsel: if he meditated on the Law and obeyed it, he would be prosperous and successful (Joshua 1:8). Truth as a guide will be essential to the generation of the Lord's return. In the last days, the arrival of the "lawless one" will be accompanied by counterfeit miracles and great deceptions (2 Thessalonians 2:9). Many will perish "because they refused to love the truth and so be saved" (2:10b). Merely knowing the truth or giving mental assent to it will not be enough; we must teach our students to **love** the truth if we want to protect them from the deception and deceit that will flourish in the last days.[7]

Truth is a sanctifier. Jesus said, "Sanctify them by the truth; your word is truth" (John 17:17). When we embrace Jesus' teaching, His word will purify us and make us holy: "Now that you have purified yourselves by obeying the truth so that you have sincere love for each other, love one another deeply, from the heart" (1 Peter 1:22). That is because God's word acts like an umpire: "For the word of God is living and active. Sharper than any double-edged sword, it penetrates even to dividing soul and spirit, joints and marrow; it judges the thoughts and attitudes of the heart" (Hebrews 4:12). We must remind our students that God's word has a cleansing, purifying power; it will penetrate their hearts, disentangle those confusing thoughts and emotions, and bring real hope!

Truth is a liberator. Jesus connected truth to His teaching and His teaching to freedom, worship, and love. "Jesus said, 'If you hold to my teaching, you are really my disciples. Then you will know the truth, and the truth will set you free'" (John 8:31b-32). Along with Jesus' teaching, the Spirit of Truth will teach us all things, even the truth of what is yet to come (John 16:13-15). Truth is vital to the kind of worship the Father seeks—the true worshipers will worship in the Spirit and in truth (John 4:23)—and it is indispensable to maturity in love. When anyone obeys God's word, love for God is truly made complete in him (1 John 2:5), and when we love, we are to remember it is with actions and in truth (3:18).

Jesus is truth. The Spirit is truth. The Father is truth. God's word is truth. God is a guide, a sanctifier, and a liberator. Nothing is more important to a human life. Our students will spiritually die without it. The bedrock of our faith and the foundation for our hope, truth should therefore be the first cornerstone of every Christian school.

---

[7] Four times in the Olivet Discourse, (Matthew 24:4, 5, 11, 24), Jesus warns against being deceived.

WHAT IS THE MESSAGE?

It is amazing how easy it is to lose sight of the core message of the Bible. It is found in the words of Jesus. "'The time has come,' he said. 'The Kingdom of God has come near. Repent and believe the good news!'" (Mark 1:15).

When Jesus said the time had come, He was talking about the period of time since the Fall of Adam and Eve to that moment when He was actually announcing the Kingdom for the first time. Ever since the Fall, when God prophetically told the serpent, "he will crush your head, and you will strike his heel" (Genesis 3:15b), the world had been awaiting the Redeemer, the one who would defeat the devil, overthrow his kingdom, and rescue mankind. That person was now in the flesh, in Jesus. After many thousands of years, the time had finally come. The very Kingdom of Heaven itself was at hand!

Jesus was announcing the Kingdom of God, which is the rule and reign of God, the government of God Himself. When Adam surrendered his position to the devil, the whole world came under the control of the evil one, the one Jesus later called the prince of this world (John 16:11). A prince is one with authority to rule over a jurisdiction, a realm, or territory. And the devil's realm was the earth and the heavenly places. We see this when the devil tempted Jesus in the wilderness: "The devil led him to a high place and showed him in an instant all the kingdoms of the world. And he said to him, 'I will give you all their authority and splendor; *it has been given to me,* and I can give it to anyone I want to'" (Luke 4:5-6, emphasis added). Who gave the Prince of Darkness this authority? Adam did when he sinned and gave up his position as a co-ruler with God. The evil one has controlled all the kingdoms of the earth ever since.

So when Jesus came saying, "The Kingdom of God has come near," this was incredibly good news because He was proclaiming that a new government, the Kingdom of light, had finally come to replace the kingdom of darkness that had enslaved the whole world. **God's Kingdom** was near, it was "at hand," meaning it was accessible to mankind and the prostitutes; the demonized and the tax collectors were falling all over each other to get into it. A new King had come to power to engage in a war on behalf of His people, to overthrow this ruler of the kingdom of the air (Ephesians 2:2), who ruled this present evil age (Galatians 1:4), and to bring in a new order, a new life, and an entirely new age for all who believed in Him. It was the most stupendous proclamation in all of human history!

Jesus followed His announcement of the Kingdom with the words: "Repent and believe the good news!" To understand what He meant, parents, Bible teachers, and pastors need to rescue this word "repent" from how it has evolved over the hundreds of years since the time of Jesus.

In our day, the word "repent" has been defined narrowly to mean "confess your sins." And while repentance definitely includes this concept, it is actually a far larger, far richer concept. Repent, which in Greek is "metanoia," literally means change ("meta") your mind ("noia," "nous"). It means change the way you think in your heart about things which will then change the way you behave. It means get a new mindset. It means change your worldview, the framework from which you have been seeing and doing everything until now.[8]

It was as if Jesus were saying: "The world has been under the control of the devil. As a result, every aspect of your thinking and your behavior has conformed to that reality. But now a new King is here. I have come to bring in my government, my laws, and my way of life. Therefore, repent and believe in me. Change your worldview, your way of thinking about everything, including your behavior, and conform your life to this new reality from now on!"

This great proclamation, this fabulous good news of the Kingdom, a Kingdom that is both here and not yet here, should always be at the forefront of our teaching. It is the main message. It is the

---

[8] The paragraph is a summary of a teaching by Ken Fish from his series *The Kingdom of God in Presence and Power*, 2012. See his website, //http:kingdomfireministries.org/.

central organizing principle of the Bible. Out of it flows everything else we want our students to master—Christian living, Kingdom ethics, and powerful servant ministry. It is the one message our students must consistently hear in chapel services, Bible classes, and classrooms from elementary school to high school.

HOW DO WE WANT OUR CHILDREN TO VIEW THE BIBLE?

What attitudes or beliefs about the Bible are we forming in our students or our children? We must be vigilant about how we present the Bible to young people. We can never forget that the Word of God is **"good news"**! With that in view, we might also strive to keep in mind that the Bible is:

More than rules and principles. The Bible contains the Ten Commandments and numerous principles for holy living. However, if rules and principles are taught apart from the grace of God, apart from the Holy Spirit's work in our hearts, and without stressing that God's requirements are impossible for us to fulfill on our own, then young people will learn to view the Bible itself incorrectly. They may see it negatively because the rules are impossible to keep, or they may see it falsely and believe that merely by working harder they will be able to do what it says. Neither is acceptable.

Two Testaments, One Story. From the core prophecy of Genesis 3:15b ("he will crush your head, and you will strike his heel"), through the formation of Israel, the covenants, the monarchy, and the prophets; from the good news of the Gospels to the stunning book of Revelation where Jesus returns as conquering King, the Bible keeps its focus steadily on one thing: Jesus. He is the hero of the story. He is the "good news." Every book of the Bible, whether in the Old Testament or New, points steadily to the work and person of Jesus Christ. When we teach the Bible, we must be careful to maintain this focus.

Illuminated by the Spirit. Jesus reminded us that when the Holy Spirit, the Spirit of Truth, comes he "will teach you all things and will remind you of everything I have said to you" (John 14:26b). He will also guide you into all the truth (16:13). And John writes in 1 John 2:27a: "As for you, the anointing you received from him remains in you, and you do not need anyone to teach you." Of course, John was not saying we have no need of teachers; he was countering the counsel of Gnostic teachers who were saying that apostolic teaching was limited and inadequate. In any case, *without the illuminating power of the Holy Spirit, the Bible will not come to life!*

Moreover, without understanding the role of the Holy Spirit and His ministry to form Christ in us by grace, the believer can only conclude that fulfilling the commandments of the Bible depends on human effort alone. This is the unintended message preached in many of our churches, Sunday schools, and Christian schools today. Teachings that exhort believers to work harder, do more, read more, give more, and serve more usually come from this mindset. Such teachings misunderstand the Holy Spirit, the finished work of Christ, and the Bible itself, which quickly ceases to be the good news it actually is.

We want our children to love God and to love His Word. We want them to trust it, read it, and be excited by it. We want them to bury it in their hearts. Let's not lose sight of the fact that the Bible is always fundamentally and forever…**good news!**

EXPERIENCING TO KNOW

Students often abandon their faith after high school because they have accepted a flawed concept of God. The God they have been taught is too abstract. God is more of a concept than a real Person. When Bible teachers have to resort to bribes of candy and secular television themes to drum up interest in God or His word, they are on the wrong track. The gospel that delivered people from demons and raised people from the dead does not need Bible Bucks and puppet shows to make it more appealing. People did not rip roofs off houses in Jesus' day because He championed a new form of entertainment.

Unless students encounter God, unless they personally experience His presence and power, His active intervention in the world and His voice through the Holy Spirit, they will be handicapped in their faith. Their God will be an abstract concept, a theory. One actual kiss is worth a thousand lectures about kissing. Our universe is open, not closed, to God's intervention, and in this universe, God speaks to His people. We must encounter and experience this God to really know Him.

Let's say a student grows up on a farm. From the earliest age, she is surrounded by all kinds of farm animals—chickens, dogs, cats, horses, cattle. She pets the dogs and brushes the horses; she feeds the chickens, pigs, cats, dogs, horses, and cattle every day. The smell of farm animals is in her bones; she has experienced them in all kinds of situations. She has collected eggs from the hen house, cleaned up horse manure, bathed the dogs, and witnessed all kinds of animals giving birth to their young year after year.

This goes on for eighteen years.

At last, this young lady goes to college. On the first day of class her philosophy professor, with a sneer and an arrogance that knows no bounds and with what only appears to be impressive reasoning, says emphatically to all present: "Students, the first thing you should know is this: there is no such thing as farm animals. Belief in farm animals is make-believe. Serious intellectuals like ourselves know that farm animals simply do not exist."

To those who have never experienced farm animals for themselves, who have never touched, smelled, fed, named, bathed, or played with farm animals, the professor's arguments would be persuasive. After all, he is the expert. His students would likely abandon their "faith" in farm animals rather quickly. But to the young lady who has spent all her life on a farm and has encountered farm animals in all kinds of ways, his statements would be utter nonsense. Without a moment's hesitation, she would conclude: "My professor is insane," and indeed, she would be correct. Anyone who cannot see the obvious has lost the good of reason (Romans 1) and veers toward a kind of insanity.

Have our students encountered Christians who have been filled—not merely sealed—but filled with the Holy Spirit as Stephen was in Acts? Have they been taught to encounter God in lavish worship? Have they ever witnessed miracles or the spiritual gifts in action? Have they seen the healing of a disease or affliction, the deliverance of someone from pornography, the dramatic conversion of someone who has been suicidal, or the sudden and unexplainable gift of money when a father had just lost his job? Have they actually **encountered** this amazing and active God of ours?

Perhaps we need fewer simplistic Bible stories and more proclamations of the Kingdom. The Bible proclaims the Kingdom, but the Kingdom is the reality, the thing that is really here. It came with Jesus and has been extended through His disciples through the power of the Holy Spirit poured out at Pentecost, which is the day the Church was created. That should tell us something: the Church was born in, through, and by the Holy Spirit. And it is through the Spirit that the proclamation of the Kingdom by the Church continues: "But you will receive power when the Holy Spirit comes on you; and you will be my witnesses" (Acts 1:8a). Power for what? Power to do exactly what Jesus did.

We are called to carry on the ministry of Jesus. Our students are called to carry on this same ministry. When Christian school leaders and parents are able to bear witness to this reality, our students will experience God for themselves, Jesus will become more real in their lives, and their faith will be stronger to withstand the onslaughts coming from the increasingly hostile secular colleges and universities.

THE CORNERSTONE OF VIRTUE

"Moral excellence or goodness." "Virginity, chastity." "Moral strength or courage," "manliness."[9]

Common to these definitions of "virtue" is a concept unknown in our day, the idea that virtue is a kind of **power**. The virtuous are those who have the moral power to govern themselves and to dramatically alter the social, cultural, political, and spiritual landscapes of their world.

When students embrace truth, virtue is not far behind. Since Jesus is the truth, when we abide in Him, His goodness becomes ours. Virtue, then, is the one infallible sign that a person is vitally connected to the Lord. It proves that truth is truly directing a person's life. In other words, truth is catalytic for a moral chain reaction: truth produces virtue, virtue is power, and power changes people, cities, and nations.

Much has been said in Christian schools about promoting "character." Teachers encourage students to pursue "character traits" through self-effort and practice until the students acquire them. We might stress instead the cornerstone of **virtue**, the more positive side of character, something all students can develop with God's grace. It is the transforming power of the Holy Spirit that cultivates virtue— God's very own nature—into the hearts of our students until they own

---

[9] "Virtue". *Dictionary.com Unabridged.* Random House, Inc. 05 Dec. 2015. Dictionary.com http://dictionary.reference.com/browse/virtue; "Virtue." *Merriam-Webster.com.* Merriam-Webster, n.d. Web. 5 Dec. 2015.

them for themselves. This is not to say one does not have to "work" at developing virtues, since we all have to "work out" what God has "put in" (Philippians 2:12).

Becoming virtuous is becoming "Christ-like." We see this in the only New Testament passage containing the word "virtue," Colossians 3:12-14: "Therefore, as God's chosen people, holy and dearly loved, clothe yourselves with compassion, kindness, humility, gentleness and patience. Bear with each other and forgive one another if any of you has a grievance against someone. Forgive as the Lord forgave you. And over all these **virtues** put on love, which binds them all together in perfect unity" (emphasis added).

Paul's context is important. Before this passage, Paul encouraged the Colossians to get rid of all the sinful habits produced by their old selves. They have taken off their old selves "with its practices" and have "put on" their new selves, meaning they are no longer the people they used to be. God has worked a miracle of transformation in them and in us. Maturity in Christ is about being a new self, growing in the virtues of Christ. We are to put on compassion, kindness, humility, gentleness, and patience like we put on a set of clothes, "wearing" them wherever we go.

We know the virtues have power because practicing them is so hard to do, especially with the last three virtues Paul mentions: forbearance, forgiveness, and love. Anyone who has ever had to bear with another knows this. To bear with someone who aggravates us requires tremendous power, power that includes patience, endurance, and self-restraint. Forgiveness, too, requires enormous internal power because it is so contrary to the innate demand for justice and the primitive desire for revenge when we have been wronged. Finally, love, which is as strong as death, is the most powerful force in the universe, burning like blazing fire (Song of Songs 8:6). Like the atomic force that binds a nucleus of an atom, it is the one power that "binds" all the other virtues together in perfect unity (Colossians 3:14). Love overlooks a wrong, patiently endures, and steadfastly remains kind and forbearing when the old self rages for payback. It is that awesome power which fuels compassionate sacrificial service to those less fortunate, binding up their wounds and paying for their recovery (Luke 10:33-35).

In a Christian school community, growing in the virtues does not happen by accident or from the mere passage of time. Everyone must be "virtue-conscious"—that is, focused on the Lord as the Source of all virtue—and committed to creating a culture of virtue throughout the school community. Parents must encourage a love of the virtues in their children through imaginative moral stories contained in the Bible, myths, fables, and fairy tales and, as students get older, through the biographies of great men and women. Coaches, teachers, and school leaders, besides being virtuous themselves, must also love the virtues and incorporate them into their coaching, teaching, and disciplining of students at school. This is how home and school can work together to make virtue the second great cornerstone of a powerful Christian school community.

A VIRTUE FOR OUR TIMES

A disturbing trend in our day is the formation of a kind of Christian student whose academic credentials are excellent but whose strength of soul is weak. It is a student who is intelligent and book smart, but not savvy or resourceful; grade-conscious and performance-oriented, but not reflective, insightful, or wise; obedient and studious to a fault, but timid, fearful, quiet, and unimaginative. What we have here are Christian Boo Radleys scared of their own shadows.[10]

Without a radical conversion of soul, a revised theology, or a decisive encounter with the Lord, they will never lead, never make an initiative of any significance, and never make an impact on their world, although they may test very well, hold the highest GPAs, and win many academic scholarships. We must see them as morally handicapped and ill-equipped to confront the cultural and philosophical strongholds that control the systems of this world (Proverbs 21:22).

That is why Christian education must prioritize the formation and development of virtue, why it must place moral education on par with academic instruction—not in name or rhetoric but once and for all. Three virtues are especially crucial for our times: the moral **courage** to champion the truth, the power of **initiative** to bring about change, and a Spirit-infused **optimism** rooted in a robust faith, which brings light and hope to the darkest of situations. The most important of these virtues, and the key to the other two, is moral courage.

Our students will influence no one if they remain timid, whiney,

---

[10] A sickly, home-bound character in *To Kill a Mockingbird* by Harper Lee.

thin-skinned, easily offended, and introverted. But we will continue to produce such students as long as we continue to believe that introversion is the way some students are permanently "wired" or that being easily offended is a mark of sensitivity or even a positive virtue. Regardless of their grades or the depth of their Biblical training, such students will champion nothing in any public square if they are pathologically afraid to speak in front of a group or if the first criticism from an opponent is so painful it sends them into severe discouragement and withdrawal. Therefore, the formation and development of students with great moral courage should be one of the most important objectives of our mission.

Courage is bred early, in the home through discerning and purposeful parents who are intentional in forming this virtue in their children—first, through the oral presentation of great stories that seed the children's imaginations with unforgettable images of courageous people, and second, through practice in activities that gradually present challenges. Courage comes, not surprisingly, from "encouragement," a "putting in" of courage through affirmation gained from overcoming obstacles and surmounting difficult challenges. It is not the garden-variety shallow praise for anything, even for merely showing up for practice. Ultimately, that kind of praise will prove discouraging, and students accustomed to it will surely collapse at the first serious obstacle or challenge.

Because they are in partnership with the home, school leaders should honor and reinforce the virtue of courage in our schools. At the elementary level, teachers should continue to structure students' moral imaginations through classic moral stories drawn from parables, myths, and Biblical literature. At the junior-high and secondary levels, this training must continue; more opportunities than one might think are available for practicing this virtue. Practice occurs in the classroom when students face a challenging subject, like chemistry or physics, or a difficult project, research paper, or final exam. This is precisely why grade inflation, so endemic in our schools and in our culture, is so destructive; it removes difficult challenges and destroys the motivation to try harder and make work even better than what students previously thought possible.

In so many other ways students can practice courage in a school environment. It takes courage to say no to temptation. It takes courage to redirect a conversation that veers toward gossip, slander, and criticism. It takes a lot of courage to disagree with a friend, fast from social media, admit wrongs, or take responsibility for one's actions. It takes courage to overcome several bad grades in a row. It takes courage to do the right thing when everyone else is doing something different or to champion the truth in a hostile environment, knowing that criticism and abuse will surely come. It takes courage to risk offending someone who does not realize she is deceived. It takes courage to take a stand for the Lord or tell a Muslim about God. In athletics, students need courage when they face a larger, faster, better opponent, when they have to endure a series of grueling practices, or when they must continue to play the game under extremely adverse conditions.

Opportunities to breed courage abound in not only extra-curricular activities like athletics, but also in fine arts, drama, worship, or special interest clubs as long as teachers, coaches, and leaders have been trained in the virtue themselves and consistently encouraged to make this virtue a priority in their programs. That is to say, courage must be a school-wide core value if it is to be uniformly established in students' hearts.

THOUGHTS ON ATHLETICS

When looking at almost any sport in America today, one cannot avoid the conclusion that athletics are just another platform for self-promotion and self-glorification. Examples abound: the defensive lineman, after a routine tackle, who rises from the pile thumping his chest and strutting in the open field for all to see; the tennis champion who can only congratulate herself for winning; cheerleaders who pose for pin-up posters and wall calendars; and basketball stars who appear to be trying to outdo one another by having the most tattoos.

What has been lost in these hyper-narcissistic times, in this gooey therapeutic culture, is the virtue of sportsmanship and the concept of the noble champion. As a result, the wisdom and beauty of athletics have been lost. Christian schools celebrate and promote athletics because they are a platform for developing mature, humble, and gracious men and women who understand that their gifts are not for honoring themselves but for serving others—the very opposite of self-promotion and self-glorification. Borrowing a phrase from former football player Joe Ehrmann, the football field, and by extension, the basketball court and outdoor track, serve as "the last classroom of the day," meaning they are *moral and educational* environments as well as athletic.[11]

A Kingdom approach to athletics recognizes that sports are an

---

[11] Ehrmann, founder of "Building Men and Women for Others," specializes in leadership training for business, sports, and educational leaders. See his website: http://www.coachforamerica.com/what-we-do/bmom. The quotation is from his In SideOut Core Seminar.

excellent training for life. Just as in life, we find in athletics winners and losers, leaders and followers, those giving commands and those obliged to obey them. We find champions and heroes, underdogs and difference-makers, and great dynasties that rise and fall.

In sports, as in life, we observe mistakes with terrible consequences and plays executed to perfection. We see people who panic and players who persist through pain, teammates who are tested and trained to give everything they've got for a cause that is just. We see teams who lost but should have won and teams who deserved to lose but won anyway.

In sports, as in life, we find a concentrated focus toward a common goal, plans of attack and defense, times of holding the line or pouring it on. We find virtues of hard work, self-sacrifice, personal responsibility, and fearless courage. We see perfect equality and fierce competition, talent that disappoints and average ability that breaks games wide open.

In sports, as in life—indeed, in the life of faith as well—there are lost chances and missed opportunities, surprises, turnovers, and reversals of momentum. We see up close confidence and intimidation, fear and faith, grief and exaltation. In sports, as in life, we learn that sometimes winning comes at a very high cost, or in losing, if we are gracious, we are sometimes honored even more.

Christian schools can never, ever cave in to the world here. We run sports programs intentionally, not because everyone else has a program or because athletics bring income, but because we understand how they help us to accomplish our mission, which is to promote virtue, change lives, and help young people come to a proper and sober knowledge of themselves as men and women on their way to becoming future husbands, fathers, wives, and mothers. This can never become merely fine-sounding rhetoric on our promotional brochures. Christian athletic programs exist to teach and model virtuous behavior, and in doing so, to exhibit a view of the athlete, the coach, and athletics in general that is redemptive and Kingdom-minded.

HALLOWING WHAT WE LOVE IN
SYMBOL, CEREMONY, AND RITUAL

After the flag ceremony and the opening prayer, the awarding of merit badges and advancement through the ranks, the lights darken and the audience's attention shifts to the screens on the sides of the altar. Inspirational, patriotic music plays as the majestic image of an American eagle appears, flying in slow-motion through white-capped forests among a chain of mountains. The magnificence of this powerful creature, a symbol of the Eagle Scout, sends shivers down the spine and brings tears to the eyes.

The master of ceremonies invites all Eagle Scouts in the audience to stand for a long applause. Video tributes from seasoned men in the troop honor the young man. An honor guard escorts the scout and his parents to the front, where the scout is to stand at attention for the remainder of the ceremony. He recites the Oath, Law, and Pledge. His father removes the boy's scarf and replaces it with a new one representing the rank of Eagle. Friends, scout masters, and parents gather around the scout to pray. The senior scout leader then challenges the new Eagle to spend the rest of his life upholding the values of scouting and serving others.[12]

Symbol, ritual, and ceremony are the ways a community honors and passes on what it holds dear—the timeless truths and core values for which that community stands. God did not create man to rule

---

[12] Ideas for this ritual come from Troop 437 in Richardson, Texas, a Troop that represents traditional scouting at its finest.

strictly by law and propositions. He also made man as an imaginative, picture-making, subordinate maker in His image, a natural artist who is essentially poetic. Genesis 2 shows Adam using his creative imagination to express himself in language, then to bring order to his realm by naming the animals, and finally to praise the beauty of his wife, Eve. His actions demonstrate that man is a symbol-making creature, who orders his world and lives by the symbols he constructs. Symbols (and the rituals/ceremonies that express them) "bind up reality" for us, helping us to define and order our world.[13]

All that we love and value needs expression in arresting symbols and in the rituals and ceremonies that mediate them if we ever hope to pass them on. Like the symbol of the soaring eagle in the scouting ceremony, the right kind of Christian imagery profoundly moves us, reminding us of what is good, true, and beautiful and anchoring them deep into our hearts. If Christian educators and parents are called to the formation of the soul, then symbol, ceremony, and ritual are not options—they are the very means for reaching the heart, for "talking" to it.[14]

Unfortunately, our churches, still in the grip of an idolatrous rationalism, along with the many Christian schools which have come from them, no longer understand these deep truths and therefore are falling short in preparing students for life in the world and in the Kingdom of God. Students graduate from our schools armed with many fine propositional truths gleaned from Bible studies and a Christian worldview, but carry few of the powerful symbolic pictures of the faith in their hearts. It does not need to be said that when the symbols of a community die, when the rituals and ceremonies that enshrine our values become boring and meaningless, the community and the truth for which it stands, also dies.[15]

How do we get out of this bind and escape the depravity of our own symbols? We need to create a new symbolic landscape for our times. This is the task of the artist who is thoroughly Christian: to wrap ancient truths in fresh, living symbols that appeal to a new generation.

---

[13] Leanne Payne, *The Healing Presence* (Westchester: Crossway, 1989), 119.

[14] James K. A. Smith, *Imagining the Kingdom: How Worship Works*, Volume 2 of Cultural Liturgies (Grand Rapids: Baker Academic, 2013), 6; and, *Desiring the Kingdom: Worship, Worldview, and Cultural Formation*, Volume 1 of Cultural Liturgies (Grand Rapids: Baker Academic, 2009), 28, 54, 59.

[15] Payne, *The Healing Presence*, 128-131.

If they have not done so already, Christian schools might begin by identifying the distinctive symbols of their particular school communities. This is no small thing; it takes prayer and discussion and revelation from the Lord since it is He who has brought together the leaders, teachers, parents, and students who make up our separate schools. Our school communities form for different reasons and for different purposes and values. Each school community must, therefore, capture the core values and truths that the Lord has uniquely revealed to them and then prayerfully consider how they might express those values in ways students can understand and truly believe.

One school, whose property contains a lovely grove of oak trees, identifies its core values, whatever they are. Playing upon a distinguishing feature of the property the Lord gave to them, they identify the oak and its roots as the principal means for expressing their values. That imagery then controls every instance where the school communicates those values—in parent education meetings and chapel messages, and especially on the quotations stenciled throughout their halls and on the walls of their gymnasium. Another school, whose main offices are housed in a stately mansion that came with their property, feels drawn to the imagery of cornerstones, whereas a school with a classical focus anchors its core values in the form of Corinthian pillars. Symbols focus and express our mission. These roots, cornerstones, and pillars stand for something; they have meaning. They express what the community loves and how it defines its purpose.

Since our Christian schools are committed to forming character through the perfection of virtue, we must do a better job of making the virtues more imaginatively compelling and more desirable. We might start with the priceless virtue of purity. Instead of calling in an army of professional "sex-ed" speakers, as schools often do, or showing popular videos about STD's and the dangers of pre-marital sex, we might promote instead chasteness and purity by actually honoring them in ways students can understand. Can we not more imaginatively celebrate the sanctity of marriage, (thereby countering once and for all the false oxymoronic worldview behind the concept of "pre-marital sex") and then exalt the glory and power of purity in the chaste young man or woman? Or have we forgotten that purity is a power which comes from obedience freely chosen out of a sincere love for God? Why do we seem so weak in our ability to celebrate the heroic virtues revealed in these courageous life choices?

And what of other great Christian truths? When a young man graduates from our schools, what symbolic pictures have we given him of fatherhood, marriage, work, family or true masculinity?[16] Are only a few feeble Bible verses on the various "topics" the best we can do? We need to profoundly rethink our methodologies here. "If we—and if the alumni of Christian universities—are going to be 'prime citizens of the kingdom of God,'" writes James K. A. Smith, "who *act* in the world as agents of renewal and redemptive culture-making, then it is not enough to equip our intellects to merely *think* rightly about the world. We also need to recruit our imaginations."[17] That is because the heart is the place where action originates.

Creating a new symbolic landscape may require abandoning outworn or superficial traditions that no longer have any meaning beyond promoting popularity or fashion, such as homecoming and the senior prom, or reinvigorating aspects of our current traditions so that they more powerfully speak to a new generation, such as graduation and perhaps even our awards ceremonies.[18] This is how we keep alive what we love and cherish.

A Christian school is a picture-making, symbol-loving community which expresses what it loves in symbolic language and practices. These symbols and the ceremonies/rituals that accompany them become a vital part of the rich formative education of each new generation of believers. We communicate what we love by loving it. Virtue grows by celebrating it. And, as in the Eagle Scout ceremony, honor is taught by honoring. And the way we teach what we love and honor is to enshrine them in memorable practices of the school community. In this way, they become not merely abstractions or "character traits" for which students ought to strive, but powerful, meaningful, and lasting images in the heart and soul.

---

[16] Ibid., 131.

[17] Smith, *Imagining the Kingdom*, 6.

[18] Perhaps the Awards Ceremony should be modernized and expanded to include the idea of multiple intelligences. See Kathy Koch, *How am I Smart?* (Chicago: Moody Publishers, 2007). Leadership, design, academic, and moral excellence should also be honored and rewarded!

THE CORNERSTONE OF FAMILY

When we reflect on the cornerstone of the family, we need to keep in mind the ideal, the real, and the restored. God, being three persons in one, is by nature a community, and He has expressed this nature in the institution of the family. A father, mother, and their children reflect the image of the Father, Son, and Holy Spirit. That is the ideal. However, the family exists in a fallen world. In many ways and to different degrees, families fall short of God's ultimate design and purpose. This is true of all families, Christian and non-Christian.

We all are broken images of God. Parents, although Christians, will parent out of their brokenness if they have not been healed and restored. A mother may have grown up with an abusive father who sowed fear and intimidation of men into her soul. Without healing and forgiveness, she will continue to relate to her husband from that unhealed place. A father, whose own father may have neglected him, will not know how to parent his sons if he does not acknowledge his own deprivation, forgive his earthly father, and ask for God's wisdom, healing, and grace. If he is not restored, his children will remain un-affirmed, insecure, fearful, and wounded. Even though parents might be solid believers and regular church-goers, if one or both parents remain unhealed in some area, the children will suffer damage. This is the sad, but true reality. Children will manifest different degrees of dysfunction and immaturity, which they then bring with them into our schools.

The restoration of a family depends, first, on the degree to which each parent collaborates with the Lord. With God's grace and a parent's cooperation; with God's truth and a parent's obedience; with the humility of Jesus and the virtues God's Spirit imparts to both parents, God can restore parents, children, and families. Through encounters with God, dads can become more affirming of their children and more loving toward their wives. With God's grace, moms can learn to love and respect their husbands without feeling inferior and discover how to create warm, nurturing home environments for their children. Through revelation, repentance, forgiveness, and healing, Christian parents can reach their ultimate common goal—to love their children with the love they themselves have received from God so that their children become "whole, truth-centered, secure lovers of God and others."[19]

Restoration of our families continues through relationships with others. Families do not exist in a vacuum. God's plan to restore families requires them to participate in a Christian community. Through a family's relationships with others, God is able to heal and restore parents and children through the different measures of grace He has distributed throughout His Body. We see this principle in Ephesians 4:12: God apportioned His grace to different leaders "to equip his people for works of service, so that the body of Christ may be built up until we all reach unity in the faith and in the knowledge of the Son of God and become mature, attaining to the whole measure of the fullness of Christ." While this verse applies specifically to the mission of the Church, the principle also applies to families in community: we are blessed, healed, and restored by God through the grace given to others.

Along with the Church, a Christian school community can be a significant source of healing and restoration for children, parents, and families. In partnership with the school and in close relationships with other families, Christian school parents can serve as surrogate parents capable of imparting wisdom and virtues into other children. Dads can sharpen themselves with other dads and mentor many other sons besides their own; moms can support and encourage other moms in addition to mentoring each other's daughters. By bringing the rich resources of its parents, teachers, and leaders together, the Christian school community becomes a tight-knit extended family and a powerful redemptive force for each of its members.

---

[19] Quote is by Mark Gordon Fee in his teaching series, "First Loved to Love." See First Loved Ministries at www.firstlovedministries.org.

The family is God's primary means of forming persons. Healed and restored from its fallen ideal, the family can become a child's first and primary experience of healthy relationships and true community. Centered upon the marriage covenant between a man and a woman, the family can be a child's first and primary experience of real love. The family can be the means by which parents introduce their children to the Lord and validate their place in the Church and in the Kingdom. In families, restored parents can affirm their child's unique design, special calling, and specific destiny in the world.

Fortified by truth and redeemed by virtue, the family reflects the very nature of God and serves as the bedrock of all civil society. It should, therefore, be an honored and vital third cornerstone in every Christian school community.

A CULTURE OF ENCOURAGEMENT

We may not realize it, but encouraging others is **hugely** important to God. After the early church scattered because of persecution, a new colony of Christians appeared in Antioch. Leaders in Jerusalem decided to send Barnabas, whose name means "Son of Encouragement" (Acts 4:36), as the first leader to visit this new group. True to his name, Barnabas encouraged the new believers and then brought Saul there (Acts 11:23). Saul and Barnabas then taught the fledgling church for an entire year (Acts 11:26). Later, the Holy Spirit decided to send Paul and Barnabas on the first missionary journey (Acts 13:1-2), and the rest is history.

School leaders need to seriously reflect upon these texts. The first leader to visit the new church was an encourager. The leader who brought Paul to the group was an encourager. The leader who stayed at the new church for a year was an encourager, and the leader who went on the very first missionary journey was an encourager. In fact, Paul and Barnabas' return journey on that first trip was conducted solely to encourage the new believers in the churches they had just founded: "Then they returned to Lystra, Iconium, and Antioch, strengthening the disciples and encouraging them to remain true to the faith. 'We must go through many hardships to enter the kingdom of God,' they said" (Acts 14:21b-22).

Many hardships—true indeed. And that is why Christian school communities are vitally in need of encouragers, those good, wonderful saints who are "full of the Holy Spirit and faith" (Acts 11:24b), who come alongside us when we are discouraged or tired or disillusioned and impart life to keep us going. Many of the good works God calls us to do cannot be done without them.

A Christian writer was halfway through his first book when his project hit some roadblocks. He gave the manuscript to a friend who read it and liked it. That encouragement kept the writer going and soon his book was finished. After that, he started a sequel but again he got so stuck and discouraged that he could not make any progress. All his imaginative energy seemed gone. Once again, his friend sought him out to encourage him to keep at it. The writer was named Tolkien. The book was *The Lord of the Rings*. And the friend who was the fire-starter, the encourager without whom the book would never have been finished, was C. S. Lewis.[20]

Later, Tolkien gave high praise to Lewis for his role in the completion of the book: "The unpayable debt that I owe to [Lewis] was not 'influence' as it is ordinarily understood, but sheer encouragement. He was for long my only audience. Only from him did I ever get the idea that my 'stuff' could be more than a private hobby. But for his interest and unceasing eagerness for more I should never have brought *The L. of the R.* to a conclusion."[21]

If the Lord thought an encourager was essential to the first Christian community and the first missionary journey, and if a few encouraging words by C. S. Lewis produced a work of genius which has now blessed generations of readers, then we need to much more highly regard this great gift of encouragement. In doing so, we should also resolve to hate its opposites—judgment, accusation, criticism, and blame—and see them for what they really are: sinister, evil efforts to crush human hearts and steal from the people of God the good works God has called us to do.

We need an army of encouragers. We need encouragers among teachers to remind them that their work is valuable and producing fruit, although many will never see it. We need encouragers among parents too so that they will persevere in faith for their children and never lose sight of hope. We need encouragers among students, who face so many hardships and pressures today in an ever darkening world. And we need encouragers among school principals and deans and headmasters and board members to remind them of that

---

[20] Alister McGrath, *C. S. Lewis: A Life* (Carol Stream, Ill.: Tyndale House Publishers), 197-199.

[21] Quoted in McGrath, 199.

encouraging word from Hebrews 6:10: "God is not unjust; he will not forget your work and the love you have shown him as you have helped his people and continue to help them."

HELPING FAMILIES CONQUER PERFECTIONISM

One of the most entrenched mindsets in many Christian families is the bondage of perfectionism. Sometimes students and parents talk about this vice as if it were a natural part of one's personality, simply the way a person was "wired." Generally, it develops in the student who is desperately trying to please a parent, usually the father, who explicitly or implicitly sends the message that the child must perform in order to be loved. Very often it is the parent's own insecurity, fear, and lack of self-acceptance that drives the whole process.

We might see this condition in the student who believes that anything less than a perfect GPA means failure. Or we might see it in the one who thinks he or she must excel at everything extra-curricular. It appears more subtly in the student who is simply actively involved in everything—several sports, the student council, the worship band, while also carrying a part-time job and achieving high honor roll status every semester.

Perfectionism is a denial of the fallen nature of man and a rejection of the grace of God. It promotes a fourfold illusion: 1) that perfection is actually the goal (and not excellence or learning); 2) that self-effort alone will attain it (apart from grace); 3) that once perfection is attained the parent will be satisfied; and 4) that the student will then feel loved. All four beliefs are wrong. Perfectionism is a way of earning a parent's love by works. It is actually a desire for **conditional** love. It is a sign of a **love deficit** in the child who has failed to achieve the virtue of self-acceptance.

Perfectionism is rooted in pride and very often accompanied by overwork, competition, great anxiety, and sometimes even depression. It fosters the kind of mindset that restricts the student from ever attempting anything new for fear of falling short. As a result, perfectionists are more often than not, joyless, driven, works-oriented performers who are incapable of peace and rest because there is always something for which to strive, always a mountain to climb, always something else they can do. Perfectionists are incapable of lasting happiness because they are cut off from the deep inner joy of personal well-being.

The cure is not easy. It involves actions of applied Christianity. For the student, healing begins with confessing and repenting of the pride behind the striving and the belief that one can do all things. Then the student must learn to be okay with obstacles and setbacks, and learn to see low grades or failures as opportunities to improve rather than as marks of failure or condemnation. Students desperately need to know that their value and well-being are not dependent on anything they "do" but flow out of accepting God's love and being at peace with who they are, limitations and all. And, since perfectionistic students are often cut off from grace, they need to recapture the joy and grace that come from an active and sincere personal relationship with the Lord.

For the parents, love, acceptance, and forgiveness will do much to undo all those unrealistic expectations and disappointing frowns that came when the student missed the mark. Parents also need to look deeply inside themselves to check their own insecurities, fears, and perfectionistic tendencies. Perfectionists breed perfectionists. Our own failures need to be honestly acknowledged and sincerely confessed before our children can be set free.

The long road to restoration begins with parents and students re-patterning the way they respond to challenges and the ways they understand and react to failure. The great virtue of self-acceptance is the goal here, that deep inner peace and well-being that comes from knowing we are loved and honored for who we are and not for what we do.

PLACING OUR CHILDREN IN STORIES

A human life is a tapestry of rich and colorful stories. These stories validate us as individuals and situate us in our world. Placing our children in the moral, historical, and spiritual contexts which have uniquely shaped their lives is vital to their identity and well-being, to the meaning and purpose of their lives.

In our world, truth and reality exist in a fog of confusion and obscurity. Because we act from the heart more than from the conscious mind, parents must use the language of the heart—stories—to cut through this confusion with the moral, historical, and spiritual truths stories contain. Early in their child's life, parents should deliberately use imaginative stories to shape the child's moral imagination to help the child understand the way the world really is. Two foundational truths of our world are especially important for all moral training which will follow: our world is designed and created by a good and loving God, but it is fallen and therefore contains the presence of both good and evil. Because of these realities, a child's choices are supremely important, literally a matter of life and death. Thus, imaginative stories showing choices and their consequences will help prepare the child for moral action later on.

Parents should use the "first" story of Adam and Eve to show their children the nature of God, the fall of our first parents, our own sin nature and the nature and reality of evil, but also the exciting promise of our redemption. Reinforcing this initial story are endless fables, fairy tales, poems, songs, and stories from our Western tradition. Parents might use the famous fable of "The Boy who Cried

Wolf" to emphasize the need for telling the truth and being responsible and trustworthy. Or they might use the myth of Icarus and Daedalus to teach the wisdom of trusting one's parents and exercising self-control. "Rumpelstiltskin" shows the value of keeping a secret and the pitfalls of pride. The fairy tale of "Cinderella" is useful for showing the value of humility, to teach the redemptive truth that good triumphs over evil, and to point children toward the ultimate reality that a real King will marry us someday in the most enchanted Kingdom imaginable. Because so much of our Western tradition is also the story of Christianity, sources from this tradition are full of truth and excellent for shaping the moral imaginations of young people.

Stories, then, first inform children about the true nature and reality of their world. However, as the children get older, parents should then place their children into the true stories of their origins. These stories should be rich in ethnic, religious, historical, and geographical continuities. A former barmaid in Prague married an American who then settled in an Iowa farming community. But she was lonely and missed her dear friends back in the old country. Through her several letters back home she succeeded in getting three girlfriends to join her. One was named Mary, who—after she joined her friend in Iowa—met and married a bricklayer from Budapest. He and his only brother had just recently decided to split up in Nebraska. The brother went west to find his fortune in California managing fruit orchards. The bricklayer went east and settled in Iowa. Mary and the bricklayer became the children's great-grandparents on their father's side.

Placing children in the stories of their origins is a testimony to God's amazing design and timing and a powerful reminder of the children's exceptional value and destiny. The Italian grandfather on their mother's side is still living and full of vivid stories of his upbringing. When he was five, he lost his father, who was a boxer, to a brain tumor. The family suffered a sudden loss of income, and then had to move to a smaller home where they struggled to put food on the table. Other stories: his time in the Great War, the funny story about how he learned he was color-blind, his hard work raising a family, working long cold hours as a bricklayer in snowy Boston. And the brick home he built with his own two hands in the fading hours after work and on weekends, the very home where their mother grew up and which is still standing on the corner of School Street and Lexington Avenue in Lexington, where Revolutionary War virtues and values have long shaped generations of rugged Americans.

If it were not for a lonely barmaid, two brothers parting ways, a bricklaying great-grandfather in Iowa, and a resilient Italian-American grandfather in Boston, the children would not exist. These are the thrilling facts that make up the real-life narratives that have shaped the children's lives.

A child's destiny is only fully comprehensible when parents consistently place their children into the ongoing spiritual stories of the past, present, and future. These are the equally real and amazing God-stories happening to the family and children right now—the stories that solidify to our children the implacable truth that God is real. That day in elementary school when their father came home with an envelope containing five thousand dollars precisely when the family needed it. The photo-copy of the actual check in each of the children's bedrooms for ten thousand dollars that just came "out of the blue" after that. That incredible day when both family cars were sold in an afternoon to one buyer who moments before had gotten lost in their neighborhood and just happened to see the sign after he and his wife prayed for an opportunity to bless someone. That day when the daughter randomly stopped at the gym where she just happened to meet an old coach who offered her a job which funded her last two years of high school. The other daughter who earned a full scholarship at precisely the right time to a university which only recently created the degree program exactly matching her design and calling. That time when the son, at fourteen, built a tool shed with his own two hands, and the high-end furniture maker next door who saw it going up, and then offered him an apprenticeship, bringing the son a handsome income and teaching him a life-long trade. True God-stories like these testify to the reality of the Lord's presence and activity in the children's lives and encourage them to trust in His leadership and His Word for the future.

Without moral stories forming the imagination early on, children will be deficient in their perception of the world and indifferent to the power and consequences of their own choices. Without family stories later, especially in adolescence where the search for identity is particularly acute, children will not have the best contexts for understanding themselves or their place in the world. They are not lonely, isolated selves in a meaningless universe, but separate and individual persons created in the image of God and placed in a family shaped by long lines of fascinating ancestors. And finally, without the amazingly interconnected God-stories of the present, stories that prove God is real, our children will lack the most important framework of all: the supernatural contexts which reveal purpose and destiny. Without stories, children will lack truth and meaning and have no testimonies of God's goodness, timing, presence, and power. They will have no stories to tell of their own, no stories to pass on to those after them.

THE CORNERSTONE OF PURPOSE

When we anchor our lives in the Truth, which means when we obey the Truth, we naturally grow in all the virtues of Christ. When parents grow in the virtues, in other words, when they become Christ-like, their families become pleasing to the Lord and their children receive the nurturing and training they need to become spiritually mature adults. But then what happens next?

What happens next is Purpose.

Purpose is not calling. We discover our purpose when the certainty of our design and the knowledge of our calling intersects with the release of God's grace in His perfect timing. Ephesians 2:10 is the scriptural basis: "For we are God's handiwork [our design], created in Christ Jesus [God's grace], to do good works [our calling], which God prepared in advance [God's timing], for us to do."

We are all colorful and very beautiful puzzle pieces; no two are alike but each must interlock with others to fulfill the sovereign plan of God. Regardless of our purpose, we only have meaning in relation to others. Or, to put it another way, we cannot achieve our purpose without being in relationship to others. And yet, each one of us is uniquely designed with personalities, dispositions, talents, gifts, and perspectives of our very own. We are truly works of art designed by the great Author, the great Potter. Understanding our marvelous design and possessing the great virtue of self-acceptance is a cause for joy and freedom because we feel "at home" in the world and comfortable in our own skin. We no longer need to compare ourselves with others or compete for honor. Ideally, our parents, in their love for us, are to discern, affirm, and bless this design in us, this way we should go (Proverbs 22:6). When they fall short of this responsibility, only a relationship with the Lord will put us in touch with who we really are.

Our calling, our works, have long been decreed. We do not search for them and we do not try to make them happen. They are not discovered but revealed as we grow in the knowledge of God, as we become more perfect in Christ: "But when God, who set me apart from birth and called me by his grace, was pleased to reveal his Son in me so that I might preach..." (Galatians 1:15-16a). As Jesus is revealed in us, we discover what we were born to do. In Paul's case, it was to preach. In our case, we "hear" our special calling in union with the Lord. In other words, our sense of calling is proportional to our knowledge of God.

In spite of our design and calling, we accomplish nothing apart from God's grace. We are not in a fifty-fifty collaboration. It is all or nothing. Everything we do is by grace and not by us, for if our works depended on us, we would get the glory and not God. That is why, sometimes, Jesus has to deconstruct a life before He can actually use it. Just as Peter, who was confident of his own goodness but ignorant of his self-reliance, had to fail and then be humbled before he was called by God to feed the sheep (John 21:17), we too must confront our weaknesses and realize our need for God. We must become, like Jacob, "leaders with a limp," leaders who know their weaknesses and are certain only of their complete dependence on the Lord. As Jesus said, "apart from me, you can do nothing" (John 15:5b).

Design, calling, and grace always depend on God's timing. The concept of timing implies it is something we can know, which means we must be able to recognize and listen to God's voice and know something about how He works. Philip, who heard an angel tell him to walk along a certain road and approach the Ethiopian eunuch's chariot (Acts 8:26, 29), is an example. Cornelius who, while praying one afternoon, heard an angel tell him to go find Peter (Acts 10:3-4), is another. And Jesus, who emphasized several times that "My sheep listen to my voice" (John 10:27), is a third. All three testify to the reality that we live in an open universe with a good Father, a mighty Lord, and an ever-present Spirit who are always talking to us. Of course, to hear God speak implies we have chosen to remain very close to Him through an immersion in the scriptures, faithful obedience to His commands, and participation in Christian community.

Purpose, the fourth and final cornerstone of a school community, completes a coherent, logical, and cohesive sequence of long-standing and everlasting core values: **Truth** is our infallible guide, **Virtue** is our confident hope, **Family** is our first and eternal community, and **Purpose** is our divine mission in the world.

WHAT IS A KINGDOM EDUCATION?

Jesus' great obsession was the Kingdom of God. The prophets announced it, Jesus taught about it, and His disciples carried it forward. And the most fundamental of prayers, The Lord's Prayer, reminds us that we are to pray, "your Kingdom come, your will be done, on earth as it is in heaven" (Matthew 6:10).

As we "pray heaven down" into our schools, we begin to discover Kingdom templates for everything that we do. We begin to receive the wisdom of God for everything from administration to student life, to athletics, academics, and family education. That is because God dearly loves us and longs to reveal His ways to us through His amazing wisdom, which is freely available to all (James 1:5).

A Kingdom education is one that takes place in a worshipping Christian community through a close partnership with parents to call forth and affirm God's unique design in all students, training them to do the good works God created them to do. A Kingdom education trains not merely the intellect, but the whole person—body, mind, will, emotions, and spirit—in a secure learning environment that promotes curiosity, wonder, exploration, and discovery. It encourages home and school to collaborate in creating and maintaining a hope-filled culture of life that prizes spiritual growth and vitality, personal responsibility, servant leadership, and giving back to the community.

The great enemy of a Kingdom culture is the mindset that says "we want a king like all the other nations." This idea comes from 1 Samuel 8 when the elders of Israel approached the prophet Samuel and said, "You are old and your sons do not follow your ways; now appoint a king to lead us, such as all the other nations have" (1 Samuel 8:5b). When Samuel approached God about this, God said, "it is not you they have rejected, but they have rejected me as their king" (8:7b). At a time of crisis and when the leader was weak and vulnerable, Israel surrendered the very thing that made her unique among the nations of the world—leadership by God Himself!

In our schools, this mindset is subtle and dangerous because it masquerades as the voice of reason, tradition, and practicality. "Every school has cheerleading (or football, or a certain curriculum, or a school band), so we should develop a similar program." Really? Is that what the Lord is telling your school? Or does He hope to reveal to you a never-before-seen program or activity for bringing young women together for fellowship and service to the community? Or school leaders might say, "At our other school we always did it this way," never pausing long enough to let God reveal a better idea, a more efficient, more righteous, and less expensive way.

Classical, traditional, and University-Model® schools are showing the signs of creativity that come from exciting Kingdom ideas: the University-Model® itself, which has brought parents back into the educational process in a powerful and effective partnership between home and school; the development of a modernized classical curriculum with a Biblical worldview focus; initiatives to restore the liberal arts; the adaptation of the English house system to build fellowship and community; in addition to student-led worship bands, exemplary parent education programs, and outdoor leadership programs.[22]

What other amazing Kingdom ideas are on God's mind right now that He longs to reveal to us? To your school? A sincere love for the wisdom of God, robust faith, and a commitment to individual and corporate prayer will bring heaven down into our schools and fill them with redemptive new ideas for whatever we seek to do or build. When this happens, Christian schools will once again become the head and not the tail, and soon, as the Queen of Sheba did in Solomon's day, educators will come from miles around to marvel at the wisdom God has graciously given to us and to find out why we are so successful at what we do.

---

[22]Lucas Christian Academy (Lucas, Texas), Wylie Preparatory Academy (Wylie, Texas) and Veritas Academy (Austin, Texas) have developed effective programs in student-led worship, the House system, and parent education respectively.

THOUGHTS ON THE FINE ARTS

Leaders in traditional, classical, and University-Model® schools have a fantastic opportunity before them: to mentor and train those specially gifted young people, those rare seers among us, the sensitive ones, the artists! If we can pause just a little, just enough to hear and see the value of art and the artist to our mission—if we will be open to revising our thinking and changing our assumptions and practices, the artist-who-is-Christian can make a comeback, as opposed to the ubiquitous "Christian" artist afraid of his own imagination and content to produce shallow, uninteresting work of dubious value.

Since God Himself is an Artist and we are made in His image, we are all subordinate "makers" in His image. Adam's naming the animals, his using the first poetry in human history to praise his wife, Eve, or even perhaps the first couple's sewing of fig leaves together to cover themselves after the Fall are examples of the natural artistic gifts God has given to man. The Fall does not take those intrinsic gifts away, though it has corrupted them. The good news, however, is that in Christ all our natural artistic gifts are restored.

There are profound truths here. Before the Fall Adam used his artistic powers to order his world and to praise beauty. After the Fall he used his creative powers to cover himself, lie, and hide from God. In this perversion we find the clue to the artist's restoration: to "uncover" man, to tell the truth of our existence, and to point the way back to God. Perhaps here we might also find a mission statement for a fine arts program that is truly Christian: **"to develop artistic programs that would encourage and train artists to make sense**

of our world by pointing to the truth about man and God and praising what is truly beautiful."

Such a mission statement rests on three plain facts. First, the created world is astonishingly beautiful.[23] It was so beautiful that when God was laying its foundations, the morning stars sang together and all the angels shouted for joy (Job 38:7). And Wisdom herself, assisting God at the creation of the universe, "was filled with delight day after day, rejoicing always in his presence, rejoicing in his whole world and delighting in mankind" (Proverbs 8:30b-31). Beauty is simply the wisdom of God made visible. Throughout the wisdom literature, personified Wisdom is a craftsman and a builder, and elsewhere in scripture, those filled with wisdom are prophets and artists. Bezalel, Oholiab, and others were given wisdom by the Spirit of God (Exodus 28:3; 31:1-6) for artistic expression in gold, silver, bronze, stone, and wood. And when we recall from Psalm 104:24 that God Himself created all things in and through wisdom, the link between the Spirit of God, wisdom, beauty, and artistic power becomes obvious.

Second, beauty has both **evidential power** capable of pointing us back to God as well as **sacramental power** causing us to actually encounter Him.[24] We have only to turn to Psalm 19:1-3 to know that the heavens and skies display a universal speech and knowledge—they declare the glory of God and proclaim the work of his hands—or to Romans 1:20 to learn that God's power and nature are clearly seen, being understood from what has been made. These facts alone should stir us to rethink our commitment to the arts. Like nature herself, human works of art can exhibit these same powers; they can become

---

[23] In his Commentary on Genesis, Victor Hamilton replaces "good" in the creation story with "beautiful." See Victor P. Hamilton, *The Book of Genesis Chapters 1-17*, New International Commentary on the Old Testament (Grand Rapids: Eerdman's, 1990), 120.

[24] Thomas Dubay, *The Evidential Power of Beauty: Science and Theology Meet* (San Francisco: Ignatius Press, 1999), 14; and Oswald Chambers, *My Utmost for His Highest*, February 10 (New York: Dodd, Mead and Co.: 1935): "The people of God in Isaiah's day had starved their imagination by looking on the face of idols, and Isaiah made them look up at the heavens; that is, he made them begin to use their imagination aright. Nature to a saint is sacramental. If we are children of God, we have a tremendous treasure in Nature. In every wind that blows, in every night and day of the year, in every sign of the sky, in every blossoming and in every withering of the earth, there is a real coming of God to us if we will simply use our starved imagination to realize it."

platforms through which God can speak to change the hearts of people and nations. When Abraham Lincoln met Harriet Beecher Stowe, author of *Uncle Tom's Cabin* in 1862, he reportedly said, "So you're the little woman who wrote the book that started this great war," a statement testifying to the power of art to change the destiny of a nation.[25]

Third, beauty is intimately related to **worship**. Not in the way our popular culture has understood it, however. We do not idolize beauty as the modern artist might, or because of his outrageous humanism only worships himself, some hybrid of himself and technology, or even his own procreative powers. Having evidential power, beauty opens a window into heaven. The artist creates a beautiful work which draws us in and captures the imagination of our hearts, pointing beyond itself to the transcendent which then evokes admiration, love, and then worship of God, the "one and only," the ultimate source of all that is one, good, true, and beautiful. For this reason, Christian fine arts programs not grounded in adoration and worship and disconnected from virtue will fail.

In his Nobel Lecture, Alexander Solzhenitsyn contrasted the artist who was independent of any higher power with the artist who was conscious of God. His description could serve as a starting point for an understanding of the artist we should want our students to emulate:

> Another artist, recognizing a higher power above, gladly works as a humble apprentice beneath God's heaven; then, however, his responsibility for everything that is written or drawn, for the souls which perceive his work, is more exacting than ever. But, in return, it is not he who has created this world, not he who directs it, there is no doubt as to its foundations; the artist has merely to be more keenly aware than others of the harmony of the world, of the beauty and ugliness of the human contribution to it, and to communicate this acutely to his fellow-men. And in misfortune, and even at the depths of existence—in destitution, in prison, in sickness—his sense of stable harmony never deserts him.[26]

---

[25] See https://www.harrietbeecherstowecenter.org/utc/impact.shtml.

[26] Alexander Solzhenitsyn, "Nobel Lecture," 1970, in *Nobel Lectures in Literature 1968-1980*, Ed. Sture Allén, (Singapore: World Scientific Publishing, 1994).

Rather than producing "Christian" artists, we might instead mentor and train artists who are Christian, which is to say, thoroughly human because we have put them deeply in touch with the "harmony of the world" by pointing them to the Source of that harmony, the Creator of that world. Re-envisioning the artist and the role of art in our schools would benefit all our students. The capacity for art to enrich and nourish the soul; the demands that art places upon each of us to stretch our vision and alter our ways of seeing ourselves and our world are among the several benefits that renewed programs in the arts can encourage and teach.[27]

We should no longer allow a lack of funds, other priorities, only a few interested students, or inadequate classroom space to suppress faith for art and worship programs in Christian schools. We must show some aggressive leadership here and much faith. Building competitive arts programs *with worship at the core* will produce the artists, the seers, and the singers who will champion the good, the true, and the beautiful, and redirect the eyes of the world toward the Lord and, ultimately, toward hope and change.

---

[27] Dubay's *Evidential Power of Beauty* would be a good place to start.

IN REST WE SEE ... AND THEN DO

One of the great paradoxes of our faith is the relationship between our purpose, the "good works" we are called to do, and our faith, the trust we are to have in the Lord who enables us to do them. But the relationship is only an apparent contradiction. A conversation between Moses and the Lord in Exodus 33 resolves the paradox. For individual believers confronting stress and restlessness and for Christian schools who have a tendency to pile on student activities and programs until all the poor moms are exhausted, the secrets of the Kingdom revealed in this text will be invaluable.

The Lord had just given Moses and the Israelites a purpose: "Leave this place, you and the people you brought up out of Egypt, and go up to the land I promised on oath to Abraham, Isaac and Jacob, saying 'I will give it to your descendants.'" (Exodus 33:1b). But God refused to go with them because the people were rebellious—He would send His angel instead (33:2). This did not settle well with Moses who wanted no one but God to go with them. In protest, Moses replied to the LORD, "You have been telling me, 'Lead these people,' but you have not let me know whom you will send with me. You have said, 'I know you by name, and you have found favor with me.' If you are pleased with me, teach me your ways so that I may know you and continue to find favor with you. Remember that this nation is your people" (33:12b-13).

Tremendous revelation and power come when we press God to know Him more. The conversation absolutely changed God's mind. Remember what Moses had just asked; it was for God to teach him

His ways. God's reply does not seem to answer that request, or does it? God's answer was: "My Presence will go with you, and I will give you rest" (33:14b). Moses begins to think out loud about the implications of God's reply. Then he said, "If your Presence does not go with us, do not send us up from here. How will anyone know that you are pleased with me and with your people unless you go with us?" (33:15b-16a). And then Moses poses the greatest rhetorical question of the Bible: **"What else will distinguish me and your people from all the other people on the face of the earth?"** (33:16b, emphasis added).

There it is, the question of all questions: what is the one thing that sets God's people apart from everyone else on the planet? The question is rhetorical because God had already answered it: God's people are at **rest** and they are at rest because **God is actually with them.** God is not a theory; He is a real presence. Whenever God is around, His people, if they believe and trust Him, will be at rest. They will know and experience shalom.

Because of what Jesus did for us on the cross, God's answer is further qualified: God's presence is not only with us but now literally in us through the presence and power of the Holy Spirit. When we receive the Spirit Jesus gave us, the gift the Father promised, we enter God's rest and receive the peace of the Lord. Anxiety, striving, fear, works—all these disappear at a fundamental level in our souls when we finally fully trust in the real presence of God in and with us.

Rest, then, is the indispensable middle link between faith and purpose. Jesus made this clear in a series of logically interrelated statements showing the relationship of each to the others. In John's gospel, Jesus makes the connection first of all between faith and purpose. Before we were born, God created the good works we are to do in our lives. This is the work God requires of us or, if you will, our "purpose." To know this purpose, we obviously must have faith. When the crowds anxiously pressed Jesus with the question, "What must we do to do the works God requires?"(John 6:28b) Jesus was emphatic: "The work of God is this: to believe in the one he has sent" (John 6:29b). The "works of God" are performed not by our "doing" anything at all, but by faith.

In Matthew 11:28-29 Jesus then links faith (belief) and rest. "Come to me, all you who are weary and burdened, and I will give you rest. Take my yoke upon you and learn from me, for I am gentle and humble in heart, and you will find rest for your souls." Faith in the finished work of Christ means we no longer need to strive to get good on our own; we now share in the salvation Jesus won for us and the wonderful rest that comes with it. God's promise of rest to Moses and Jesus' promise of rest to all believers, therefore, are aspects of the same truth—rest is the infallible mark of the people who have placed their trust in a living God.

The most intriguing link in the faith-rest-works sequence is the link between rest and the good works we are to do. Due to the works-driven ethos of "busyness" and activism so common in our day, it is a relationship largely misunderstood or simply forgotten by many believers. We must remember that Jesus was perfectly in sync with the Father and always conscious of the Father's presence with Him. As a result, Jesus always operated from the place of rest where He could both see and hear what the Father was saying. Several scriptures testify to this. Jesus did not at first act at Cana (John 2:1-11) because his "time" had not come. How was He to know that time? He would know it when the Father told Him so. As it turned out, His time was soon after He said this! When the Jews criticized Jesus for "working" on the Sabbath, Jesus replied: "Very truly I tell you, the Son can **do nothing** by himself; he can **do** only what he **sees** his Father doing, because whatever the Father does the Son also does. For the Father loves the Son and **shows him** all He **does**" (5:19-20a, emphasis added). How did the Father show Jesus all this? Jesus was in the wonderful "rest" of the Father's presence: "I am telling you what I have **seen** in the Father's presence" (8:38a, emphasis added). What happens in the Father's Presence? Rest! What happens when we are in God's rest? We **see** and **hear** and then **do**!

How do we do the works God requires? The work of God is to believe. What happens when we believe? We experience the real presence of God and find rest for our souls. What happens when we are in rest? We see and hear what the Father is doing. Our purpose, our work, whatever we are to "do" individually or collectively for God is not something we figure out or do on our own; it is something God reveals to us when we believe in Him and enter His rest.

PRAYER CULTURE

CONDITIONS FOR BLESSING?

We think we need a school bus. Or we pray earnestly for a certain kind of curriculum, or a really bright teacher to teach physics, or maybe we just need chairs for our chapel, or some free weights for our athletic program. We think we need material things and we do of course, and so with our focus on what we need, we pray earnestly to receive them.

But as Christians, we are a community before we are anything else, before we do a single thing together. This means something more fundamental than our material needs must always be addressed first and that is, once again, our relationships with one another.

If we invest in the people we've got, God will send us the people we need. This applies to other resources as well. We say, "Lord, we need this," or "Lord, we are running out of money," while all along the Lord is trying to tell us that we have a far more pressing need to address, that we have a broken relationship somewhere. A parent and an administrator are angry with one another and not speaking. A group of moms is criticizing and slandering the school on Facebook because of a new dress-code policy. Two board members have different visions for the school and one is threatening retaliation if his demands are not met.

If we fix our broken relationships, if we summon all our energy and give our full attention to bringing understanding, repentance, forgiveness, and reconciliation where they are needed, *then, from the Lord's standpoint*, we are now in a position to receive from Him. We are in the zone of His abundant blessing.

When our relationships (in a family, church, or a school

community) are pleasing to the Lord, we rest in the zone of God's miraculous provision. God will generously give revelation (what to do), wisdom (how to do it), and direction (where to go) for whatever He has called us to do.

We must never forget that God holds in His heart the perfect divine templates for whatever we are to do or build. Are we starting a school? Assembling an English department? Composing a board of directors? Are we forming a family, setting up an efficient office, trying to craft an exciting lesson, or hoping to get our finances in order? Whatever it is, the Lord has the perfect divine template, which is essentially His way of doing that particular thing, for each of these objectives. And He is most willing to reveal these to us, provided that our relationships with one another are sound. Sound relationships are the circuit through which God sends His revelation and His resources. **Relationship before Revelation, Revelation before Resources**—these are the conditions of blessing. If our relationships are right, God will reveal His plans, and His resources are soon to follow. He will generously give us all that we need—the bus, the chairs, the physics teachers, and the sports equipment—whatever we need to complete our mission.

It works like this: when the Lord sees His people acting like His people, acting like Him; when He sees us loving, forgiving, and reconciling with one another, He gets excited. He says, "Look at that school community down there. See how they love one another! They are treating one another in a way that pleases Me. Therefore, I am going to send them more people and more resources because I want others to experience the same love, acceptance, forgiveness, and freedom that they have. I will release to this school community whatever they need to accomplish what I have asked them to do!"

When we commit to protecting our relationships with one another, we will walk in divine favor and blessing. We will receive the resources we need. Most of all, we will fear no obstacle, setback, tragedy, or failure because God securely holds us in the palm of His hand and has promised He will never let us go!

PRAYING FROM A CENTER OF OFFENSE

Suddenly you find yourself facing an adversary. It might be a person who has something against you—you said or did something to him that was offensive. Or it might be an angry parent so upset with a policy or decision that she wants to tear down the school. Whatever the case, the adversary cannot stop spreading derogatory and hurtful comments about you or your school to others. And you have good reason to believe the criticism is having a terrible effect—others are talking about leaving the school.

You know you are supposed to pray for those who persecute you. But you are so angry you think Jesus could not have meant what He said. Still, you dutifully comply and try to pray.

You do not realize it, but you are **praying from a center of offense**. You still have anger (the surest sign your prayer is a little off) and you still are painfully aware of the damage your adversary has caused to you and/or your school. If the truth be told, you would rather call fire down from heaven on this irritating adversary and be done with it. But that would not be loving. You pray instead that God will judge the person severely and pay him back. But that is not loving either.

Your prayer is not pure. Praying from a center of offense— praying out of anger or pain, out of one's desire to have the slander and criticism stop—still has you or your needs and desires at the center. Your own pain and sense of being offended are motivating your prayer—it is quite simply a self-centered prayer. The focus needs to be on your adversary, but not in the way you have been praying.

You need to pause and let the strong emotions and desires for judgment and punishment subside so that the grace of the Lord can flow. You need to get God's heart and feelings for that person; you need to pray from the center of selfless mercy and compassion. That is something you are not naturally inclined to do. Nor are you even capable of it. It will take all of God's grace for you to pray the right prayers in the right spirit.

As God's peace begins to work in your heart, you find yourself thinking and praying for your adversary in a totally different way. Why is he so unable to let this issue go? Why is this mom not giving up her campaign to destroy the school? Then, in a place of calm repose, you hear the profound whisper of God.

"It is because your adversary feels powerless." The thought stuns you. Taking up our own causes for justice, our self-appointed campaigns to make things right, gives us a sense of power. It makes us feel important; it gives us a purpose. To one who normally feels powerless because perhaps her life is out of control in other areas, this campaign does more than seem to satisfy a need; it is like a raging addictive drug. It feels good to have power. But this kind of power absolutely destroys others and the work of the Lord.

You then hear the Lord saying, "Pray that your adversary will be encouraged. Pray she will become more secure in My love. Pray for more light in her home. Pray that she will see the bitterness and shame motivating her actions."

Your heart softens. God has shown you the pain behind your adversary's vicious behavior. You pray for God's healing, encouragement, revelation, and love. You begin to feel the well-being of your adversary is solely your responsibility. The damage your adversary has done to you, perhaps even the damage she is still causing, is no longer your focus. You have achieved an exceedingly high level of prayer: **You have put yourself and your offense aside**. All you can do now is pray for her restoration. Now you are praying from the center of love and mercy, from a place of real power, from the furnace of God's own heart. And that is a prayer God will most certainly hear and answer because it is absolutely His own.

THE PRAYER OF A RIGHTEOUS MAN (OR WOMAN)

Sometimes the simplest things are the hardest to believe. As educators in our homes and in our schools, do we believe prayer can literally change the direction of a human life, alter our present circumstances, or determine the future?

James tells us that "the prayer of a righteous person is powerful and effective" (5:16b). Then he elaborates: "Elijah was a human being, even as we are. He prayed earnestly that it would not rain, and it did not rain on the land for three and a half years. Again he prayed, and the heavens gave rain, and the earth produced its crops" (James 5:17-18).

Elijah was so powerful his prayers controlled the weather for three years. He prayed for rain and it rained. James believed his hearers had the same power. That is why he said, "Elijah was a human being, even as we are" (5:17a).

James makes a persuasive argument: Elijah was a man who prayed powerful prayers; we are men just as Elijah was a man, so we ought to pray with the same power. Why do so many of us find this so hard to believe? Is it possible we have incredible power at our fingertips, more power than we can imagine, in simple earnest prayer, both individual and corporate? Have we forgotten that when two or more come together in Jesus' name, Jesus is present among them?

Can an administrator or board member pray earnestly that her school receives all the resources it needs, including lots of money, so that the Lord's work can continue? Can a parent earnestly pray for a child who is struggling academically, or who has a serious health problem, or who finds it difficult to interact socially with other children? Can a leadership team pray earnestly that God will send more men to the school as leaders, teachers, and coaches? Can an entire school earnestly pray, pray, pray, for a new building, a new headmaster, several new teachers, more families, or a school bus?

As Christians, we would easily say yes to these questions. But what if we push this a bit further? If we pray for a child with Asperger's Disease, could that child be healed? If we pray for a young person addicted to pornography, can he be delivered? If we pray that a couple not divorce, can our prayers move God's heart to move on their hearts to save their marriage?

Just how much power do we really have? Maybe that depends on whether we pray at all and whether we pray earnestly (sincerely, consistently, and fervently). Perhaps that depends on whether we have cultivated a lifestyle of prayer. Perhaps it depends on how much faith we have or how well we know God personally. We do not have because we do not ask. And if we pray for anything in His name He will do it and God will back up His act: "And I will do whatever you ask in my name, so that the Father may be glorified in the Son. You may ask me for anything in my name, and I will do it" (John 14:13-14). "Very truly I tell you, my Father will give you whatever you ask in my name" (John 16:23b). Jesus cannot be more emphatic: we may ask Him for anything in His name!

If you are a headmaster, what are the three most serious needs or issues in your school right now? Fast and pray for each of them for ten days with your leadership team and ten days by yourself. Watch what happens. If you are a parent, what is the most serious need in your children? Is it academic, spiritual, or emotional? Fast and pray for each child over a 30-day period and you will see God do amazing things. Moreover, cultivating a lifestyle of prayer from then on will change you, your children, and your circumstances beyond what you can imagine.

Consistent, fervent, individual and corporate prayer should be the chief activity and interest of anyone building a home, a family, a church, or a school community!

CAN YOU HEAR THE WHISPER?

Many of the messages we hear in our churches today in one way or another can be boiled down into the advice to just "work harder." We are told to pray more, serve more, read more, memorize more verses, volunteer more, and do more.

And while there is nothing intrinsically wrong with this advice, it can lead us astray if we are not careful. It can cause us to make two mistakes: to think our own effort is really what matters most and to believe that productivity, in the form of measurable results, is the goal. We develop a mindset that says we need to work more to produce more because that pleases God. With this mindset, we then easily fall into habits of hyper-activity and busyness, and soon we are striving under our own efforts in everything we do, including, especially, educating our children. If we are not vigilant, we can fall into a religious performance trap that makes us and everyone around us miserable.

This performance mindset can be disastrous when it comes to educating our children. Parents with this mindset become "helicopter" parents who incessantly hover over their children and hyper-scrutinize everything they do. They take on responsibilities they are not to assume. They turn in work when their children forget. They sometimes complete difficult assignments when their students feel overwhelmed. Their presence looms so large in the child's life that the child eventually feels suffocated and resentful, although at first he eagerly welcomes the help and becomes very skillful at manipulating his mother to get it.

Jesus was clear about our absolute dependency on Him. In John 15, the famous "I am the Vine" passage, Jesus says that all our fruit comes from a relationship with Him: "No branch can bear fruit by itself; it must remain in the vine. Neither can you bear fruit unless you remain in me." (John 15:4b) Then He says quite bluntly: "Apart from me, you can do nothing" (John 15:5b).

Earlier in John's gospel, a crowd of people asked Jesus: "What must we do to do the works God requires?" (John 6:28b). Did you hear that? What must we **do** to **do** the works God requires? The people were thinking in terms of **activity**. They were thinking works, performance, something they could control. But Jesus was thinking in terms of **intimacy**. His answer had to be incredibly shocking to the works-oriented people of that time: "The work of God is this: to **believe** in the one he has sent" (John 6:29b, emphasis added). Everything we are to "do" we do out of faith and intimacy with the Lord.

Matthew 11:28-29 shows us more clearly why faith in Him is so important for us as co-partners with our children's teachers or as educators in Christian schools: "Come to me, all you who are weary and burdened, and I will give you rest. Take my yoke upon you and learn from me, for I am gentle and humble in heart, and **you will find rest for your souls**" (emphasis added).

Rest for our souls. That includes minds that are not oppressed, anxious, or always compulsively thinking, thinking, thinking, but at rest. It includes wills not always active, striving, working, working, working, but at rest. And it includes emotions not always elevated, anxious, worried, frantic, or fearful, but at rest. A parent whose soul is truly at rest, a parent walking in peace and great patience, a parent who understands the difference between encouraging and enabling, is the parent and teacher her children actually need. The disposition and condition of soul in a parent will either liberate or handicap a child.

Faith produces the blessed rest that we need to hear the gentle whisper of God. "Then a great and powerful wind tore the mountains apart and shattered the rocks before the LORD, but the LORD was not in the wind. After the wind, there was an earthquake, but the LORD was not in the earthquake. After the earthquake came a fire, but the LORD was not in the fire. And after the fire came a gentle whisper. When Elijah heard it, he…went out and stood at the mouth of the cave" (1 Kings 19:11b-13a).

We can't hear a whisper when we are constantly moving, surrounded by incessant noise, or distracted. Elijah himself was alone in a cave. In **rest**, we hear God's words. We hear His directions. We hear His will for our lives for that day and for every day. Then, after hearing Him, we "do" what He says. Those who are always striving, always working, always performing, always laboring under their own power might be missing the marvelous whisper of God—the words, counsel, and direction of God, which are the basis for all that we are to "do."

THE GREAT WHISPER OF GOD— APPLIED

Just what does it mean to hear the whisper of God? To hear God direct our steps and order our time? What does that really look like in daily life? What does it look like for students under pressure? For moms working with a challenging curriculum? For dads who don't have enough time?

Students: The pressure is on. You have a difficult paper to write and your mind is all knotted up. You sit down at your desk and put away your phone. No texting tonight. The paper is due tomorrow. As you sit there struggling for an idea you feel this nudge: "Get up and go for a walk." No audible voice, just a hunch, an impression. "No way," you tell yourself, "I have work to do and finally enough time to do it." But the nudge persists. "Go for a walk." The urge is so unusual and so strong, you give in to it and out you go.

While walking you start to notice things. Trees, sounds of birds, a breeze rustling the tall grass. The more you look, the more your mind clears, and right about the time you become aware that you are actually enjoying the walk an idea for your paper comes, full blown, right out of the blue. You were not even thinking about the paper. In fact, you were not thinking at all; you were just walking and noticing things. At once you turn around, go home and write the entire paper in one sitting. This is a student who can hear the whisper of God.

Moms: Your daughter is caught up in the Rhetoric Stage of a classical school curriculum and all this is quite new to you. You feel way behind all those other moms who seem to have it all together, and you have been getting anxious when you try to work with her on homework. One morning as you take time to pray, you open your Bible to the book of Daniel. Daniel? What's that got to do with anything?

But in the first chapter your eyes zero in on this passage: "To these four young men God gave knowledge and understanding of all kinds of literature and learning" (Daniel 1:17a). You are dumbfounded. God gave four Hebrew boys who did not know the literature and language of the Babylonians the ability not only to learn the language but to master the literature in that language? No way. And when the boys were taken to the king, he found them ten times wiser than the wisest men in the kingdom?

You get on your knees and quickly turn this word of the Lord to you into prayer: "Lord, please give me that ability to help my daughter. Teach me. Show me how to parent and teach her. Give me the ability to learn just as you gave Daniel and his friends that ability!"

That evening, looking for light bulbs at the grocery store, you run into another school mom in the same aisle. She has older kids and has been through the model and the curriculum before. She has tons of books to lend. She has so much peace. She is encouraging and willing to come over and show you how to do it. You discover she lives only two blocks away. And she assures you that you will get the hang of Rhetoric in no time. This is what happens when a mom hears the great whisper of God!

Dads: Driving home from work your mind is full of all the things you have to do. That leaky faucet. The trimming you left for another time. Looking at Fox News on the Internet.

You pass an ice cream shop and the thought comes to you: "Take your son out for ice cream tonight." "Not enough time," you say to yourself and drive on. "I've got work to do!" But as soon as you have settled the matter, you hit a red light. Then another. And then another. "This is weird," you say to yourself. "I always make these lights." When the light turns green, you just "happen" to notice a billboard for Nike shoes. A chill goes down your spine. You begin to wonder if God is whispering to you, and in a language you really understand. **"Just do it"** the billboard says, and when you get home you can't get your son into the car fast enough. This is how a dad might hear the amazing whisper of God.

REFLECTIONS ON PRAYING FOR OUR SCHOOLS

Jesus had just cursed a fig tree. The next morning, when His disciples saw that the tree had withered, Jesus responded with a powerful message on prayer. Three aspects of that message are instructive for those who wish to make prayer a priority in their schools.

The Power. Jesus said, "Truly I tell you, if anyone says to this mountain, 'Go, throw yourself into the sea,' and does not doubt in their heart but believes that what they say will happen, it will be done for him" (Mark 11:23). We already know from James that "the prayer of a righteous person is powerful and effective" (James 5:16b), but just how powerful do we believe our prayers can be? The mountain image is proverbial for any impossible task or insurmountable obstacle. Jesus uses exaggeration here (or does He?) to encourage us to believe that prayer can alter any "landscape" in which we find ourselves.

What are the most insurmountable obstacles facing your school right now? Is it a lack of money? Is it an immediate need for a larger building or land at an affordable price where you might build a building? Is it a lack of strong teachers or the need for an experienced headmaster? Aggressively take your need to the Lord in faithful prayer with two or more others (Matthew 18:20), and power from heaven will come to remove any obstacle.

By Faith. Jesus prefaces His remarks with the simple statement, "Have faith in God" (Mark 11:22a). Then He introduces the mountain image and concludes by saying: "Therefore, I tell you, whatever you ask for in prayer, believe that you have received it, and it will be yours" (Mark 11:24). In other words, Jesus brackets the point about moving mountains with two statements about **faith**. Faith elicits the power of God to change our circumstances and remove obstacles. What amazing things could happen in our schools if all stakeholders prayed with this same level of faith!

Faith implies knowing enough about the goodness of God that we can approach God confidently with no doubts. Leaders must, therefore, spend time with the Lord to know and trust Him enough to take care of whatever threatens their mission. This is not always easy to do amid the responsibilities, distractions, and pressures of leading a school. However, it is by far the most important priority, the one activity we must protect at all costs.

Fix Your Broken Relationships! Jesus concludes His teaching about prayer with an exhortation to forgive those who have offended us. "And when you stand praying, if you hold anything against anyone, forgive them, so that your Father in heaven may forgive you your sins" (Mark 11:25). Here Jesus is tapping into a concept found elsewhere in the scriptures, which is the idea that God may not hear our prayers if we choose to treat others badly. "When you spread out your hands in prayer, I will hide my eyes from you; even when you offer many prayers, I am not listening" the Lord says in Isaiah 1:15a. Why will God not listen? "Your hands are full of blood…Take your evil deeds out of my sight" (Isaiah 1:15b-16a).

How many of our prayers is God **not hearing** right now because we have not extended forgiveness to those who have wronged us or not asked forgiveness from those we have wronged? God will hold back an answer for a single grudge. He will close the doors of heaven for one refusal to forgive. He will block our path and even perhaps actively oppose us if, in our pride, we continue to criticize and judge others, imagining we are superior (James 4:6).

Which of the several pressing needs in our schools would we like to remain unmet, preferring instead to allow the bad relationships we know about to continue? How much more is God willing to do for us if we would drop everything to mend them? There really is a causal relationship between the way we treat others and the blessings we receive.

BUILDING A FURNACE OF PRAYER AT YOUR SCHOOL
(For Hugh)

My house will be called a house of prayer for all nations.
(Mark 11:17b, emphasis added)

Set aside a small building, a room, or even a temporary tent if that is all you have. Do not call it a chapel. Call it a Furnace of Prayer.

Then systematically change the mindset and culture of prayer that currently exists in your school community. Point out how dull we have become, how full of unbelief we have at times become in our drippy, cliché-ridden, routine prayers before leadership and board meetings, before the start of a school day, at mealtimes, or the beginning of classes. We have lost the concept of the incredible power God has given to us in prayer! We have lost the faith that prayer can move mountains!

Then start teaching each of the different people groups in your community everything you know about prayer: how to do it, why, what it will bring, how it will determine the future. Use God's word to build faith for prayer. Teach your young people how to turn scripture into prayers. Teach older students how to pray any of the several apostolic prayers by adapting them to actual circumstances in the school.[28] Teach the teachers and parents to intercede and petition the Lord for issues in their spheres of authority as well as for general issues in the school

---

[28] As, for example, in Ephesians 1:15-16 and 3:14-15.

such as finances, material needs, and more teachers.

By doing this you will be building a furnace of prayer and power at your school. And it will absolutely change your destiny. You will see astonishing and sometimes rapid changes. You will feel a difference on campus—the spiritual climate will shift. You will see transformation and conversions; you might see healings and miracles because now you are tapping into the bedrock reality of the presence and power of God in your midst. This is not a theological concept. It is reality. The King is present among His people (Matthew 18:20).

Encourage moms and dads who have some spare time to invest it in prayer. Convenient times are after drop-off in the morning or thirty minutes before pick-up at the end of the day. Encourage students to visit the prayer house during their lunch hour, before or after school, or perhaps during a study hall once in a while. Invite teachers and staff to spend time praying for their needs; let your leadership teams and board members gather there on a regular basis to quietly go before the Lord and listen for His guidance and direction. Having a place to pray is better than having no place. One person praying is better than none. Many people praying is better than one. Prayer absolutely moves God's heart and causes Him to act on our behalf.

Pray for all aspects of the school. Pray for the schools in your area, including the public schools. Pray for a spiritual revival in your city or region. Pray that the crime rate will fall in your city, pray for the sick in the local hospitals, pray for the fatherless, pray for the Lord to raise up harvesters and evangelists in your churches, and pray for the leaders in all the churches in your region. Pray for our country and the President as we are exhorted to do (1 Timothy 2:1-2). Pray and teach your students to do the same. They need to see adults in serious prayer and they desperately need to see a real God in real time who listens and responds to His people.

Pray also for larger things: the state of Israel, the future of Jerusalem, the salvation and restoration of the Jewish people (Romans 10:1). Our students need to become citizens of the world. Pray conversions to Christ will occur among Muslims. Pray for the Christian martyrs throughout the world and for Kingdom ministries to flourish and make a difference in oppressed nations. Students need to focus much more on the world outside their cell phones and computer screens; they need to shift their attention away from themselves and toward the needs of others. We must encourage them to learn about current events. Without this worldwide dimension to their faith, they will be handicapped and limited in their effectiveness in the Kingdom of God.

As we spread a culture of intercession throughout our schools, let us keep in mind four deeply encouraging truths about prayer:

1. The power of two or more believers praying and agreeing together on an issue is greater than we think (Matthew 18:19-20).

2. God will give us whatever we ask for in prayer if we ask, seek, and knock aggressively in faith (Luke 11:9-13; Matthew 7:7-9).

3. Faith the size of a mustard seed will move mountains (Matthew 17:20).

4. Although we are in a constant spiritual war, our weapons have "divine power to demolish strongholds" (2 Corinthians 10:4b).

Therefore, we can actually take back enemy territory and establish justice in our neighborhoods and in our schools if we remember to "always pray and not give up" (Luke 18:1b).

BRINGING THE FUTURE INTO YOUR SCHOOL: INDEPENDENT, SYSTEMIC PRAYER CELLS

The ministries, churches, and schools spectacularly thriving today are doing so because their leaders are intense and zealous for prayer. Serious prayer. Aggressive systemic prayer that storms heaven and cries out to God to come down with power. Prayer that pulls the future into the present.

Since we know when two or more are gathered the Lord Himself is in their midst, we can confidently form prayer cells in each sphere of authority at our schools, knowing that the Lord is with us and will hear our every petition and need. This approach to school-wide prayer consists of **independent, systemic prayer cells**.

Every school community contains different but interrelated spheres of authority. Teachers are a sphere of authority with a unique vantage point. The board is a sphere of authority with a different vantage point. The leadership team is a different sphere with a different perspective while the school staff, coaches, parents, and students are additional spheres of authority, each with its own perspective on the issues and needs of the school.

The idea behind independent, systemic prayer cells is to have members in each sphere of authority independently praying for the school from their unique perspective in smaller prayer cells during a specified period of time. That is what makes the activity systemic: since the interconnected spheres of authority comprise the perspectives of the entire community, the entire community will be covered in prayer when members of each of the spheres pray.

Spheres of authority should be divided into smaller prayer cells of five to seven people to make interaction and prayer more efficient. Teachers, for example, might group themselves into prayer cells by combining two grade levels, whereas the board and school leadership team might be a single prayer cell each. Parents might form cells with parents who have children in the same grade. Students might group themselves into several smaller cells within their particular class depending on its size. Likewise, the office staff might become a cell, the financial team another cell, and coaches perhaps one or two more.

Prayer cells then agree to meet on their own for concentrated prayer a specified number of times within a restricted time period, say three to five months. In their first meeting as a cell, they should discuss and then list the main prayer topics for their sphere and perhaps a few more general prayer topics for the school as a whole. For example, a 7th- and 8th-grade teachers' prayer cell might sense that helping junior high students manage social media, or guiding them through the challenges of adolescence, or showing them how to make their faith their own are critical prayer needs. They might add to this list more general concerns of the school—its finances, its need for additional teachers or staff, or its need for new facilities.

With their list compiled, and still in their first meeting as a cell, they go to prayer. Prayer cell members may pray in any way that suits the group rather than according to a specified formula. The prayer group gives each problem or prayer need to the Lord and asks for His resources, wisdom, and direction. Most likely each person in the group will gravitate toward particular items on the list so that by the time the prayer is finished, a number of different prayer perspectives will have been shared, thus covering the topic or need thoroughly.

The groups are independent in the sense that each prayer cell is free to meet and pray whenever it is convenient within the specified time frame. If the period is three months, a cell might pray early in the first month at someone's home, later in the second month at a park, and a final time in the third month at the school itself. Having independence means each group has fewer schedules to coordinate and more flexibility to meet whenever it can. And praying as a cell a set amount of times in the entire period assures a thoroughness of prayer for their particular needs. Having all cells in each of the spheres praying this way thoroughly covers the needs of the entire school.

Prayer should never be forced upon anyone, although undertaking a prayer project like this will definitely be sacrificial. And it should be. Prayer by nature is sacrificial. It costs time and energy. But it should never be a "program" that draws people because leaders have made them feel guilty or obligated. You want people who are free and willing to volunteer because they love the school and desire to see God bless it. Not all teachers and parents will be able to pray every time, so the cells may not be the same each time. Some participants may never have the time and that is okay. Those who cannot pray with the group should be sent a list of the prayer needs anyway so that they might pray at home. If such concentrated systemic prayer becomes an annual tradition and the entire community sees God answering their prayers, perhaps over the years there will be more buy-in from those who initially did not catch the vision.

Think of a Christian school community where prayer is spotty or non-existent or routine and dry. If prayer pulls down strongholds and brings a surge of God's presence and power then such a school will be handicapped indeed. It will settle down and comfortably go to sleep. Then imagine what can happen when the entire community comes together and prays with purpose and power several times from every perspective for an agreed-upon length of time. How could God not bless it? How could its people not see God do amazing things? And if members of a Christian school prayed with this intensity year after year, how could its children not prosper or the school itself not exert a powerful influence on the local community?

SMALL GROUPS, PRAYER MEETINGS, AND GREAT AWAKENINGS

Concerts of prayer appeared throughout New England as colonists hungered for revival. Ignoring denominational boundaries, they just wanted to come together and pray. And then, suddenly, the First Great Awakening was on, and Jonathan Edwards and a firebrand named George Whitefield were evangelizing the American colonies and the world with astonishing results. In England, a man named John Thornton was converted under Whitefield's ministry. Two years later, Thornton linked up with another well-known evangelical named Henry Venn, and together they formed a small community of believers who became known as the Clapham sect.[29]

In the late 1970s, a small, tired group of evangelicals disillusioned with the church started meeting in a home in southern California. They were worn out and dry as a bone after years of serving in their ministries with negligible results. They worshiped and prayed and cried out to God for revival and revival came.

Nine years later a man started a prayer group with five people. They had a heart for India at the time. In their meetings, they would spread out maps of Asia on the floor and pray. Sometimes only three people showed up for the meeting.

Fifty years after Thornton was converted, the man who would become "the greatest social reformer in the history of the world,"

---

[29] See Eric Metaxas, *Amazing Grace: William Wilberforce and the Heroic Campaign to End Slavery* (New York: HarperCollins, 2007), 182-189.

William Wilberforce, was at the center of the Clapham group who now functioned as a small community of Christians dedicated to social reform.[30] Together they supported dozens of ministries and organizations for orphans, slaves, and the dispossessed. With the support of the Clapham community behind him, Wilberforce succeeded in abolishing the slave trade in England. The rest is history.

By the late 1990s, the small group of tired Christians meeting in a home in southern California had become a worldwide evangelical renewal movement whose influence is still being felt today. Hundreds of new churches, beautiful, intimate, new worship music, a new emphasis on the Kingdom of God, and a national ministry for men were the fruit of that one small group.[31]

And what used to be five people in a tiny Tuesday night prayer meeting is now an organization that serves more than 16,000 indigenous missionaries throughout Asia. They run 54 Bible colleges serving 9,000 students in ten countries. Today, that small prayer meeting that started more than forty years ago has become an international evangelistic organization called Gospel for Asia.

There is no such thing as "merely" a small group of praying believers. God seems to love Gideon-style small beginnings. Very often throughout history, God has used individuals in committed relationships—like-minded believers in small groups—to birth some of His greatest Kingdom works. In groups like this, anything can happen. Every small group of Christians—whether it is a Bible study, a service group, a prayer group, or simply a social fellowship—can become a platform for God to break in and then bring forth a work that could significantly change the social, political, and spiritual landscapes of our world.

---

[30] Ibid., *xvii*.

[31] I am referring here to the Vineyard Movement, a worldwide network of approximately 1,500 churches. From http://www.vineyardusa.org/site/about-vineyard.

PROTECTING CULTURE

GUARDING THE HEART OF THE SCHOOL COMMUNITY

Because the Lord intends that we all prosper, He is excited to place us in relationships and communities for our good, but also so that we can positively influence others. Therefore, we must periodically examine ourselves to ensure that our behavior is pure and faultless so that we will never compromise the Lord's great name or weaken the community by being the cause of strife or division.

In 2 Corinthians 12:20, Paul identifies eight sins that will hurt others and tear people apart: quarreling, jealousy, outbursts of anger, factions, slander, gossip, arrogance, and disorder.

Quarreling between members instantly divides a school community. If not quickly addressed, it will produce factions and scores of wounded people. Jealousy tears apart relationships through resentment, suspicion, and rivalry. Anger, as for example when an offended parent fires off a scathing email to a teacher, introduces threat, intimidation, accusation, and blame into a relationship of equals. By choosing to send the email and avoid a face-to-face meeting, which takes a lot more maturity and even more courage, the angry person loses the opportunity for the Lord to check his escalating sinful impulses through interaction with others. Angry people act the way they do because it gives them an illusion of power. That is precisely the deception; it is power all right, but power that destroys.

Factions are small rebel groups that form through gossip and criticism to challenge leaders or other groups within the community.

Sometimes they form because of the sinful influence of just one disgruntled person with an ax to grind. Believing themselves to be the vanguards of justice, they sometimes exhibit a mob spirit (think of diatribes on Facebook) which then gives the devil a powerful foothold into the community.

Other sins are equally destructive. Slander and reckless words pierce human hearts. Gossip separates close friends, and arrogance destroys confidence, trust, and equality. Even a seemingly weak problem such as disorder is no small thing. Disorder generates chaos, and chaos breeds confusion, doubt, and disagreement. When we choose to sin in these ways, we are appallingly destructive even as we convince ourselves that justice is absolutely on our side. We give the enemy the legal right to hurt those we are called to love and forgive. By doing this, we absolutely destroy what God holds dear.

Gossip is destructive to both the hearer and the tale-bearer: it "separates close friends" because it "betrays a confidence," and therefore, fans the flames of a "quarrel" (Proverbs 16:28; 11:13; 26:20). We know that "the words of a gossip are like choice morsels; they go down to the inmost parts" (18:8), meaning their words are fantastically tantalizing and capable of penetrating the deepest parts of our souls. Such "morsels" are very difficult to ignore.

A warning found in Isaiah applies here: "If you [Israel] do away with the pointing finger [blaming and accusing others] and malicious talk," (and instead treat others the way they deserve to be treated), "then your light will rise in the darkness, and your night will become like the noonday" (Isaiah 58:9b, 10b). When we put an end to the sinful ways we treat one another, the Lord will satisfy our needs, guide us, and strengthen our frame (58:11). Physically, emotionally, materially, and spiritually, we will prosper.

It has been said that in a conflict people always have two choices: accusation or intercession. We can choose to be a part of the problem by listening to the Accuser of our souls and pointing the finger of blame at others, or we can be healers, reconcilers, and restorers of broken relationships by choosing to pray for all concerned.

Virtues that flow from the Wisdom of God are powerful antidotes to gossip, slander, anger, factions, and strife. James 3:17 lists seven virtues that directly build up relationships between members of a community. Anyone possessing this "wisdom that comes down from heaven" becomes pure, peace-loving, considerate, submissive, merciful, impartial, and sincere.

Purity acts like a protective shield against the contamination of gossip, slander, and hearsay. A peace-loving person will strive to establish harmony between warring factions. A considerate person spreads kindness that melts obstinate hearts. One who is submissive honors community leaders, enabling their work to continue. One who is merciful covers over offenses that cause division and pain. Someone who is impartial judges fairly in disputes and one who is sincere promotes confidence and trust, which in turn create depth and intimacy. If we value people at all, or if we care about the relationships we have with one another, then we simply cannot do without these virtues!

We must decide how we will act **before** conflict ever occurs. It is a choice. Will we choose to protect the Lord's investment and guard the heart of the community as well as the hearts of the people in it, or will we choose to be willing accomplices to its destruction? Do we desire the Lord's grace and favor or the devil's fire?

> The tongue is also a fire, a world of evil among the parts of the body. It corrupts the whole body, sets the whole course of one's life on fire, and is itself set on fire by hell. (James 3:6)

THE BAD REPORT

"'We can't attack those people; they are stronger than we are.' And they spread among the Israelites a bad report about the land they had explored. They said, 'The land we explored devours those living in it. All the people we saw there are of great size. We saw the Nephilim there (the descendants of Anak come from the Nephilim). We seemed like grasshoppers in our own eyes and we looked the same to them'" (Numbers 13:31b-33).

This passage from Numbers tells the story of the Hebrew spies who went in to spy out the land and then came back and spread a bad report about it among the people. Keep in mind that the land they explored was the land God promised to give them. It was indeed a land flowing with milk and honey. They even brought back a huge cluster of grapes they had found growing there; the cluster was so big two men had to carry it on a pole between them (Numbers 13:23).

In spite of this explicit factual evidence, the spies' fears got the better of them. In their report to the people, they began to exaggerate and distort what they saw there. Their bad report spread fear among the entire Israelite community to such an extent that everyone began to grumble against Moses and Aaron, the God-appointed leaders of the community. "And they said to each other, 'We should choose a leader and go back to Egypt'" (Numbers 14:4). They even talked about stoning them (14:10). Stoning *Moses*? My, how distorted their thinking had become!

This is how a single bad report can inflame an entire community and bring the leaders under severe oppression. What the grumblers and fault-finders did not realize was a point of enormous importance: in grumbling against the land and the leaders, the people were grumbling against God Himself. Their punishment was never to see the Promised Land—everyone who grumbled died during the forty years of wandering in the desert.

With this story in mind, school leaders might first reflect on a series of questions. Do you believe your school is a work of the Lord? Is your school caught up in the great story of God? Do you have stories of His unmistakable intervention in your affairs from your founding to the present day? Do your parents have stories of how God provided for their needs? Do you know of people that He raised up at just the right time to give their time, energy, and resources? Has God ever provided you with land or a new building? Can you cite instances when the Lord clearly brought teachers, leaders, board members, outstanding families, and administrators to your school? If so, then can any of us tolerate continued grumbling and complaining?

If leaders believe they are indeed participating in a real work of the Lord, then they will take seriously grumbling and complaining in their community. When we complain and grumble about the school to others, we speak against something the Lord really, really cares about. Are there some things the school does not yet have right? Of course, and there is so much work yet to do. But there is a right way, a Godly way, to address issues, and there is a seriously wrong way to talk about them also. Spreading bad reports is wrong. Even if one is seeing a legitimate problem, it is not good to spread the bad report to others not involved to enlist them in the cause. Gossip, which is speaking negatively about others when they are not present, and slander, which is maligning another's character, are wrong, too. Along with grumbling and fault-finding, these sins against the community are most displeasing to the Lord.

Spreading bad reports is always wrong and always sinful. When we sidle up to others and spread bad reports about teachers, parents, leaders, the school, whatever—we are in fact thumbing our noses against God. We are placing ourselves in opposition to a work the Lord has established. We are in fact setting ourselves squarely against what God wants to prosper. Not a smart place to be. And definitely not a good thing for the school.

The take-away from all this is easy: **accept no bad reports**. Not on Twitter, not on Facebook, not from another person directly. And what we say to those who are doing so is simple. We should look them straight in the eyes and say firmly and clearly: "**We don't do that here.**"

HAVE YOU BECOME A JUDGE?

Only one man has the right to sit in the Judge's seat and that is Jesus. That is because He is the only perfect human being, the Son of Man, and of course, God Himself.

When our pride or need for power creates the illusion that we deserve to sit in that seat ourselves, and then we do so and begin to judge and criticize others, seizing on their faults, pointing out their sins, and judging them for their actions—what in Isaiah 58:9 is called the "pointing finger,"—the grace in our lives stops flowing at that very moment. It stops because we have removed ourselves from our proper position as dependent creatures and have become something we are not—little self-appointed deities.

A famous myth tells the story of Daedalus and his son Icarus who were imprisoned in a tower by King Minos. To escape, Daedalus made a set of wings for himself and his son and fastened them with wax. With the pairs of wings, the two flew up and out of the tower.

Now the father had counseled his son to stay near him, flying neither too low near the sea, which could wet the wings, or too high near the sun, which could melt the wax. Unfortunately, the freedom and exuberance of liberation went to his son's head. Leaving his proper position at his father's side, he soared higher and higher. He flew so high the sun melted the wax. The wings fell off, and Icarus plunged into the sea that now bears his name.

On the one hand, this story says much about teenagers—their exuberance sometimes, their lack of self-control, their disinclination to listen to the wisdom of their elders—and we can learn much from this as parents. But the myth also describes what happens to anyone who chooses to leave his proper sphere of authority. We end up "falling" and hurting ourselves.

When we criticize or judge another, we give the enemy permission to exercise his diabolical authority. We give permission for the devil to harm others through us. We become divisive and sinful; we destroy relationships and invite discord into whatever enterprise we take on. And so, criticizing our spouses, we essentially give the enemy free reign to hurt them. Harping on our kids permits the devil to attack them. Judging teachers or principals or board members or anyone over us, for that matter, can bring them under severe demonic oppression. Do we really want this to happen to those we are called to love? Do any of us really understand what we are doing to others, to ourselves, and to the community when we set out on our own petty campaigns for justice?

It might help us to realize why we like criticizing others in the first place: it is because we ourselves feel small and powerless. That is one reason we have such a hyper-focus on our rights. It sometimes explains why teachers have a hyper-focus on standards. It explains why parents have such a hyper-focus on the goodness of their children. Because we ourselves feel small, we latch on to whatever we think gives us value or significance. We become self-appointed critics and judges in an effort to obtain power and significance.

The truth is, we have not experienced the fullness of the Lord's love. Judging and criticizing others comes from our deep hunger for significance (it goes back to the Garden and our first parents), which makes us believe that the only way we can be someone is by putting others down and elevating ourselves. It gives us the illusion that we possess a power and a value we do not actually have.

Grumbling, complaining, gossiping, and judging come from the illusion that we are somehow in a superior position in relation to others. We are not. We are equal members of the Body of Christ and equal stakeholders in our communities. The way we get free is to repent and then take responsibility for those we have hurt. We need to humble ourselves, ask for their forgiveness for harassing them, and then willingly choose to step down from Jesus' throne and return to our proper sphere, the place where we can receive His wonderful grace once again.

TWELVE WORDS EVERY STUDENT, PARENT, TEACHER, AND LEADER SHOULD KNOW

Since, as parents and educators, we are building Christian school *communities* and not merely schools, relationships with one another become supremely important. We should be wise, therefore, to understand the range of conditions that can compromise our interactions with one another. The following twelve words identify some of the most insidious sins that can separate people and tear apart communities.

Boasting, which is too much praise for oneself, and **arrogance,** "an attitude of superiority,"[32] absolutely destroy relationships (or prevent them from occurring at all) because they create inequality—one person thinks and acts like he is better than another. Sincere communication, the foundation for all healthy relationships, cannot take place when one person is always talking about himself.

Egoism, or too much concern for oneself (narcissism), and **egotism,**[33] talking about oneself too much, do exactly the same thing—they destroy communication and upset relationships between equals. The self-centered person is unable to listen to another because he is too driven and impatient to talk about himself. Others will always

---

[32] "Arrogance." *Merriam-Webster.com.* Merriam-Webster, n.d. Web. 6 Dec. 2015.

[33] "Egoism." *Merriam-Webster.com.* Merriam-Webster, n.d. Web. 6 Dec. 2015. "Egotism." *Merriam-Webster.com.* Merriam-Webster, n.d. Web. 6 Dec. 2015.

be ignored, slighted, or dishonored when an egotist comes into the room.

Hypocrisy is in a class all its own. Hypocrisy destroys truth and therefore confidence and security in relationships. A hypocrite is a false person, one who appears to be what one is not. Relationships are built on trust and trust on truth; hypocrisy destroys trust because one person in the relationship, the hypocrite, is false in his words and in his deeds. We see this when people wear happy faces at church while in fact, they are deeply hurting, or when a politician calls himself a family man while carrying on an affair. We see this in the alcoholic parent or in students who play the religious part at school but never truly make their faith their own.

Disobedience, presumption, and **scorn** compromise relationships because they create unsafe environments where those relationships might exist. Each is a threat of some kind. Disobedience, not following rules or commands, threatens leadership. Presumption, which is overstepping one's boundaries, threatens order while scorn, which is "open dislike or derision,"[34] threatens peace because it creates conflict and causes strife or injury. How can two people work together if one constantly criticizes the other or does not respect another's boundaries?

Even seemingly small vices like **impatience and obstinacy** can profoundly affect people in a community. Impatience, irritation when confronting opposition, and obstinacy, stubbornly holding on to an idea or perspective in defiance of reason,[35] obviously threaten stability and productivity. Impatient people create pressure, haste, and anxiety while obstinate people delay or impede progress. Trying to work with either will be frustrating, time-consuming, and costly in one way or another.

Finally, **vainglory**, a word not used much anymore but which means pride in one's accomplishments, and **vanity**, excessive pride in one's appearance,[36] compromise communication because, like boasting, one person is hyper-focused on himself. Relationships

---

[34] "Presumptuous." *Merriam-Webster.com.* Merriam-Webster, n.d. Web. 6 Dec. 2015. "Scorn." *Merriam-Webster.com.* Merriam-Webster, n.d. Web. 6 Dec. 2015.

[35] "Impatience." YourDictionary, n.d. Web. 6 December 2015. "Obstinate." *Merriam-Webster.com.* Merriam-Webster, n.d. Web. 6 Dec. 2015.

[36] "Vanity." *Merriam-Webster.com.* Merriam-Webster, n.d. Web. 6 Dec. 2015. "Vainglory." *Merriam-Webster.com.* Merriam-Webster, n.d. Web. 6 Dec. 2015.

require give and take, equal degrees of sharing and listening, which depend on the virtues of humility and self-control. Conversation is impossible if one is always bragging about his exploits or, like the poor Narcissus, always admiring himself!

These twelve words have a common root: they are derivatives of **pride**, the chief sin of Lucifer, the root of every vice and the bane of healthy relationships and true community.

GRACE(S) FOR RESOLVING CONFLICT!

Regardless of how difficult or insurmountable the problem seems to be between two people, we must never forget that God gives us grace for resolving conflicts. Walking in this grace requires that we follow the way of love, think the best of one another, and do all we can to quickly repair the relationship. The following strategies will be helpful to anyone who cares about resolving conflict.

Go to the person directly. This obeys the principle found in Matthew 18 that we go to our brother individually and show him his fault, hoping he will listen. This means we do not involve others who are not a part of the problem. When we spread our problem to those not involved we defile them and create more problems. Although it will require much courage, going directly to the person is the right thing to do.

Resolve to speak the truth in love. This implies that we know the truth and are not filling in gaps in our knowledge with our own assumptions, guesses, or expectations. We speak only the truth that we know. However, truth is never enough in a dispute nor is establishing truth the ultimate goal. Protecting one another's hearts is the goal. Seeking reconciliation is the goal. We are a Christian school community; God really cares about our relationships with one another. We preserve our relationships and the community as a whole when we resolve to speak the truth in love with the right spirit, when we are more concerned about the other person than with being right.

Ask questions to achieve a common understanding of the problem. We ask questions for understanding, clarity, and confirmation, and not as a lawyer would with a litigious spirit. The other person is not on trial. When we are attempting to resolve conflict with someone, we are not adjudicating a case but seeking to understand in a spirit of humility (not control) and hoping for repentance, forgiveness, and reconciliation. These are the goals that please the Lord and bring on His grace and power.

Contain/control your emotions and your words. This is actually a working out of speaking truth in love. Love does no harm to its neighbor (Romans 13:10). Pray and spend time listening to the Lord before the meeting. Ask Him to order your emotions and give you peace. Don't even have the meeting until everyone is calm and emotions are more subdued. Accuracy, clarity, and truth get obscured in emotionally charged conversations. Self-control is very often the single most important ingredient to a successful meeting between two adversaries, and that is why sometimes conflict resolution requires the presence of a wise mediator who can make this happen. One slip of the tongue, one surrender to an emotion can ruin the entire meeting and delay reconciliation and healing.

Expect the Lord to break into your meeting. Oswald Chambers says we are to never calculate without God.[37] We forget we live in an open universe. God can break in at any time. God can break in and change the hardest of hearts if we walk in faith (believing He is present), in wisdom (His way of doing things), and in love (His heart for ourselves and others). When we pray, remembering that the prayer of a righteous person is powerful and effective (James 5:16), we are inviting the Lord to enter the conflict. Because we can count on His presence and power in our midst by the Holy Spirit, who is "God with us" today, we can expect Him to reveal hidden facts or motives, clarify confusing actions or outcomes, and provide miraculous solutions to the problem.

Seek to restore justice. Those in conflict might need to repent and extend forgiveness before a solution can reveal itself. Since justice has been violated in some way, justice must be restored, and the person responsible for causing the conflict must receive correction so that he experiences a change of heart. This might require that he see the damage he caused and the people he hurt so that he feels genuine godly sorrow for what he has done.

Leaders and/or the cultural architects in our schools need a range

---

[37] Chambers, *My Utmost for His Highest*, "Don't Calculate Without God," July 5.

of skills, interests, and abilities to keep relationships healthy. They need to have a heart for family ministry overall and for parent education, in particular, to keep parents knowledgeable and confident as co-partners with the school for their child's education. They need to have a pastor's heart for the teachers and staff to provide encouragement and counsel for when circumstances become difficult. But most of all, they need wisdom from the Lord and confidence that His grace is available to resolve conflicts, preserve the relationships, and protect the unity of the school community.

RESOLVING CONFLICTS AT HOME AND SCHOOL: AN OVERVIEW

Jesus did not mince words when it involved broken relationships. The Sermon on the Mount, where He addressed the topic, was probably delivered in Galilee, seventy miles from Jerusalem and the temple. Jesus was saying that if someone were offering a gift at the altar of that temple, but realizes his brother has something against him, he should leave his gift, travel the seventy miles back to Galilee, fix the relationship, and then travel the seventy miles back to the temple to offer his gift (Matthew 5:23-24). In other words, Jesus urges us to radically drop everything and sacrifice whatever is necessary to repair a damaged relationship. That should give us an idea of how important good relationships are to Him!

Jesus follows that teaching with the command to "settle matters quickly" (Matthew 5:25a). If we don't, matters will get worse. Our adversary might turn us over to the judge, who may turn us over to an officer who has the power to throw us into prison. The point Jesus is making is quite clear: if we fail to settle our disputes at once, they will quickly escalate and we will have to pay a most severe penalty—we will become progressively less free. Is it easier to quench a fire as soon as one smells smoke or an hour afterward when the fire is raging and half the house is already destroyed?

So, Jesus is asking three things of us whenever we have a broken relationship. First, we are to value that relationship highly; second, when it is broken, we are to do whatever we can to fix it; and third, we are to fix it quickly, or it will escalate. No advice could be more practical and more helpful for parents and leaders in Christian schools. We are compelled to fix our broken relationships and keep them healthy.

However, the book of Hebrews cites a fourth principle to keep in mind with respect to troubled relationships. "See to it that no one falls short of the grace of God and that no bitter root grows up to cause trouble and defile many" (Hebrews 12:15). A single person with a bitter root judgment against another and who will not confront the offending person can defile many and absolutely destroy a Christian community.

We have all experienced before how one person with an unresolved issue, instead of confronting the person responsible for creating the problem, chose instead to vent frustrations to others who were not involved in the case. When this happens, the writer of Hebrews says, "many" people can become defiled. Those who have been defiled will then take sides on the issue, creating more strife and division and setting even more people against one another to such an extent that it takes leaders weeks to resolve all the problems and hurt feelings.

Our fights and quarrels, James reminds us, come from the evil desires battling within us (James 4:1). We all struggle with our sin nature, different degrees of brokenness and pride, different family histories, religious traditions, and degrees of education, different levels of experience and maturity. Any of these conditions can bring us into conflict with others.

Thankfully, we have clear guidelines on what to do when we have an issue with someone. First, we are to go to the person directly and express our concerns (Matthew 18:15). If it is a teacher, we should go to the teacher, one on one. If it is a parent, we should call up the parent and ask to meet so that the issue can be worked out. If an administrator said or did something that was offensive, or implemented a new policy with which we disagree, we should schedule a meeting quickly to talk it out and gain understanding, while also making up our minds that even if we disagree with a decision and express that disagreement in the right ways to the right people involved, we will still support it once it has been made, trusting that the Lord will work it out either way.

We don't go around the person who has offended us; we don't spread our issue to others not involved; we don't make excuses for why we do not confront the person; and we don't grumble and complain to others on Facebook out of our own frustration. These kinds of actions **defile others and harm the community.** When an issue arises, we drop everything to repair the relationship; we try to settle matters quickly so the issue does not escalate; and remembering to always *"speak the truth in love,"* we go directly to the person who has offended us and work out the problem face to face. This is how mature Christians resolve their differences and preserve their unity and their mission.

RESOLVING CONFLICTS 1: ACHIEVING A COMMON UNDERSTANDING

Settling conflicts involves three phases: first, the two sides need to achieve a common understanding of what happened and why; second, they need to seek repentance and forgiveness for the wrongs committed; and third, they need to seek reconciliation and commit to the restoration of the relationship. Full resolution of a conflict—between parents and the school, a teacher and an administrator, or a teacher and a student, should move through these phases with the ultimate goal always being the restoration of the relationship.

Both sides in a conflict must first seek a common understanding of the problem. Since everyone in the community should already be committed to seeking a change of heart in students who break the rules or in adults who get caught in disputes, all involved in a conflict need the same set of facts and an understanding of the motives, choices, and actions that caused the conflict in order to bring about reconciliation and restitution.

So many issues become conflicts because one or both sides in disputes do not have the same information. This is especially true with issues involving students. All semester long a student has been turning in sub-standard work; his record also shows several missing or late assignments. The day before, he failed to turn in a rough draft for his research paper. The parents insist that in the past too much time with a girlfriend has been the problem but that problem has since been resolved. Their son broke up with her two weeks ago. They don't know why the paper was not turned in. The son insists that he was not aware of the due date. When the parents meet with the boy's teacher, the teacher produces the son's five-page handwritten note (written in a study hall) to a new girlfriend whom he has been seeing for the past two weeks. The student failed to do the work, lied to his teacher, deceived his parents, and found a new girlfriend. At last, everyone is now operating from the same set of facts!

Admittedly, sometimes the facts are not easy to pin down. A student is accused of plagiarism. The teacher had defined plagiarism for the class that week. But the parents think it is only a case of sloppy scholarship—their son knew he was quoting a source but simply was too lazy to cite it. They are certain he had no intention to deceive. Resolving that fact might affect the type of correction the student receives from the school. Two student papers are identical; it is clear one student copied from the other. Which student is it? Did the one student permit his friend to copy the paper or was he unaware that copying was going on? When the evidence is circumstantial, and students are not forthcoming, leaders must make the most reasonable judgment that they can and move on.

When there is a lack of communication, especially between school and home, parents tend to fill in the vacuum with their own conclusions. That is why frequent communication at every step of the resolution process is crucial. However, it is also true that given our sin nature and conflicting desires, especially our deep sense of entitlement and natural desire for justice, we are quick to make assumptions, judgments, and accusations along the way, clouding the facts and complicating matters even further with rabbit trails that lead away from resolving the main issues. Yes, a teacher's methods may be erratic, but that discussion is for another time because the issue right now is plagiarism and dishonesty. Yes, the student missed the teacher's verbal directions about an assignment change, but the assignment sheet online, which the parents were diligent to consult, did not reflect that change. And so on.

It is also important that everyone involved respects the reality of privileged perspectives. Very often there is one fact in someone's situation about which the other person knows nothing. Parents may have all the facts but one—the one held by the head of school or the student who has witnessed everything but has remained silent.

Teachers may look at the data on a particular child, but without knowing details of the child's home or personal life, conditions which may reveal the motives behind the low test scores or incomplete work, their assumptions and their remedies may be premature. Approaching initial meetings with humility and an open mind, keeping the possibility open that all information might not yet be on the table, is a wise approach.

Motives are more difficult to establish. A teenaged boy comes from a good home, with godly parents who are actively involved in the school community. To the best of everyone's knowledge, he is a typical boy, guilty only of small isolated acts of foolishness in the past. His heart is good, his grades are very good, and his moral sense has always been excellent.

But now he stands before the headmaster having been caught skipping on the day of standardized testing. The facts are clear. The day before the testing was to begin, the boy was told by his teacher he needed to be at school at a certain time to take his exams. Disobeying the teacher, he was discovered on the day of testing to be with public school friends at the State Fair. A phone call to parents revealed that he had lied to them in order to get spending money.

What would cause a good student from a good home to flagrantly disobey a teacher, lie to his parents, and skip school? Simple questions can reveal the root system of the motivations behind the deeds—it comes out that the student has severe, even debilitating test anxiety to the point that he cannot sleep the night before and completely locks up during test time. The year before on testing day he called in sick. The fear has been growing since junior high when he failed several tests. Parents discover that their son's fear of taking tests had become so strong that it eclipsed the child's moral judgment and led to his skipping school and even lying—something he had never done before.

When the facts, circumstances, and motivations have been established this step is complete. It is when all sides in a dispute can say, "This is what happened here and why." At that point, both sides can enter Phase 2 of the reconciliation process, the repentance and forgiveness stage.

RESOLVING CONFLICTS 2: REPENTANCE AND FORGIVENESS

It is surprising how handicapped and even paralyzed we can be when it comes to facing and resolving conflicts. It is a rare moment when people in conflict dig in, face the problem, and then come out victorious on the other side. That is because we have devised many clever, subtle, and not so subtle ways to rationalize our cowardice and our fears. "That headmaster is too busy," we say to ourselves. Or, "It just won't do any good to address that teacher because she never listens." Or, "That parent is always unreasonable and bullying, and he has probably already made up his mind."

As a result, we fail to hold others accountable for their actions. We also fail to resolve the actual issue and then repair the damage, which is why very soon the problem begins to fester. The offended one, rather than summoning the courage and good sense to initiate a conversation with the offending person, begins to tell others who are not involved with the issue all about it. This makes the teller feel very good; it gets it off her mind and usually wins sympathy from the hearer. However, telling others proves to be inflammatory and even hurtful to them; hearing only one side of the story and poisoned with the teller's biases and hurts, stirs their sense of injustice. A campaign of slander catches fire. The Accuser of our souls now has full permission to damage other people and injure the community even more.

When this happens, it is vital that those resolving the conflict reach Phase 2, where they must walk the perpetrator and victim through the stages of repentance and forgiveness. Choices have consequences usually in the form of hurting and humiliating others; the perpetrator must take responsibility for causing the injury, repent, and ask for forgiveness, while the wronged must extend forgiveness to the offender and move on. Yet we know repentance and a contrite heart cannot happen on demand. Neither is forgiveness easily extended. It takes time for both to occur and leaders must allow for it. A forced confession does no good and remorseful statements that occur only because the perpetrator happened to be caught have little value. How do we know repentance is authentic?

It is authentic when one sees godly sorrow in the offending person. That happens when he or she really sees up close and feels remorse for the pain he has caused another. That is why it is important to avoid endless one-on-one discussions and instead get all parties to meet together in the same place at the same time. Leaders need to create a safe environment for the victim to tell his story objectively, so that the offender can see, hear, and feel firsthand the damage he has caused to the other's heart. Once it appears the offender is truly sorry and the offended is willing to let it go and forgive, leaders need to bring the two adversaries together and work through the process of confession and acknowledgment, which in many cases is back and forth from both sides. One expresses remorse for his actions and the damage he has caused, the other forgives him and asks forgiveness for his sinful response.

It is important to keep in mind that repentance must occur at the level of the offense. Teachers, especially, but parents as well, need to understand this principle. Repentance should occur without shame, undue guilt, or humiliation. The fruit of repentance should be freedom and joy. If a student punches another student in the restroom, he does not repent in front of the entire class, but only to the one he has offended. When a football player punches a referee (yes, this happens in Christian schools), he has sinned at a very public level and has embarrassed the entire community. Therefore, he needs to own his offense at that level. If one person has been offended, then the offender goes to that person. If several have been injured, the offender apologizes to them alone and so on.

Phase 2 ends when the two adversaries are no longer adversaries but back to zero in their relationship, with neither holding anything against the other. However, the process is still not finished. Leaders must now bring correction/training and perhaps restitution to replace what was lost and clear the debt. That is Phase 3, when the two sides attempt to fully restore their relationship by fixing what was broken. Most conflicts never reach this stage. But what a glorious moment when they do!

RESOLVING CONFLICTS 3: CORRECTION, TRAINING, AND RESTITUTION

In every home or administrator's office, there should be a sign that reads: "You are not in trouble. You are in **TRAINING!**" This sentiment places disciplinary work in its proper perspective. Intimidation, punishment, and fear must give way to formation, sincere correction, and hope whenever someone in the school community injures another. The goal is to bring conviction to the offender's heart and point him in the right direction while compensating the victim for the wrongs suffered. Both correction and compensation, Phase 3 in the conflict resolution process, involve the offender making restitution.

Several scriptures, mostly in Exodus and Leviticus, outline the principle of restitution. "If a fire breaks outs and spreads into thornbushes so that it burns shocks of grain or standing grain or the whole field, the one who started the fire must make restitution" (Exodus 22:6). If someone commits a fault, he must repair the damage. Sometimes he must pay back double for something he stole. Sometimes he must add a percentage to the full amount. Restitution must come from the best of his flock and so on.

We must think of injuries suffered in various conflicts as a kind of theft. When one person wrongs another—as when a parent slanders a teacher, or a student lies to another student, or a teacher insults a student or an entire class—from the victim's perspective, something has been lost, something has been taken or stolen from him. That is why, in the healing and restoration phase of conflict resolution, the principle of restitution (in Hebrew the word means to make whole) is so important. Restitution is not punishment but an obligation undertaken by the offender to restore the other person to the level that existed before he suffered harm.

Slander and gossip damage a reputation and wound a human heart. Lies are a form of injury and perhaps even a kind of hate: "a lying tongue hates those it hurts" (Proverbs 26:28a). Theft or destruction obviously takes away costly property, while breaking school policies ruptures relationships and destroys trust. In each case, in order for a return to the status quo—relationships healed and damage repaired—the offender must make restitution of some kind.

Restitution is simply the application of justice to injuries or wrongs. If an athlete injures another's reputation, he needs to honor the victim and restore his reputation in the eyes of others. If a student breaks a window on the school bus, he needs to pay for a new window and its replacement. If a student steals money from the lunchroom, he must return the same amount, plus perhaps more to compensate the school for the inconvenience and loss of time. If a group of junior high students leaves the lunchroom in chaos, they need to clean it up themselves and apologize to the staff. If a teacher has insulted or judged another teacher or administrator, the teacher needs to take responsibility, apologize, and do whatever it takes to repair the damage he has caused.

Requiring student offenders to make restitution can be wonderfully redemptive. First, taking this step at all sometimes is the trigger that finally touches the offender's heart, even as it heals the victim's heart which is so crying out for the wrong to be made right. Second, it frees the offender from undue guilt and shame as he exchanges his role of destroyer, which is negative, to that of restorer, which is positive. All of this is necessary in order for both to be healed so that the relationship can move on. Third, if leaders conduct this process skillfully with fairness and compassion, they will be providing a mini-object lesson for all involved, giving them an unforgettable, real-life picture of the right way to mediate and heal broken relationships.

Resolving conflict in this way is demanding and exhausting, usually requiring several meetings (difficult to do with our busy schedules) to do it right. However, with patience, long-suffering, and self-sacrifice (essentially, the application of the virtues in James 3:17), the effort will prove to be wonderfully redemptive in the end.

TEACHER CULTURE

THE POWER OF A GREAT TEACHER

Gather a group of adults together and get them talking about the greatest teachers in their lives. Soon you will hear words like: "friendly," "caring," "loving," "encouraging," "compassionate," "warm," "kind," "humble," and "inspiring." They will eagerly tell you how those teachers helped them grow in confidence, courage, determination, value, and hope. You will hear them describe, perhaps even with tears, how they were motivated to work hard, achieve, and overcome challenging obstacles while under their leadership.

You will discover why these rare teachers made them feel intelligent, capable, important, safe, and special. You will understand why as students they eagerly desired to take their classes and why some continued to take classes with the same teachers again and again. You will be shocked to know these teachers were so powerful that when their students became adults some actually selected their professions because of them even though their classes were actually quite demanding and difficult. Then you will understand how great teachers light fires. How they fan the flames of confidence and hope. How they convince their students to believe they could succeed. You will know that the great teachers are those who consistently draw out of their students the wealth of talents, skills, and desires woven into them by God.

Some parents will choke up when trying to describe the influence of their greatest teachers. Many can easily remember even minor details from moments with them. Others will readily recall how those teachers served as examples of how to teach or manage others or even parent their own children. Parents will insist that these teachers affirmed and valued them as unique individuals but also taught them unforgettable lessons about many other things besides the subject matter. They taught lessons about life.

Good teachers equip and encourage students to believe they can meet and overcome any obstacle without fear of failure, without being discouraged by momentary setbacks. Good teachers unlock God-given ability and release God-given potential because they recognize God-given design. In doing so, they encourage their students to want to become better through application and effort. In many ways, good teachers set students free to become who they were meant to be. The power and the impact of such people can last for generations.

A handful of teachers like these can change the culture of the entire community. By merely being themselves they become the standard for all other teachers to follow. Their widespread good reputations become catalytic for the continued growth of the school. Parents will sacrifice whatever they can to enroll their children in their classes. High tuition will not dissuade them. Distance from their homes will not matter. They know that such teachers can absolutely change their children's lives. Therefore, leaders in traditional, classical, and University-Model® schools should challenge their teachers to become the *best* teachers they can possibly be, by God's grace.

A TEACHER'S INTIMACY WITH JESUS AND SELF-AWARENESS

Teachers cannot give what they do not have. They can only give what they have received. To receive anything requires humility, and that virtue comes from Jesus and the impartation of His grace and wisdom. **The single most important element in the making of a great teacher is his or her ongoing intimacy with Jesus.** The degree to which a teacher is intimate with the Master is the degree to which that teacher will be a whole human being and a powerful influence on young people.

As we grow in our knowledge of God by continuing to obey His commands, God reveals to us the truth of who we are, and that revelation is always painful and very discouraging. It exposes and strikes down the illusions we have believed about ourselves. We all are broken images of God, the result of growing up in a fallen world under the control of evil. Like Abraham, we too must leave our country, our people, and our father's household in order to discover and then possess the new identity God has for us (Genesis 12:1). That is, we must throw off all the shaping influences of our upbringing, what Peter called the "empty way of life handed down to you by your ancestors" (1 Peter 1:18b).

Then, in exchange, God gives us His love and goodness through the Holy Spirit, who sheds abroad the love of God in our hearts (Romans 5:5). The very Spirit that was in Christ becomes our possession. Like a personal trainer, the Holy Spirit reveals to us our true selves without masks, without fig leaves. The Spirit of Adoption frees us from our fears and puts us in touch with the love of the Father (Romans 8:15). The Spirit of Life energizes our souls (Romans 8:2). The Spirit of Truth renews our minds, making us more perfect in Christ (John 14:17). The Spirit of Holiness purifies us (Romans 1:4). The Spirit of Wisdom and Revelation teaches us the secrets of the King and His Kingdom (Ephesians 1:17).

As we "keep in step with the Spirit" (Galatians 5:25b), we experience wholeness and well-being. Centered in Christ, we become freer, more authentic, and more loving. We begin to feel at home in our skin. We believe we have a place in the world. Inevitably, because we have been fundamentally transformed at the core of our being, our relationships begin to change, because in this process we learn to see others differently also. As we become more like Christ and as our relationships become more wholesome and good, we become more effective teachers and more powerful witnesses for Christ.

Scripture tells us that being able to love is a function of having been forgiven. When Simon complained that a sinful woman was anointing Jesus with expensive perfume, Jesus replied with a story about two men who owed a man different amounts of money. Both debts were canceled, Jesus explained, so which of the two men will love the man more? "Simon replied, 'I suppose the one who had the bigger debt forgiven'" (Luke 7:43).

Jesus agreed and then listed the lavish acts of love given by the woman. He said in conclusion, "Therefore, I tell you, her many sins have been forgiven—as her great love has shown. But whoever has been forgiven little loves little" (Luke 7:47).

Without experiencing ongoing forgiveness through a real, living relationship with Jesus, we lack self-awareness and have no way of overcoming our natural brokenness. We, therefore, teach out of that brokenness and fear instead of out of wholeness and confidence. We may be Christian teachers but **we remain unhealed ones** and therefore we are capable of doing great damage to others, often without our knowing it.

Teachers are good to the extent they are real. But only Jesus can turn us into real people. Therefore, the greatest way to becoming a great teacher is to walk closely with the Lord, listening to His voice, obeying His commands, and keeping in step with His Spirit who empowers us to become whole—and in that way, we become a fragrance to God and a gift to others. We become what Oswald Chambers called "sacramental personalities," those rare saints who spread the fragrance of the knowledge of God to others wherever they go.[38]

---

[38] Chambers, *My Utmost for His Highest*, "The Delight of Sacrifice," February 24.

TEACHERS AND CORE VALUES

Much has been said about training students in the virtues, but rarely does action move beyond the rhetoric. Is merely teaching students "about" them the best we can do? There is a huge difference between a student learning about boldness in a twenty-minute chapel presentation and that student being trained by someone who is zealous to develop that virtue in him over time according to a specific plan.

Christian schools need a more carefully thought-out global approach to training students to embrace and love the virtues, not through moralistic Bible verses or simplistic chapel teachings but through mentors who disciple students to prioritize intimacy with the Lord so they can grow in wisdom and the gifts of His Spirit. If teachers and coaches do not **intend** to disciple students in the virtues, students will never possess them. Only a total **culture of virtue** can bring this about. Coaches, teachers, staff, parents, and families must move together in the same cultural atmosphere until virtuous language and habits become unconscious and natural throughout the community. Assemblies, parent meetings, information meetings, orientation meetings, and board meetings need to consistently reflect this same culture of virtue.

Those who should teach the virtues are those who actually possess them. Because the virtues of God are liberally distributed in His people who collectively represent Him, all the adults in a school community can potentially be in-the-flesh models of specific virtues. However, the classroom teacher's role is vital. Because the teacher has the most consistent contact with students, the teacher is the principal means for students to see the virtues displayed.

Administrators can help teachers become more intentional in modeling the virtues in three ways. First, they must help teachers to see their roles as mentors tasked with the responsibility to disciple their students not only academically but also morally and spiritually. Then administrators need to give teachers core values/virtues training that will help them to know how to do this. Finally, leaders need to hold teachers (and coaches) accountable for developing concrete plans for weaving the virtues into daily classroom activities and procedures. The virtues need to be an organic part of the class, not tacked on to existing material. Since the teacher loves and demonstrates a particular virtue or set of virtues already, this should be easy and natural to do.

Let's say a teacher noted for enthusiasm determines to impart that trait to her students for a year. She puts posters on the wall illustrating it. She associates the trait with any class content that she can and talks about it often. She tells students why she loves it so. She demonstrates it herself so that students can "see" it. She has students rate themselves on their degree of it. Whenever she can, she points out threats to that virtue—apathy, boredom, laziness—and warns against their dangers. The teacher consistently and purposefully models enthusiasm in the natural daily conversation of the class.

The teacher might also create exercises that will expose her students' need for enthusiasm or require them to practice it. In an English class, she might select a tedious reading or an activity that is pure drudgery and then coach the students through it, teaching them how to generate the enthusiasm they need to overcome the obstacle. Seeing long, tedious assignments as a way to practice this trait is a powerful way to make the trait real. Or, she simply looks for the natural places in the class where this virtue is expected. A difficult test, a hard stretch of homework, a research paper, are all occasions where the virtue can be discussed and applied. Soon it becomes clear that she is not merely developing in her students a single virtue; she is teaching them a valuable life lesson—a positive way to approach any hard task or difficult obstacle.

At the end of the school year, because the teacher has "framed" her class with this virtue, students will associate the teacher with it and be a little more disposed to desire it for themselves, especially if they have seen what it is and have been honored for demonstrating it. And whenever students recall this teacher in the future, they will think, "She lived and breathed enthusiasm!"—a sure indicator that the teacher has made a real difference.

If every teacher in the school could represent just one virtue in this way every year, would not the collective impact on the school community be tremendous? Moreover, if the parents themselves could receive the same training from school leaders so that virtues practiced at the school would be reinforced in the home, then this growing culture of virtue could be very powerful indeed.

EXERCISING AUTHORITY, BEING AUTHORITARIAN, AND TRUTH

Ever since the great social revolution of the 1960s, when it became fashionable to distrust "the establishment" and not trust "anyone over 30," the concept of authority has become ever more blurry. Today, anyone exercising "rightful" authority will sometimes draw the charge that he or she is being "authoritarian." In other words, the mere exercise of authority is a bad thing.

Being authoritarian implies a coerced submission to authority where obedience is strongly enforced, even compelled. In our day, it is associated with being tyrannical, controlling, and repressive. Think of a screaming, overbearing athletic coach and you get the idea.

Exercising authority, however, is very different. It means "rightful" authority, the idea that one has power granted by law to prescribe rules or give orders. Here, think of any civil magistrate, like a county judge whose authority is legal and necessary for the ordering of civil society. Being authoritarian, then, refers to the way or manner in which one rules while exercising authority speaks of the right, responsibility, and duty to rule.

Because these two concepts are so blurred in our day, those exercising true authority will often be criticized for being authoritarian. The mere application of discipline and structure to establish order will generate this criticism. Following principles or policies as they should be followed might bring on accusations of legalism and tyranny. High grading standards, strict fairness in discipline, and no cutting of deals or shortcuts will sometimes invite abuse from parents who think that merely by trying his best, their child should be handsomely rewarded. Our times are so confused that parents end up criticizing the very teachers their children need most—the ones unapologetically exercising godly authority with firmness, fairness, and wisdom.

Fear of exercising authority often shows up in tentative language. Listen to leaders and public speakers today. Rather than confidently stating simple truths or propositions as they must always do, leaders have become evasive, vague, apologetic, and conciliatory, afraid of saying the wrong thing because they don't want to come across as being authoritarian and offending someone. And so, leadership is becoming more about not offending people rather than simply telling the truth and motivating others in a worthy cause.

Speaking about the nature of truth and its proclamation, William F. Buckley, in *God and Man at Yale* wrote: "...truth can never win unless it is promulgated. Truth does not carry within itself an antitoxin to falsehood. The cause of truth must be championed, and it must be championed dynamically."[39] Buckley is saying that the mere presence of truth in the public square is not enough to combat error and falsehood. Why? Because anyone who attempts to bring correction in the public square invites hatred, insults, and abuse (Proverbs 9:7-8). Just as Wisdom struggles to be heard out in the streets (Proverbs 8:1-3), truth competes with deception, error, and falsehoods from the world, the flesh, and the devil in the same arena. To champion truth, therefore, requires a very special type of person. It takes a man or woman of exceptional courage and boldness. It requires leaders to exercise their rightful authority courageously, with all goodness, and without fear.

---

[39] William F. Buckley, *God and Man at Yale* (Washington: Regnery Gateway, 1986), 141.

ENCOURAGING A GROWTH MINDSET

One of the most valuable things a parent, teacher, or an administrator can instill in a student besides knowledge of a subject area is a basic attitude or stance about approaching a subject—and even life itself—in a way that will bring success. That attitude is what has been called a "growth mindset" or an "overcoming mindset." It is characterized by grit, determination, and perseverance when addressing a challenging problem, and a belief that sees failure as a temporary condition rather than a permanent one.[40]

We tend to forget the one common exhortation to the seven churches in the book of Revelation is for God's people to conquer, to overcome: "To the one who is victorious, I will give the right to eat from the tree of life, which is in the paradise of God" (Revelation 2:7). The more practical working out of this attitude is expressed in a popular book by Carol Dweck called *Mindset: The New Psychology of Success*, a book which, though secular, contains much truth for leaders in traditional, classical, and University-Model® Christian schools.

Contrasting the growth mindset, which sees intelligence and personality as changeable, with the fixed mindset, which sees them as permanent and unchanging, Dweck argues that *"the view you adopt for yourself* profoundly affects the way you lead your life." The fixed mindset, she claims, "creates an urgency to prove yourself over and over," while the growth mindset relies on the fact that "your basic

---

[40] Carol S. Dweck, *Mindset: The New Psychology of Success* (New York: Ballantine, 2006), 6-7.

qualities are things you can cultivate through your efforts," because "everyone can change and grow through application and experience.[41]

Dweck discovered that students with fixed mindsets often were afraid to try new things for fear of failure. Believing one has to prove himself over and over often generates this fear. Students with growth mindsets, however, were eager to accept new challenges and grow because they had a passion for learning that enabled them to leap over setbacks, which they viewed not as failures but as challenges to overcome.[42]

Students would tremendously benefit from having this mindset not only when facing the typical academic problems at school, but also when facing spiritual challenges. Confronting a difficult assignment in a subject that does not come easy, dealing with lower scores than expected on a standardized college entrance exam, or falling short of perfection even in a subject or activity in which the student excels are all ways students might benefit from adopting this mindset.

Spiritually speaking, struggling with a personal sin, choosing to maintain faith when God does not seem to be talking, or dealing with great hurt and loss indicate that a growth mindset is, at root, a faith mindset. As we trust the Lord, we can keep moving through setbacks, disappointments, and unmet expectations because we know God is a good Father and in the end, all things will work together for our good.

Creating a home, classroom, and school-wide culture which promotes a growth mindset should be a priority of everyone in the school community. This would mean, of course, that teachers, administrators, and parents would have to adopt this way of thinking themselves. Regardless, every sphere of the school's culture, from the classroom to the chapel to the athletic field, should encourage this positive, overcoming spirit, this refusal to give up, this limitless courage to work harder until the student solves the problem or overcomes the obstacle.

---

[41] Ibid.

[42] Ibid., 31-34, 39.

SHAPING CLASS IDENTITY

Seasoned teachers know that every class has the potential to express itself in a unique corporate identity, a special "personality." This special identity is a combination of student demographics understood and managed by the wisdom and maturity of the instructor. It is something that can be discovered and encouraged or suppressed and ignored. When it is affirmed, students will actually be eager to come to class because there is a special charm, a sweetness, something ineffably good about being there.

This class "chemistry" comes from various combinations of extroverts and introverts, males and females, athletes and artists, and other elements like student age and maturity levels, family dynamics, intellectual abilities, and so on. Even such things as the physical look of the classroom, the time of day the class meets, the relationship of the class to the lunch hour, or to other classes can come to bear upon this. Mature teachers will discern and understand the elements that shape the mood of their classes and then adapt their approaches and methods to tease out this personality in a way that is healthy, positive, and good.

Building a class identity begins when the teacher is dedicated to creating a safe place for everyone. Safety leads to freedom and freedom leads to self-expression. When students feel free to let their guards down and drop their masks, when they feel free to "be themselves," their individual and collective creativity and originality naturally come out. Creating this safety requires the teacher to be confident and bold in setting firm boundaries. It also requires the teacher to be well-planned and organized, to control reckless and destructive comments, and to correct the more undisciplined students early on rather than tolerate unacceptable behavior until it becomes toxic.

Teachers also must have the spiritual discernment to "see" each student's goodness and God-given design and then call it out. Praise, encouragement, and humor go a long way here. The student with a genuine sense of humor, the one who thinks creatively, the one with the engineering mind, or the student with the positive, happy personality should be affirmed in natural, unflattering ways, whenever each particular gift reveals itself. In this way, the teacher "blesses into being" the gifts in each one and in doing so gives each student his or her special "place" in the classroom.

In this environment, students cannot help but prosper. Besides feeling deeply valued, they will feel they belong to something larger than themselves—they will understand themselves as part of a group, something which produces feelings not unlike those one feels when belonging to a close-knit team. In a small way, in such a class, they will experience *participation in genuine community*.

Students in classes like these will be tremendous players in classroom dynamics all year long, and they will return with pleasure to visit years after they graduate because they shared an experience and sense of belonging found in few other places.

DETERMINING LEADERSHIP
MINDSETS WHERE WE WORK

Think of yourself as a leader at whatever level in your school or organization right now. Maybe you are a parent, teacher, or an administrator, or perhaps a director or board member. Wisdom from Proverbs will help you determine the quality of your leadership mindset.

1. Are you someone who can easily take advice or do you come across as a know-it-all? If you can take advice, you can justly be called wise and will always be open to change and growth (Proverbs 13:10). If you are a know-it-all, most likely other workers experience a sense of competition and intimidation around you, making them unwilling to share ideas freely—the very thing you need for growth and progress!

2. Do you love instruction? Do you love to grow and expand the knowledge of your craft or strengthen your sphere of influence? If not, as the Proverb says, "Whoever scorns instruction will pay for it" (13:13a)—that is, you will be costly to yourself and to your organization. In order to be a continual blessing to those around us, we are obliged to keep growing, to remain open to new ideas and be willing to accept challenges and change. This is especially true for teachers who have taught for many years and for parents who might think they have little to learn after raising one or two children.

3. No matter what your position or title, can you accept commands? This actually ties in with having a desire to grow. "Whoever scorns instruction will pay for it, but whoever respects a command is rewarded" (13:13). Those who can accept commands are those who do not scorn instruction; they have the humility to do what they are told and the desire to improve themselves. As a result, they prosper and contribute to the prosperity of the organization overall.

4. Are you able to take correction without condemnation? If so, then you will always be in a position to grow, improve, and widen your range of influence. The result might surprise you— you will be honored: "Whoever disregards discipline comes to poverty and shame, but whoever heeds correction is honored" (13:18). People who can receive constructive criticism and take correction indirectly demonstrate their commitment to the organization. By acknowledging their flaws, mistakes, or limitations and being willing to remedy them, they improve and become more productive, a change which adds more to the organization and ultimately brings them success and honor.

5. Do you spend time seeking out and learning from others who have greater knowledge, skill, or wisdom? This means you do not see your intellect or abilities as "fixed" and unchanging but as capable of growing and developing through effort and determination.[43] "Walk with the wise and become wise, for a companion of fools suffers harm" (13:20). Others will either stretch us to make us better or pull us down to make us worse. They will bring to us honor or shame.

The one common denominator in each of these texts from the Proverbs is the virtue of humility. When students have this virtue, they will improve rapidly and grow in confidence. When parents have this virtue, they will be able to acknowledge serious parenting mistakes and make course corrections in time to save their children. With this virtue, teachers will never stagnate and the impact of their instruction will be greater. They will become more influential. When administrators and board members possess this virtue, they will listen to counsel from

---

[43] Ibid., 7.

outsiders who at first might seem to know less. Humility makes a person teachable, open to correction, able to take commands or advice from others, and willing to learn and grow in order to make himself and his peers better at what they do.

HOW PERSONAL BROKENNESS
AFFECTS TEACHING

Great teachers have "presence." There is a gravity or magnitude about them—one knows when they are in the room. They have an aura of respectability and carry themselves with authority. They have great power and influence. Their words matter and people listen to them. Because of this, they are honored and respected.

Presence is a mysterious combination of personal well-being, self-acceptance, faith in God, and wholeness. It is more than charisma. It includes experience, skill, emotional and spiritual maturity, and wisdom. One does not come by it easily or instantaneously. It is the mark of persons richly souled and in secure possession of their true selves. Their very lives are the will of God. They bless others wherever they go because they are walking in those "good works" God planned for them long ago (Ephesians 2:10).

Many things can eclipse a teacher having this kind of presence. Every person has a wound, a blind spot, a limitation, and a weakness of some kind, and teachers are no different. Personal brokenness very definitely affects teaching, and that is why when we are healed and restored, our teaching naturally improves. The more we mature in love, the more compassionate, merciful, forgiving, and just we will become, and any one of these virtues cannot fail to change the way we teach and relate to others.

An insecure teacher will crave affirmation from students and will be tempted to compromise the integrity of the class to do so. Timid or fearful teachers will shy away from setting standards and confronting students and parents when needed. Angry teachers will carry anger and blame into the classroom and might over-emphasize rules and regulations. Their classrooms will be rigid and stifling. Proud teachers, thinking they have nothing to learn, will never grow, but they will always believe they are the best at what they do and they can become very good at criticizing others.

Teachers who have no personal boundaries will generally be reluctant or unable to set boundaries; they will treat students unfairly and tolerate their bad habits instead of confronting them. Their students will never grow up. Teachers gifted with mercy, without the necessary checks and balances, will fail to hold the line in terms of school and class policies and might not be willing to confront problems as quickly and forcefully as they should, causing them to fester.

Teachers who might have been over-disciplined growing up might become lax and under-disciplined as adults. Emotionally needy teachers might resort to mothering students while wounded and unhealed teachers might appear unfriendly and cold-hearted. Teachers who have been controlled and stymied or who have experienced tremendous injustice in their personal lives will seek justice by becoming tyrants who will over-control their students in the name of having high standards. Teachers who have been hurt will hurt others. **We teach and act from the grid of our own brokenness.** That is why the healing of the soul always produces a better person and a better teacher.

As we are healed through an active personal relationship with Jesus and through consistent involvement in a community of believers who hold us accountable—and whose spiritual gifts are for our edification—we grow in presence and power. We become fuller, richer, stronger souls. We become more loving, less selfish, and more open to giving and serving. We learn the great Christian virtue of self-acceptance. We no longer fear others or are intimidated by stronger people. Our relationships grow stronger because we ourselves are stronger. We become free and that freedom absolutely comes out in our teaching.

No one ever fully arrives at this. In fact, the best teachers know they will learn something more about themselves, their students, or their teaching, in general, every year, and they are eager to incorporate and apply that new knowledge quickly for the next term. Humility does that and growing in the knowledge of God does that. This is why humility is the one indispensable virtue of a great teacher—this virtue allows the Lord to expose and then heal the natural brokenness that prevents us from being whole men and women, mature Christians, and effective teachers.

A TYPOLOGY OF TEACHERS

Teachers are the nuclear fuel of a school's culture. Their performance individually and collectively year after year shapes local public opinion and defines the school as friendly or mean, challenging or easy, ancient or modern, legalistic or liberating. A single outstanding teacher will bring many families to the school. A single substandard teacher will be the reason they leave. Because teachers have enormous power to shape a culture and forever alter a student's life, administrators must be vigilant and wise in their selection and training of this most important people group in their schools.

Economies obey the laws of supply and demand. The most in-demand teachers will get hired with competitive pay. Those not so much in demand will fare less well. Our schools, however, are governed by higher laws, the laws of the Kingdom. The best teachers are the ones the Lord brings after faithful prayer—regardless of the market. Our Christian school leaders can decide which law they wish to follow. It all comes down to faith. An administrator with little faith will hire teachers according to economic necessities. Leaders have made many mistakes because they hired teachers out of fear and desperation. If administrators have great faith, they will wait until the Lord brings the teachers He wishes to send. He may not send them according to our timetables. The "best" teachers are those who come after administrators have spent a lot of time on their knees.

We must qualify "best," because if we do not understand Kingdom ways we can be disappointed. The "best" teachers are the ones sent by the Lord, irrespective of their skill or maturity. We cannot assume that because we have prayed, the Lord will send us the most outstanding people. The Almighty has His own purposes.

Very often, sending His very best is exactly what He does. The just-recently-retired Marine Corp pilot, who feels called to help the younger generation. The engineer who feels an unreasonable urge to abandon a lucrative career to teach a worldview class. The former home-schooling mom who is infinitely more competent than her public-school counterparts because she is a woman of faith, passion, and wisdom even though she does not have a degree in her field. God can and often does send amazing men and women as a result of faithful prayer.

Sometimes, however, the teachers God sends do not seem to be those with the experience, maturity, or skills we might desire. God works in very strange ways sometimes. He might send a teacher we may need to let go at the end of the year but who has gained a great deal of personal insight about herself in the process. Failure very often is God's means of training us. He may send teachers that will rub some long-standing and well-loved parents the wrong way, causing them to leave the school. That teacher, then, could be His catalytic instrument for great change for the families and for the school. He might send apparently good teachers who experience tremendous personal, financial, and spiritual hardship for a few years and then find better jobs elsewhere. In those cases, God has brought them to train and test them for more difficult roles later.

Through prayer, God might also send strong or weak teachers because He wants to change something in us or in our schools. He might send a very strong teacher to call the school to higher teaching standards. He might send a less able teacher to urge the school to refine its teacher orientation program. He might send a teacher with nominal teaching skills but who in a few years will become a director or dean of some other area. He might send a parent who might teach for a year, taking in the school's culture and traditions, because He is training a future board member who will then become the next headmaster. Our job is to pray and discern whom God is sending. We have to choose our teachers by faith knowing that very often we do not know what God is doing until we see or hear about the results much later.

Still, obviously, administrators are duty-bound to find and train great teachers. If they intend to build a positive school culture they need to find teachers who have a combination of experience, emotional and spiritual maturity, professional skills, and liberal doses of that mysterious ineffable quality called "presence." They also need to know which types of teachers to avoid and which types they are able to work with and improve. The following typology of teachers may help. In general, teachers will exhibit a blend of negative and positive characteristics derived from five general types.

The Critic. Generally unhappy much of the time and sometimes even tyrannical, this type of teacher chooses to express personal frustrations and unhappiness through constant criticism of students, parents, or administrators. This teacher is dealing with great pain but does not know what to do about it. He or she may not even be aware that personal pain is causing the negative behavior. A bad marriage, a disappointing child, a stunted career, and/or anger at God are among the several backstories which could explain the behavior. This person suffers from bitterness of soul. While the Critic may be professionally very good, even excellent, the constant general negativity of this kind of teacher is toxic and destructive. The teacher must be affirmed in his (or her) excellent qualities but confronted about his disposition. Just as teachers need to know a student's background in order to best help a student, administrators should know something about a teacher's background to help the teacher. A wise, compassionate, and patient administrator needs to sit down with the teacher, point out the behaviors, explore the causes, and suggest a plan of correction as soon as possible.

The Minimalist. This type of teacher suffers mainly from a defect in will. Getting hired seems to be the summit of her efforts. She sits down often, teaching from her desk. She manages class activities more than she teaches. Free time is often spent on her cell phone. She lacks passion and drive and, for that reason, displays little motivation to change bad habits, challenge herself, or learn new skills. She (or he) will become irritated when called to improve because she believes she is doing fairly well already. She sees her work in terms of a job for her personal benefit rather than as a ministry to and for others. As a result, her product is mediocre: the best students grow little and the weaker students do not get the help they need. Correction is very difficult because it takes many classroom visits, bold, specific suggestions for change, constant monitoring, and narrow timetables. Very often, the

Minimalist suffers from a weak self-concept; he or she has been unaffirmed and/or wounded, and her brokenness shows up in a sluggish will or in a lack of motivation. There are more teachers in this category than we should like to think.[44]

The Controller. In this type, over-control and a veneer of toughness in the name of high standards mask deep insecurities. The control is protective; it creates distance between students and the teacher who often comes across as unfriendly, detached, and cold. In reality, this type of teacher has an impoverished view of self and does not know how to relate to students except when he or she is in control. Such teachers therefore "need" the protection that comes from a rigidly structured environment even while they eagerly desire to be accepted. Their classrooms are often humorless and unexciting. Students may learn and even prosper because the structure alone is beneficial, but they do so with little freedom or pleasure. Administrators might find empirical data gleaned from student/parent questionnaires along with pointed teacher evaluations as points of departure for correction and change. Since this type of teacher also lacks a healthy self-concept, encouragement and praise can help unlock the problems and spur improvement.

The Mercy-Minded. Grade inflation and enabling are the pitfalls of the mercy-minded. Well-meaning and often with beautiful hearts, this kind of teacher sometimes acts from a place of "unsanctified mercy," when firmness, decisiveness, and courage are what is truly needed. Such teachers feel great sympathy for those who struggle. They cannot bear to see a student fail. Both are wonderful characteristics desperately needed in our schools. However, such teachers can be so mercy-minded they will alter standards to accommodate weaker students, sometimes giving special privileges and options other students do not have. This can weaken students even more. Such teachers do not realize that by enabling these students they create an unfair learning environment for all. As a result, they fail to reach objectives and deadlines. Their mercy is not tempered by wisdom; their emotions are not balanced out by fortitude. Administrators can help them with encouragement and close

---

[44] A need in the Body of Christ is for effective pastoral care ministries programs designed specifically for Christian teachers.

monitoring, using a specific growth plan that holds them accountable for structuring their classes well and staying true to course objectives.

The Unforgettable. These are the difference-makers in a school community. These are the teachers who change lives. They exhibit professional excellence and spiritual maturity. Because of their intimacy with God, they become "sacramental personalities"— everyone who comes in contact with them walks away encouraged, enriched, affirmed, or inspired.[45] This teacher is a master of her discipline, displaying a repertoire of skills and creative methods that will motivate the most difficult class. She is affirming, positive, warm, and enthusiastic, but also able to blend firmness and fairness, fun and hard work, control and freedom. Her course is thrilling and difficult, but students are eager to attend and will still be seeking her out years afterward. Parents will literally wait for years so that their children can take her classes. He or she is the kind of teacher administrators eagerly desire: **a creative, mature, highly-trained professional called by the Lord to disciple others.**

---

[45] Oswald Chamber's term. See "The Delight of Sacrifice," in *My Utmost for His Highest*, February 24.

TEACHING TIPS #1

Talking is not teaching. A common assumption among teachers is that simply talking about their subject matter means they are teaching it. Not so. Talking is talking but teaching is a combination of **skills** and creative **methods** exercised to carry out a **plan** which fulfills an **objective**. The intent is for students to "get it," to pick up the information, skill, or concept the teacher requires. The intention is to meet or exceed the standard or objective. Teaching, therefore, includes holding students accountable for what is taught and encouraging them to take responsibility for learning it.

Teaching definitely is not the mere management of class activities, a cobbling together of small groups, worksheets, skits, power point slides, or board work. It is a carefully-planned, objective-driven sharing and impartation of knowledge through specific and diverse methods, followed by practice, correction, and progressive degrees of evaluation.

Your word is your bond. Since learning is based on trust, teachers need to be trustworthy and do what they say. If they create a policy and state the consequences for breaking that policy, they need to do exactly what they say and follow through. Teachers in the habit of making promises and then breaking them will eventually acquire the "boy who cried wolf" syndrome and will no longer be trusted. Students will disregard their words. This, of course, is a character issue for the teacher who needs to remember to let his "yes" be "yes" and his "no" be "no."

Never make excuses. We are modeling the behavior and character we wish to impart to our students. If we do not want them to get through life by making excuses, we should not make excuses. We are not absolved of having to display the character traits that we value. If a teacher thinks punctuality is important, then the teacher needs to be punctual. If a teacher thinks thoroughness is a valuable trait, she needs to show it. If a teacher promises something and cannot deliver, the teacher needs to apologize or give a reasonable explanation, but not an excuse.

Avoid habits of compromise. Over the course of a year, students can wear teachers down. If teachers are not vigilant and strong, they may imperceptibly compromise on small matters. This is the beginning of a slackening of standards and an unraveling of classroom order. Students will notice and take advantage of it. Signs of compromise include increasingly altering deadlines, allowing entertainment or time-fillers to replace teaching, bargaining with students over difficult assignments, and not holding students accountable for obeying school policies.

Give students your full attention. Teachers who give students their undivided attention communicate value to their students and become responsible stewards of a finite and dwindling commodity—time. Conducting personal business, texting friends, or checking one's phone calls during class is irresponsible. Walking around and observing when students are working or listening when they discuss issues in small groups can give the teacher valuable insights on how students are faring. Students working quietly on assignments or tests is not automatic "time off" for the teacher—the teacher still needs to be available, interested, and involved in what students are doing.

TEACHING TIPS #2

Admit wrongs. We make mistakes. The way we handle our mistakes (taking responsibility, not making excuses, nor denying that we erred) will have a powerful impact on those students who are intently watching us and are quick to evaluate the kind of adults that we are. That is to say, our character is on the line. Making mistakes does not diminish our authority. We must own our mistakes and correct them to **maintain** our authority. Humility is the key. Humility is the virtue that can admit wrongs, ask for forgiveness, and then do what it takes to restore the status quo.

Few rules, simple rules. Excessively rule-bound teachers can create a stifling learning environment that students will find discouraging. Rules should exist to create order so that freedom will occur. Teachers should keep rules to a minimum and make sure they are simple, clear, and enforceable. Adam and Eve were forbidden to eat from only one tree in the garden. Jesus said all the law and commandments rested on two commandments. Rules exist to provide a life-giving and productive classroom where all students have the liberty to grow.

Turn weaknesses into strengths. Every teacher, from the novice to the veteran, will benefit from frequent, objective, and detailed teacher evaluations. We all have strengths and weaknesses. We can always grow in some area, always expand our wisdom and knowledge. Polishing lecture skills, organizing a good lesson, selecting creative and effective methods, asking good questions, or just sticking to the point in a class discussion are skills which we can always improve.

Celebrate a growth mindset. Create an overcomer's mindset at the very beginning of the course. When a particularly difficult assignment or test comes up, take the opportunity to talk about grit, perseverance, and overcoming that obstacle; that is, use the circumstance to discuss some real life lessons. This overcomer's mindset says that failure is momentary and that each student can improve with a good plan, lots of encouragement, and hard work.[46] Difficult assignments will expose beliefs and fears students have about themselves. When challenging class circumstances reveal these beliefs, the teacher can focus on encouraging students and teaching them how to move past the obstacles.

Your expertise or your influence? Teachers communicate so much more than information and knowledge about a subject matter. They are always conveying a certain orientation, right or wrong, to life, to the world, and to God. Students are longing to know how life really works, how to live out their faith in a world which is so confusing. They are looking to their teachers to provide answers. In a way, they are looking for surrogate parents. They are always attentive to how we speak, how we think, what we say, how we live and respond to challenges, whether we are walking the walk at all. Your greatest impact on a student may not have anything to do with your teaching. Your attitudes, faith, authenticity, and love—these will make the greatest impact.

---

[46] Dweck, 32-34.

WHAT IS A STUDENT?

Each student is a marvelous, mysterious, utterly unique creation of God. Each student is also a terribly flawed mixture of weaknesses and limitations all wrapped up in a sin nature that easily inclines him to do the wrong things at the wrong times for the wrong reasons, often while taking great pleasure in doing so.

Students have fears, biases, and different degrees of knowledge, deception, and confusion. They come from intact families and broken families with parents who themselves are hurting, damaged, and still under the influence of a culture antithetical to common sense, wisdom, and truth. They come from different religious traditions with widely differing—sometimes even competing—beliefs and various degrees of error.

We know there are very few exclusively academic problems, most of them involve a character issue, a deficiency in the virtues which at root reveals disordered desires. However, character issues often show up in unhealthy home environments, which means teachers must address or at least be aware of the conditions that cause them. In our day, caring for students requires teachers to not only evaluate a student's behavior and performance but also to know something about the student's home life which, more likely than not, is undercutting the very values the teacher is trying to teach.

Fear can so shut down a student's thinking that he might appear unintelligent or confused. Relational breakdowns such as a divorce will often cause a student to become self-focused, distracted, indifferent, or lazy. Resentment toward a parent or teacher for an infraction long forgotten can affect years of a student's behavior if repentance, forgiveness, and restoration of the relationship do not happen. Intimidation, another form of fear, can make a student appear shy or incompetent. Financial troubles at home can make a student distracted, rebellious, uninhibited, or ashamed.

Students are fallen, broken images of God, and that fact alone justifies a thorough and disciplined education by teachers who sincerely love them. Love will find a way to reach the most difficult of students. Love will also strive to create a balanced learning environment—one that is not only safe, pleasant, and friendly, but also ordered, disciplined, and fair. Kind words cheer students up and pleasant words not only promote instruction but can begin the healing process in each of them (Proverbs 12:25; 16:21, 24). That is because "the tongue of the wise brings healing" (Proverbs 12:18b). Understanding this, the wise teacher can, therefore, be a powerful agent of healing for young people. As far as possible, that teacher will want to know and understand the larger contexts in which the student lives and be willing to sacrifice the time and energy necessary to help that student make sense of his world and overcome personal obstacles in order to succeed.

UPGRADING STUDENT DISCIPLINE: HEART-MOTIVES-CHOICES-CONSEQUENCES

Every junior high and high school classroom contains recognizable behavior types, each with its own challenges. However, if moral instruction is integral to the school's mission and educators want to pay more than mere lip service to it, they should understand their students from a **heart-motives-choices-consequences mindset.** This is an approach to discipline which seeks correction and change through a positive relationship and intelligent dialogue with the student rather than through traditional methods of punishment involving intimidation and fear.

Many academic misbehaviors are at root character issues involving deficiencies in virtues rather than a lack of "skills." So-called academic problems become more understandable when teachers use questions to probe student **choices**, which derive from what students actually **value** or believe in their **hearts**. Reflecting on the **consequences** of their choices can reveal what those conscious or unconscious values or beliefs really are.

Let's say a student consistently hands in substandard work, giving only the minimum effort to pass. Several causes could explain the problem. Has the student become bored, apathetic, distracted, or too busy with other priorities? A change in circumstances, perhaps a major disappointment caused by a layoff, a sickness, or a death in the family could be the cause. Because teachers are caring for minds and souls, implying a consistent relationship of some depth, the teacher needs to have a private conversation with the student to get at the root of what is really going on. Very often, success depends on finding the lie, compromise, or erroneous belief fueling the wrong behavior.

Teachers need to understand that the student has chosen to turn in substandard work. Consequences in the form of correction need to be wisely applied based on the reason behind that choice. Is the father out of town a lot and therefore not able to exert his influence and keep the child to a higher standard? That would call for training in self-discipline while conducting a few discussions about trust. Are the parents going through a divorce? That would call for encouragement and perhaps mercy and compassion. Has the student lost his favorite grandparent to cancer? One does not quickly recover from grief and sometimes grief, disappointment, or despair can show up as apathy. Or perhaps the student fears failure? Unpacking fears takes time and prayer. Fear of a particular subject matter could also generate the apathy the student feels when doing school work. Or are we to simply pass over the problem? Have the student's best friends moved away leaving him lonely and alone? Is he being bullied? Finding the cause generates its own solution, and solutions obviously can be very different depending on whether the student is grieving, despairing, angry, afraid, or lazy.

When teachers or parents are able to point out root causes, often the immediate result in the student is hope; something he may not have understood at all suddenly appears in a different light. He sees a way out. Teacher, student, and parent can then produce a plan of correction that will get right to the "heart" of the matter and solve the problem.

This approach honors the student and shows care. It encourages students to reflect on their choices, motives, values, and beliefs—precisely what we want to see happen! It allows them to evaluate their responses to ever-changing life-circumstances, to participate in a plan of correction, and to take responsibility for their actions. Such an approach is constructive and redemptive; it can absolutely change a student's life.

GOD'S STRATEGY FOR DISCIPLINE
PART 1: DEALING WITH CAIN

The story of God's dealing with Cain is instructive for how teachers, parents, and school leaders can query students to reveal issues of the heart that have caused discipline problems. In this story, which appears in Genesis 4, we find God using **a series of questions** to reveal Cain's motives, choices, actions, and their consequences.

1. "In the course of time Cain brought some of the fruits of the soil as an offering to the LORD" (4:3). *Cain, first of all, makes a* **choice** *to present a certain kind of offering to God.*

2. "And Abel also brought an offering–fat portions from some of the firstborn of his flock" (4:4a). *Evidently, Cain's offering was substandard and did not reflect full devotion to the Lord.*

3. "The LORD looked with favor on Abel and his offering, but on Cain and his offering he did not look with favor" (4:4b-5a). *There was a* **consequence** *to Cain's choice: God did not look with favor on Cain and his offering.*

4. "So Cain was very angry" (4:5b). *Cain was angry because God did not accept him (4:5a). Cain, it should be noted,* **chose** *to become angry, but this was not his only choice. He could have chosen to be contrite. Cain's choice to become angry, however, then led to the next* **choice.**

5. "and his face was downcast" (4:5c). *Is a downcast face, sadness, the result of indulging great anger? Perhaps. Nevertheless, the emotion of sadness appeared in Cain's face.*

6. "Then the LORD said to Cain, 'Why are you angry? Why is your face downcast?'" (4:6). *God's discipline involves the method of* **simple questions**. *In this passage, God asks Cain five different questions before He announces the consequences of Cain's choices.*

7. "'If you do what is right, will you not be accepted? But if you do not do what is right, sin is crouching at your door; it desires to have you, but you must rule over it'" (4:7). *God asks the third question. Then, seeing evidence of wrong, the Lord intervenes with preventative, corrective discipline. The Lord defines the correct choice of behavior and adds a warning about the dangers of choosing wrongly. God, in other words, is giving Cain a picture of reality; He is countering Cain's choices by telling him the truth—"sin is crouching at your door." He is trying to show Cain how he can be accepted.*

8. "While they were in the field, Cain attacked his brother Abel and killed him" (4:8b). *Cain ignores God's preventive discipline and* **chooses** *wrongly again.*

9. "Then the LORD said to Cain, 'Where is your brother Abel?'" (4:9a). *God confronts Cain with two more questions, not accusations!*

10. "'I don't know,' he replied. 'Am I my brother's keeper?'" (4:9b). *Cain continues to choose wrongly by lying.*

11. "'What have you done?'" (4:10b). *God asks the fifth question but notice, Cain does not answer it!*

12. "Listen! Your brother's blood cries out to me from the ground" (4:10c). *Now God supplies evidence of Cain's wrongdoing.*

13. And then God gives Cain the natural consequences of his choices: "'Now you are under a curse'" (4:11a). *Sometimes, when a person is completely obstinate, bringing in natural consequences in the form of punishment is all one can do.*

GOD'S STRATEGY FOR DISCIPLINE
PART 2: QUESTIONING CAIN

God's questioning of Cain in Genesis 4 gives us wisdom on how to discipline our children and our students. First, God asked, "Why are you angry?" (4:6b) and then, "Why is your face downcast?" (4:6c). This is interesting. God noticed the emotions of anger and sadness in Cain's face and simply asked about them. Those emotions are clues. Cain was dealing with not being accepted by God. He felt rejected. But he was not accepted because he did not honor God properly; he did not "do what is right" (4:7a). He valued the first fruits of the soil more than he valued God. This is a problem then of disordered love which led to the choice to make a weak offering, which in turn dishonored God and caused God to look unfavorably on Cain. That made Cain very angry and then sad. It was written all over his face.

Observing the emotions playing across students' faces and then simply asking questions about what we see can yield valuable insights. "I notice you are very angry. Why is that?" In many cases, simple questions like these can bring up emotions and tears in both girls and boys. The student's response can then be the basis for further questions until gradually the parent or teacher gets to the "heart" of the matter. That is the goal, after all, since it is out of the heart that we make choices.

God's third question tried to correct Cain's understanding by properly framing reality for him: "If you do what is right, will you not be accepted?" (4:7a). Doing what is right leads to acceptance, not rejection. God is showing Cain the solution to his problem. God is showing Cain how to be accepted. One is accepted when one does what is right. Sometimes this simple truth gets lost when disciplining students or our own children.

God's last two questions are: "Where is your brother Abel?" (4:9a) which Cain answers with a lie, and then, "What have you done?" (4:10b) which Cain does not answer at all. Every parent, teacher, or administrator has experienced similar reactions from students. How hard it is to speak the truth! God's questions have the effect of revealing the extent of the depravity in Cain's heart. Questions are useful, then, because they are "heart-exposing."

Behind every choice is a motive, and behind every motive is a value system that is either confused or clear, right or wrong. A student gets caught cheating on a quiz. A series of questions reveals that the student cheated because he ran out of time to study. He ran out of time because he made a series of choices to watch science fiction movies night after night up in his bedroom when his father was away on business and while his mother was too occupied with the other children to look in on him. The pleasure of watching the movies out-ranked the perceived drudgery of doing his homework.

Simply throwing a Bible verse at this problem does absolutely nothing for the student or for the problem. The student already knows he did something wrong. He already knows he broke a commandment. Wise and insightful school leaders know there is much more to reveal here. The goal is to get the student to reflect on the choices he made over time, which led to the consequences of running out of time, which led to a moral decision to cheat.

Questions provide answers which give evidence of character. Student discipline issues need to be addressed with questions that reveal values, motives, choices, and then consequences. The Bible is not unimportant in this process; after all, the method of questioning itself is a Biblical method. This is one way we can use the Bible, in addition to using various scriptures elsewhere in the process to help the student understand the choices he has made so he can eventually take responsibility for his behavior and change it.

STUDENT CULTURE

HAVE FUN, DO YOUR BEST, AND BE A BLESSING

Schools and students need a motto, a succinct catch-phrase that encapsulates the essential mission of the school. "Have Fun, Do your Best, and Be a Blessing" is a great place to start. Each component represents both a standard for behavior and a claim on a different aspect of the student's soul.

Have Fun. Every Christian school, but especially college-preparatory schools, need to remember to promote the idea that school can be fun. Hard work does not have to be spiritless. Learning is not, by nature, dull. Going to school does not have to fill students with dread. They can have fun. They can discover that learning is fun too. Even drudgery can be met with a positive mindset. Instead, fear, pressure, and stress have become the norm. These conditions should be countered with sound counsel about: 1) believing that the Lord has a plan for each student and will work it out (the virtue of faith); 2) making good choices each day (the virtue of sound judgment); and 3) striving for a balanced life when choosing activities (the virtue of discretion). Fun with their friends and teachers, fun with classes and activities—in a culture of hard work, serious study, and difficult challenges—is not only possible but expected from people who live out "good news." School will not always be fun, of course, but the idea is to maintain the attitude and disposition that encourages students to enjoy learning, to love challenges, and to enjoy their classmates and teachers, while not taking themselves too seriously.

Do Your Best. To do one's best requires a healthy self-concept, good judgment, and a realistic view of life's circumstances. The standard is never perfection, but always excellence with the proviso that although circumstances change and sometimes students are able to devote more time to their studies than at other times, doing their best is all they are expected to do. Generally, the result will be positive; at other times it may not be, and that needs to be okay once in a while. Balanced students know that setbacks and disappointments are not the end of the world. Of course, learning is the goal, not performance. Consistent application, self-discipline, hard work, and a teachable spirit will produce excellence. Students will do well to also keep in mind the great prayer from Daniel 1:17a: "To these four young men **God gave** knowledge and understanding of all kinds of literature and learning" (emphasis added). This prayer, offered in faith, asks God to provide the knowledge or expertise students might lack. It is a prayer for all students but especially for those struggling with a subject area where performance is below desire, expectations, or potential.

Be a Blessing! We are all so hyper-focused on ourselves. Training students to consider others before themselves frees them from the disease of introspection, so common among young people today, and spreads encouragement and honor throughout your school. Unanticipated gifts are a kind of honor; they surprise and delight. Giving itself is certain to generate joy in the giver. Who has not felt wonderful after bringing a meal to someone who is bedridden or giving a secret gift of money to one in need? Giving to others is a good addiction and blessing others is good medicine. We all share in the blessing given to Abraham—we will be a blessing (Genesis 12:2-3). We are called to turn every wasteland, every valley of trouble into a place of springs (Psalm 84). We are called to be a gift-giving people! Encouraging students to be a blessing can absolutely re-orient their perspective, redirect their lives toward others, and dramatically revolutionize the spirit in your school.

FOUR MESSAGES FOR SPIRITUAL LIFE

Christian schools are constantly changing, and many are growing rapidly as parents and educators seek alternatives to the catastrophic failures of public education. In the midst of such change, those responsible for students' spiritual development can lose sight of the core messages students consistently need to hear. For high school students, four messages will always be relevant.

Make Your Faith Your Own. Frequent teachings on the "good news" should encourage students to own their faith as soon as possible. Simplistic messages about "getting saved" need to give way to more compelling messages on living in the exciting Kingdom of God. Our purpose is to invite students to enter this Kingdom right now, to experience not only salvation but also so much more—healing, restoration, holiness, love, and service. Just as our parents, when we were children, taught us habits of hygiene until we learned them for ourselves, students need to make their faith their own, to internalize it and live it out even when nobody is looking. Regularly praying to the Lord, meditating on God's word, learning obedience, enjoying freedom in worship, and independently practicing other spiritual disciplines are signs of true ownership. Students also need to realize that religious rituals or activities are not necessarily signs of personal faith. Going to church, attending youth groups, and going on service projects and mission trips might be expressions of faith but not proofs of it. Young people conditioned to doing them year after year may not have made an individual commitment to Christ.

Relationship, Not Religion. Christian college preparatory schools need to be careful that students' spiritual lives are not snuffed out in a climate of academic rigor. Encouraging students to encounter Jesus, to see Him as a real person, as one who is actually pursuing them because he really desires their friendship can be life-changing to those with only a cerebral basis to their faith. Relationship implies spending time with the Lord, encountering Him experientially through other people and through His creation, learning to hear His voice, and submitting to His lordship. Sensing God's presence and power through the Holy Spirit, being "full" of the Spirit and "walking" in the Spirit (Acts 6:3-8; Galatians 5:25) are vital aspects of this relationship, not options or extras. Providing students with space, time, and practice (as on retreats) to express and deepen their personal relationship with the Lord should be an integral component of any spiritual development program.

Avoid the Double Life. Three general classes of students exist in a typical Christian school. One group consists of students who have truly made their faith their own. Usually a small percentage of the student body, these students get excited about worship, and they love to pray and study God's word on their own. They live out their faith through service and interaction with other believers. A second group are those who come from nominally Christian homes but who have not personally committed their lives to Christ and appear to have no interest in doing so. They tend to sit at the very back of the chapel with their arms folded, scoffing at the service. However, they are a small group also. The third group, the vast middle majority, come from Christian homes and participate in church activities but are still worldly and carnally-minded. Students in this group very often live double lives. Because they live in Christian environments but have not made that courageous personal commitment to follow the Lord, they learn to play the part. Their faith is cultural, not personal. Their behavior at school or in church does not match their behavior with peers. Confronting this reality and exposing the hypocrisy behind it must be a consistent message to the student body each year.

God Can Heal Any Condition. Faith for healing is nearly non-existent in our churches, let alone our Christian schools. Even the simple and obvious connections between repentance and emotional or physical healing or between the forgiveness of sins, healing, and emotional well-being is completely lost on many students today because it is so poorly understood by many of their leaders. Why do we not believe God can heal attention disorders, depression, suicidal thoughts, or self-destructive behaviors like cutting and tattooing? Why do we frantically consult so many outside secular experts for these conditions, sometimes medicating afflicted students to the point of imbecility? Are there no spiritual roots behind certain physical conditions? No unclean spirits behind fevers? (Luke 4:39). No connection between forgiveness of sins and deliverance from certain kinds of paralysis? (Matthew 9:2). No healings that come by simple faith alone? (Matthew 9:22). Could it be that so many students are addicted to pornography because we do not understand that particular sin's **spiritual** roots? God is the One who heals us. Healing proves God's Kingdom is real. And if it is true this Kingdom is ever-expanding (Daniel 2:35; Matthew 13:31-32), then God's healing work among us should be expanding also. And this should enlarge our students' faith and give them great hope!

YOUR INCREDIBLE DESIGN AND IDENTITY!

Students need to know how fearfully and wonderfully made they truly are. We cannot remind them often enough of their priceless value as persons uniquely created by God, redeemed and restored by Jesus Christ with an exciting and glorious future in the Kingdom. As parents, teachers, and leaders, we must continually impress upon them the wonderfully good news that they have at least fourteen different identity expressions of their one identity in Christ. If they understand each one, they will find tremendous confidence and freedom as the people God has called them to be.

Three natural identities make up our essential nature. First, we each have a distinct and unchanging gender identity as a man or woman. Next, since we are made in the image of God, and God is the Creator, we are artists who are naturally creative, and we are rulers called by God to rule over some portion of His creation—the places of leadership God has designed for us.[47] Each of these three essential identities is found in Genesis 1:26-27. When we come to Christ, He heals us in each area, so that we can be secure and confident in our

---

[47] Scripture does not explicitly define man as an artist, but reveals his artistic powers when Adam names the animals in his effort to rule and take dominion by ordering his world. Thus, we might understand his artistic gifts as a function of his role as a ruler over creation, and not as a separate identity role as an artist. However, when Adam uses poetry in his first encounter with Eve, he appears to reveal an artistic role not linked to his role as ruler and that is simply to praise and honor what is beautiful. That most certainly is the role of the artist.

gender identity as a man or a woman and productive in our roles as artists and rulers. Transformation in Christ makes us more fully man or woman, as well as more insightful and creative as artists with more authority and skill as leaders.

In Christ, we take on two new personal identities and six new social identities—two as individuals, two as members of a new family, two as members of the Church, and two for being citizens in the Kingdom. When we come to Christ we become works of art (Ephesians 2:10), each one of us God's own unique masterpiece for all the world to see. This means we have beauty and design, purpose and destiny. It means God, as a Potter, is shaping and molding each of us into a beautiful and indestructible vessel (Romans 9:21; Isaiah 64:8), and that God as Author is turning us into poems and letters known and read by others (2 Corinthians 3:3). In Christ, we also take on a new personal spiritual identity as special servants of God (1 Peter 2:16). In this role we are to listen to His voice, obey His commands, and do the work He calls us to do through faith and trust (John 10:27).

Second, as members of a new family, we are sons or daughters with God as our Father (Hebrews 12:7) as well as brothers and sisters to Jesus who is "not ashamed" to call us brothers (Hebrews 2:11). These are our roles in God's household, roles made possible by the Spirit of Sonship who takes away our fears as He brings us confidently into the presence of our new Father. The Spirit also reminds us of our rights as sons or daughters who have a fantastic inheritance in the Lord (Romans 8:15-17).

Third, as members of the Body of Christ, the Church (1 Corinthians 12:27-28) we perform different functions (prophet, teacher, etc.), for the building up of others (1 Corinthians 12:28-31; Ephesians 4:11-13) according to the grace God has apportioned to us. However, we are also priests with an important role to fulfill in the world under the direction of our High Priest, Jesus, and that is to walk in holiness as the chosen people of God and help others (1 Peter 2:9). As priests, we offer worship to God and survey our God-given realms to intercede for those in need. Wherever we find a need or discover an injustice or a territory ruled by the kingdom of darkness, we cry out to the Lord to "come down" and intervene. In this way, we turn our valleys of trouble into places of springs (Psalm 84:5-6).

Fourth, as members of a new Kingdom, we are citizens (Ephesians 2:19) who have access to the Kingdom's privileges, secrets, and mysteries (Matthew 13:11; 17:26) and to God's secret wisdom (1 Corinthians 2:7) which is given to us by God's Spirit. However, we also function as soldiers in the army of God (2 Corinthians 10:3; Ephesians 6:11). In this role, we are called to put on spiritual armor, stand our ground, and defend ourselves when attacked (Ephesians 6:10-18), but also to wield divine power to destroy strongholds and the works of the devil (2 Corinthians 10:4). Our understanding of each of these incredible identities grows and matures as we participate in spiritual communities composed of God's holy people.

Finally, we will stir up great hope in our students when we help them to glimpse the exciting restored and supernatural identities we shall have in the coming Kingdom. There will be no marrying in the coming age because we will have supernatural bodies like the angels (Matthew 22:30) in our new identity as the bride of Christ (Revelation 19:7). We will also continue to be priests in a royal priesthood, John reminds us (Revelation 1:6), as well as rulers wielding authority over nations, sitting on thrones, judging the angels, and doing various duties in the Millennial Kingdom (Revelation 2:26; 20:4; 1 Corinthians 6:3; Revelation 2:7, 28). It is fascinating and a great wonder how our three future supernatural roles—bride, priest, ruler—correspond to our first three natural roles—gender, artist, ruler!

Truly, we are great and incredible wonders created by God. Therefore, we should always encourage our students to see who they are while also reminding them that *we become what we choose to look upon.* We become what we adore, what we worship. When our focus is fixed on Christ and not on ourselves or what we are to do with our lives, we will discover who He made us to be. When we "seek first" His kingdom and righteousness (Matthew 6:33), we will know ourselves as we truly are and we will soon develop the great Christian virtue of self-acceptance. We become comfortable in our own skin and at home in the world. We will discover and embrace the seven great essential truths of our existence, truths in which our one identity in Christ is lived out and expressed. They are nature as our true home, community as our true society, worship as our true way of life, work as our true activity, beauty as our true contemplation, wisdom as our true knowledge, and love as our true purpose. All of these essential truths of our existence have Christ as the source, Christ as the focus, and Christ as the means for us to understand them at all.

ANOTHER WAY TO UNDERSTAND LAZINESS

Laziness is a serious moral defect, but it is a more complicated problem than students or parents think. It is much more than being unwilling to do work. Consider this gem from Proverbs 24:30-34: "I went past the field of the sluggard, past the vineyard of someone who has no sense" (24:30).

Like many proverbs, this one contains a surprise. One would expect the text to say, "past the vineyard of the man who was **lazy**." How, then, does "someone who has no sense" or is lacking judgment relate to being a sluggard or being lazy? We think of laziness as a lack of effort or will, but calling it a lack of judgment implies it is something else.

Notice that this man's laziness actually created three problems for him, like heads of the Hydra: "**thorns** had come up everywhere, the ground was covered with **weeds**, and the **stone wall was in ruins**" (24:31, emphasis added). Proverbs 15:19 says a sluggard's way is "blocked with thorns," suggesting that thorns, besides being dangerous, compromise one's ability to work freely. Thorns hamper, restrict, and injure oneself and others. Weeds, however, compromise the crop itself because pulling up the weeds may damage what has been planted. And in the Parable of the Weeds (Matthew 13:24-30, 36-43), the weeds were identified as "the people of the evil one," suggesting a more sinister influence. Finally, the ruined stone wall obviously compromises safety and security. A stone wall in ruins means there is no protection for the crop.

In other words, with a sluggard around, a habitually lazy person, the labor is inefficient, the crop is unproductive, and the environment is unprotected. As a result, the entire future harvest is compromised.

In our day, perhaps students have been told they have a "time management" problem. Our use of that term implies one suffers from a lack of "skills" rather than a defect in character. We think if we could only help the child organize his time, maybe through the purchase of a planner or notepad (good ideas in themselves) or by coaching him to write down his assignments when they are assigned, we would correct the problem.

But that is not what the proverb implies. It's not that the young man lacks the skills, it is that he does not properly **value** what he should **value more highly**. He values the wrong things, like sleeping and pleasure and wasting time while not valuing the right things, like self-discipline, hard work, and consistent productivity. In other words, something is wrong all right, but not with his skills or his will. It's with his judgment and his affections, what he in fact loves. He "lacks judgment"—the ability to put the right value on activities.

Being a sluggard is a serious problem; it means someone is not in touch with reality. Loving what he ought to despise and despising what he ought to love, the man has become a sluggard, for lack of judgment, the lack of knowing the clear difference between an obvious responsibility and a temporary pleasure. He suffers from a defect in seeing the obvious. And the result is a compromise in his work, his crop, his security, and his future.

At school, at home, at work, can we really afford to coddle laziness? In students? In teachers? In administrators or bosses? Can any person work successfully at all with someone who values the wrong things and rejects the right ones?

SLEEP, DIET, AND EXERCISE: ARE THEY SPIRITUAL?

Although it is true we are becoming more health-conscious in our country than ever before, it is also true that old habits die hard and we are easily deceived. How easy it is to think that by eating right but not giving attention to our sleep, or that by exercising often but not eating well, we are actually making progress!

We have to aggressively confront the many ways our culture supports all the wrong behaviors. Students are texting and Face-booking so much they are losing the sleep they need to mentally function well the next day. Our computers, tablets, iPads, and phones have created conditions that make us more sedentary than we ever were in front of our television screens. And processed foods, full of unnatural chemicals and preservatives and high in sugars and salt, have produced an obesity problem that has been with us for decades. We need consistent parental oversight in these areas more than ever, which is not easy to do given our habits of busyness and our dual-income life-styles, which have left many children without the supervision they need to form good habits and live healthy lives.

We all need to be more aware of our unconscious choices and their consequences when it comes to habits of eating, sleeping, and working. On a certain day you find yourself moving through your day very off-key. You seem to be late for everything, and you always feel tired even after you get up. As you give it some thought, you realize the problem actually began that morning when you got up late and then had to rush to all your commitments all day long. A little more reflection tells you that you got up late because you went to sleep late the night before. And then you remember that you went to sleep late because you just had to satisfy an urge to have a late snack because you felt like you needed some comfort after you spent so much time on your computer.

How did those few minutes on the computer suddenly turn into an hour and a half? A few interesting threads on Facebook. A few headlines from Fox News and then a couple of those bizarre videos of guys wrestling alligators or sharks jumping into fishing boats. No wonder you are in a fog. That explains why you don't feel like praying for anything or anybody. And why you watched the clock in your classes or meetings and why you were irritable and lethargic. A few poor choices, like playing on the computer late at night, becoming discouraged by bad news and then snacking afterward, altered your productivity and diminished your possibilities of the entire next day.

The Apostle Paul compared the Christian life to a boxing match. He said he beat his body and made it his slave (1 Corinthians 9:27). And he did this in order to maximize his effectiveness in the world. If we want to be a people who exhibit the abundant life of Christ, then we need to let the gift of self-control manifest itself in our daily lives and bring our eating, sleeping, and exercise habits under control. We need virtues to do this—temperance, self-denial, and self-control—and these come by the grace of God and the Holy Spirit, who purifies us as we obey the truth (1 Peter 1:22).

Stop and think: Are the foods you are currently eating the best foods for you or for your family? Perhaps we should evaluate our sleeping habits? Do our students understand the value of stewarding their sleep, recreation, diet, and work for God's purposes?

There is no mystery here. Sleep, diet, and exercise are very spiritual questions indeed.

SEVEN QUESTIONS EVERY HIGH SCHOOL STUDENT SHOULD ASK

Certainly, a goal of the high school years should be to explore and experience as much as possible—academically, socially, and spiritually—in order to discover one's God-given design and calling. Serious reflection and prayer around seven key identity questions will bring insight and revelation in this process.

Do I realize I am a work of art? (Ephesians 2:10) He is the Potter, you are the clay (Isaiah 64:8). He is the Author, you are the poem. You are *being made into* the person God desires (Romans 5:3-5). It is a process that does not happen all at once, so you must be patient. One aspect of being God's work of art is the absolute certainty of your gender identity as a man or a woman. Gender is fixed and unchanging, but physical and emotional brokenness can create gender confusion and identification with the same sex. Not to worry. As you seek the Kingdom of God and walk with the King, you will become fully man or fully woman, confident in who you are, secure in your own skin, and filled with peace, joy, and well-being. In other words, you will be incredibly beautiful.

How am I creative? Since we have been made in the image of God who is the Creator, we are all naturally creative. We are makers in His image (Genesis 1:26-27). Do not think "the fine arts" here because they are only a narrow form of creative expression. We are naturally creative, which means we cannot help being imaginative, resourceful, and innovative in whatever we do. The mission of the Accuser of our souls is to injure us in precisely the areas of our greatest creative potential so that we fear the very activities and vocations that God calls us to pursue. Think of the most serious ways you have been hurt or shamed and you will realize this is true. The enemy wants you to fear challenges and so avoid the direction God created for you to follow.

Which aspect of creation am I called to rule? (Genesis 1:26-27) God made man as a co-ruler with Him over some portion of creation. Academic and vocational training prepare us to rule well. Spiritual training prepares us to rule with compassion, goodness, and wisdom. Finding our own special "place" in creation—in the family, church, state, culture, or economy—comes from an awareness of our God-given design. As our design becomes clear, we discover where our leadership is to be.

What are my areas of brokenness? Without physical, emotional, and spiritual healing we will rule badly. We will hurt people instead of help them. Being in community, that is, being an active member of the body of Christ, which is so much more than being a church goer, opens us to the spiritual gifts of others and accelerates the healing process in all of us (Ephesians 4:11-16). Understanding our identity as a son or daughter, a process initiated and completed by the Spirit of Sonship (Romans 8:15-17), removes the fears which have been sown into us since we were born.

Do I understand my role as a citizen of the Kingdom? The question implies knowledge of the Kingdom message (Matthew 4:17, 23), a message which is rare in our day. Have you understood this message? Being a citizen means all the rights, privileges, practices, and powers of the Kingdom of God are yours (Matthew 13:11). It means we think and act according to Kingdom ways, not the ways of the world. And if we are citizens, then we are also soldiers (in a battle) with weapons (spiritual gifts to demolish strongholds) in an army under the leadership of Christ (2 Corinthians 10:3; Ephesians 6:11).

Do I understand my role as a priest? We are "king-priests," meaning the realm in which we rule is the realm in which we are also priestly (1 Peter 2:9). A priest takes the needs of his people to God in intercession, asking God to "come down" or to "bring heaven down" into the priest's jurisdiction, bringing Kingdom rule to that place. Whatever valley of trouble we find ourselves in, we call on God's presence and power to make it a place of springs (Psalm 84). A person in secure possession of his identity as a king-priest will be looking for opportunities to intercede for whatever is broken in his area of rule so that it too becomes a place of springs—full of life and abundance!

Have I thought about my role in the age to come? We have been entrusted with talents which we are to put to use, now, on earth, until Jesus comes. If we are faithful with what God has given us, we will be rewarded in the age to come. "Because you have been trustworthy in a very small matter, take charge of ten cities" (Luke 19:17b). To be sure, that role is unknown, signified by the new name on the white stone Jesus will give to those who overcome the world (Revelation 2:17). Reflecting on these realities and realizing that someday we will live and work with Jesus in glorified, resurrected bodies like His own for all eternity gives us great hope!

FALLOUT OF SOCIAL MEDIA

Everyone seems willing to acknowledge the dangers of social media, but except for a small group of parents whose children have been destroyed by it, few seem willing or courageous enough to do something about it in our schools. We might start the discussion by making a few simple observations.

1. **Social media feeds upon our hunger for significance**. We were created in the image of God as artists and co-rulers. When Adam sinned, he surrendered his realm of rule to the devil. Under Satanic control we have become enslaved, sinful, and broken images of God, as well as passive, uncreative, and destructive in our separate roles. Even in Christ we still hunger to be what we were created to be. It is the deepest hunger of a human being. By constructing a phantom community and involving us in conversations where we get to be "amateur providences"[48] and brag about ourselves, social media promotes the illusion that we are important. In reality, we have become disembodied voices in textual conversations that do not matter.

2. **Social media prevents us from knowing our social weaknesses or strengths**. In a real community, we have to

---

[48] Oswald Chambers' term. See "The Dilemma of Obedience," January 30, in *My Utmost for His Highest*.

learn skills to interact with others and develop personal traits that make us sociable. In authentic social interaction, we discover who we really are—where we might be confident, insecure, weak, afraid, or truly talented. Social media allows us to appear social when in fact we might be terrified of our insecurities and often paralyzed to carry on a decent conversation of give and take. In other words, social media is a showcase for self-promotion and make-believe, without the checks and balances we need to evaluate ourselves and grow.

3. **Social media is addictive.** Because social media does not really satisfy our craving for significance, while making us believe that it does because it gives us good feelings about ourselves, it actually creates an addiction for more. In that way, it is like junk food—tasty but with no real nutritional value. It becomes an idol, which is anything we go to for comfort. And we know what idols do. With mouths that cannot speak and ears that cannot hear, idols inevitably **diminish** our humanity: "Those who make them will be like them [unable to speak, see, hear, smell, feel, or walk], and so will all who trust in them" (Psalm 115:8).

4. **Social media keeps us in a state of constant distraction.**[49] It tells us to "Do this right now instead of that." It says, "Because this is urgent, it is more important," or "Because this is about me, it is more desirable." We cannot go very long without consulting our phones for messages or checking our mail in the presence of others, and we just have to answer that text this very instant even though it transmits no thought beyond that of a grinning smiley face. We have long forgotten the simple courtesy of preferring others above ourselves, and we fail to realize how insultingly rude it is when we pull out our phones in the company of others. This happens so often now that we have become unconscious of it, though it literally sends the message that we are superior to those who have made the

---

[49] For practical ways to combat distraction and experience rest, see Ellen Schuknecht and Erin MacPherson, *Free to Parent: Escape Parenting Traps and Liberate Your Child's Spirit* (Austin: Family Wings, LLC, 2014), 88-97.

sacrifice of time and effort to be with us in that moment.

5. **Social media squanders the resource of time**. This is no small thing. Time is a finite resource we are called to steward. Time wasted on social media is time not spent on something else, like prayer, serving others, creating something, or even listening to others. We work less, think less, and accomplish less when we impulsively give in to it. And when we stay up late indulging in it when we should be sleeping, we sabotage the precious times of the following day by being more tired, less alert, and less willing to expend effort for difficult activities. Social media is an investment of time with no tangible return of any value beyond momentary pleasure.

6. **Social media is anti-community**. Living responsibly in a community requires certain virtues: deference, submissiveness, patience, forbearance, kindness, consideration, humility, and personal responsibility. We learn these by interacting with others. It also requires certain skills: the ability to listen well, to communicate back and forth, the ability to resolve conflict, and to get along with others. This too takes practice. In contrast, social media places all the focus on the user. It is ultimately non-relational. The self-infatuation, hyper-narcissism, and self-glorification generated by social media undermines and suppresses the virtues needed for healthy personal relationships and the skills necessary to get along with others.

7. **Social media diverts us from bearing fruit and doing God's will**. Social media overuse is a pathetic contrast to the petitions of one of the greatest prayers of the Bible, one we can make our very own, Colossians 1:9-12: "For this reason, since the day we heard about you, we have not stopped praying for you. We continually ask God to *fill you with a knowledge of his will* through all the *wisdom and understanding that the Spirit gives,* so that you may *live a life worthy of the Lord* and *please him in every way: bearing fruit in every good work, growing in the knowledge of God, being strengthened with all power* according to his glorious might so that you may have *great endurance and patience* and *giving joyful thanks to the Father,* who has qualified you to share in the inheritance of his holy people in the kingdom of the light" (emphasis added).

How do our social media habits compare to the mighty petitions of this great prayer? They don't.

PORNOGRAPHY ADDICTION AND GENDER CONFUSION—SOME THOUGHTS

Believers who do not understand the ministry of the Holy Spirit are fighting a modern technological war with weapons no better than sticks and stones. This is especially true when it comes to helping those who are addicted to pornography and, to a lesser degree, our young boys and girls caught in gender confusion.

Asking the pornography addict to read more of his Bible, to find an "accountability partner," or to install the latest protective software for his electronic devices is completely useless in treating the problem. He has an **addiction**! An addiction is a **spiritual** stronghold. This means, like an alcoholic, he will lie to his accountability partner and find a way around the software probably within twenty-four hours of its installation. And yet, these "solutions" appear to be the best the church can do. They are but sticks and stones. Because these solutions ultimately do not work, the addict gets worse and soon grows hopeless as he continues to live out his habitual double life while secretly feeding his growing addiction.

These methods do not work because the Western rationalistic worldview behind our faulty theology blinds us to the real solution. If an unclean spirit can be the cause of a mere fever (Luke 4:39), why do we think that a far more enslaving sin like an addiction to pornography is not? And if the roots of this condition are spiritual in nature, if this is not merely a sin but, in fact, a serious spiritual stronghold, then *only the ministry of the Holy Spirit*—the same Spirit who empowered Jesus to do miracles and who now resides in us—will be able to make the addict well. He will be forgiven for his sin, healed of the brokenness that gave rise to it, and delivered from the spirit that has kept him bound.

For hundreds of years, from the time of Moses to the time of Jeremiah, Israel struggled against Baal, the Canaanite god of sexual perversion. This filthy demonic spirit has not retired. It has not graciously left the scene. It did not politely leave when the spiritual gifts supposedly died out with the last of the Apostles. It is the spirit that drives the widespread sexual perversion in the world today, including the multi-billion dollar pornography industry. Only seasoned saints filled with power and operating in the gifts of discernment, healing, and deliverance will be able to proclaim the good news of the Kingdom to those caught in this addiction and deliver them from this demonic stronghold.

The ministry of the Holy Spirit is also vital to helping young people who are drifting into gender confusion and the gay lifestyle. When the Supreme Court declares that gay marriage is permissible, an idea which would have been unthinkable according to the jurisprudence of our founding fathers, and when the television, print, and film industries assume that homosexuality is normal and then organizations like the Boy Scouts cave in to follow suit, it is very difficult for a young person growing up in today's popular culture to know what normal even is. Everything in his world is telling him the lie that being gay is just another normal lifestyle choice.

Once again, ignorance of spiritual realities is keeping us from victory. The widespread spiritual oppression that feeds upon the wreckage of marriages and families, causing fear, pain, and confusion in the children, and the outright warfare that often strikes during adolescence are vastly misunderstood by parents and school leaders alike. We have a powerful spiritual enemy, an Accuser who seeks to infiltrate the soul by relentlessly lying to the mind so that he can kill, steal, and destroy the life Jesus died to save. If he can make young people think that feelings are true so that if one "feels" drawn to someone of the same sex he or she **must** be gay, then he has won half the battle.

Trying to prove to the student that the Bible considers homosexuality a sin, which is certainly true, will do nothing for those under the kind of deception and oppression that spiritual warfare brings. Such students need care and attention from people who sincerely love them, who know how to listen well and pray effectively, and who are willing to walk alongside them long enough to release them from the warfare and oppression that keeps them from wholeness and restoration. Such saints are rare in a good many of our churches for the simple reason that a good many of our church leaders don't believe in the real presence and power of the Holy Spirit or, even worse, think that manifestations of the Spirit are from the devil. Meanwhile, in such churches and schools, the children continue to be snatched away and enslaved. Their grieving mothers and fathers can only shake their heads in disbelief and wonder how this possibly could have happened.

Simple Biblical logic should give us hope. In a prophetic vision, Daniel saw a rock that turned into a mountain that filled the whole earth. That mountain was the Kingdom of God (Daniel 2:44-45). Ever since Jesus announced the arrival of the Kingdom on the earth, this Kingdom has been steadily expanding through God's people, who have been empowered by the Holy Spirit to do the same works Jesus did. If according to Jesus, deliverance from demons was empirical proof that the Kingdom has come (Luke 11:20), and His disciples proclaimed this same Kingdom and performed those same works (Luke 10:17), then deliverance from demons ought to be increasing as the Kingdom expands through believers today. Is it? If the demons themselves are still with us, then why should we think Jesus would withdraw from His people the very power He used to drive them out?

Truth leads to freedom. Believing that the power of God is available today for our children will heal them and set them free from pornography addiction and gender confusion.

THE CRY OF THE ADOLESCENT GIRL

The cry of the teen girl's heart is complicated and deep; she is in pain and confusion, and she is calling for help but does not know where to find it. The following "cries" or questions are common to girls who struggle in their teen years.

Cry #1: Am I pretty, am I attractive, am I okay? These may be some of the deepest cries of a teenage girl's heart. Deep down she needs to know she is not just normal but beautiful in her spirit (1 Peter 3:4) and in the way God made her, and that she has all she needs to grow up and come out all right. The main responsibility for making this happen is the dad. It is amazing how many dads are unaware of the emotional, social, and spiritual needs of their own daughters. Because for whatever reason they have not invested in their daughters over time (i.e. spent TIME with them), they do not understand them and often make some of the most cutting and hurtful remarks to them out of pure ignorance. Criticizing her looks or clothing or making fun of her ("you are too fat" or "what's wrong with you?" or "why can't you be like everyone else?") absolutely rips open her soul. From these wounds she develops an unhealthy self-concept which then creates doubt, anxiety, and tentativeness in all she tries to do, including making friends—the one thing she needs at this time in her life. Very often, to compensate for her low self-concept, she will fall into a perfectionistic trap where she then tries to "prove" her worth through her performance in the classroom or in athletics or whatever. Dads who demand unrealistic standards in grades ("Nothing less than an A is acceptable") or in sports (she has to be the MVP) unwittingly play into this perfectionism, creating further inner unrest in their daughters.

Antidote: Teenage girls need to hear lots of encouragement and consistently positive good news a hundred more times than they hear criticism. They also need to spend a lot of time with their dads, who should look for ways to enter their daughter's world so that they can understand what their girls are going through and help them find solutions to the problems their daughters are unable to solve. It goes without saying that a teenage girl's concept of God as Father will be based mainly on her experience of her earthly father!

Cry #2: I feel so alone! This cry has a number of offshoots such as: "Why don't I have any friends?" and "Why don't I fit in or belong?" and "Why do my peers ignore me?" and "Why are they so hurtful and mean to me on Facebook?" This is at root a cry for belonging, for connections, for meaningful relationships, for simple friends. But it also could be a revelation of the way she is perceiving herself. An unhealthy self-concept may have formed because she has lacked affirmation, sincere praise, and unconditional love from mom or dad. Hormonal and bodily changes add to the anxiety and insecurity even more. When encouragement, affirmation, and love are missing, self-doubt, self-criticism, and self-hatred will fill the void. And then a whole range of self-destructive behaviors (nervously plucking eyebrows, anxiety episodes, cutting, promiscuity, suicidal thoughts) are not far behind. A vicious circle gets going: insecurities and hurtful comments cause her to hate herself and feel much anxiety. So, she starts cutting to relieve the pressure, but that causes her to feel shame and more self-condemnation, which makes her now think she is bad, and therefore no one would ever wish to be her friend, and on and on and on.

Antidote: A healthy functioning family is the place where two vital needs are first met: the need for unconditional love from parents and the need to belong, both of which secure a child's identity and self-concept. Through healthy families, teen girls must know they are loved and have a place in this world—that they have both value and a role to fulfill. Once again, dads are critical to making this happen. Teen girls need to know that dad thinks the world of them, cares about them, prays for them, prays over them, spends his time with them, and cares about what concerns them. Teen girls need to know they are not secondary or an item on dad's "to do" list. Teens with loving fathers will have a strong sense of self, high confidence when confronting challenges, and the ability to make friends because they have been made secure in their dad's love long before they engage with the world.

On the other hand, teens whose parents go through a divorce suffer a great deal with abandonment, feelings of rejection, and depression—there is no getting around this. The damage is there. Girls who experience the breakup of their parents' marriage and the loss of their home and way of life need to guard against looking for that lost love in boyfriends, sexual activity, and in the unreal world of social media. Instead, they need to work through the tangled feelings, extend forgiveness, and receive care from those who are willing to walk with them during those difficult times. Here the presence of a strong, loving surrogate father figure (uncle, friend) is invaluable.

Cry #3: I can't talk to my parents! When a teen girl makes this statement, relationships with her parents have broken down long before. Her statement is actually a desire to bond with them, but she feels she cannot because she believes her parents either do not understand her world, or they are too busy, or they are out of touch because they are detached or preoccupied with their own interests. Not having this connection, she feels all alone and does not have confidence that she can find solutions to the many daily issues that come up in her life—not being included in groups, struggling with loneliness, dealing with hurtful words from peers, dealing with hormones or changes in her body, struggles with teachers or classes, and the like. So, she struggles alone and she suffers alone. Her problems remain problems because she is cut off from the wisdom of those who really can help. Or, what is worse and all too common, she consults popular culture for answers. She discovers **comfort** through the **illusion of friends** on social media, **listening sympathetic ears** on various websites, and **"wisdom"** in the lyrics of popular songs or teen films.

Antidote: Dads and moms need to frequently take the initiative to enter their daughter's world. Once again, this is sacrificial: dads and moms will lose time, but the knowledge and wisdom they can gain from just a single walk down the street, or an hour going out for ice cream, or watching a movie together will be worth more than gold. Dad's job is to listen—just listen—so she can get the words out. She needs **connection** more than a **solution**. Knowing that her dad cares and is willing to listen more than lecture or scold means the world to her. By the way, the first few times dads try to do this will be awkward, especially if dad and daughter have not related to each other in a while. But this is where dads need to break through the barrier, letting it be awkward until, after many times together, trust is restored and the daughter feels safe in sharing all that is locked up in her heart.

SELF-ESTEEM VERSUS THE VIRTUE
OF SELF-ACCEPTANCE

We know that a culture's artifacts—ideas, rituals, products, and institutions—come with worldviews attached. The popular concept of "self-esteem" is no different. Inaugurated in the early 1970s, the self-esteem movement has influenced educators and parents ever since, and the concept of self-esteem is still popular in public schools and in popular culture. The movement's basic premise was pure humanism—that "feelings of self-esteem were the key to success in life."[50] In other words, if educators and parents can help kids "feel" important and valued, nothing more was required. This one idea radically altered the educational mindsets of generations past. It has produced in our day the idea that just for showing up a child receives an award or that everyone gets a trophy or that nobody is to lose because that will produce bad feelings, and so on.[51]

This mindset is the secularized and corrupted form of what used to be a robust Christian virtue, the virtue of self-acceptance:

> The virtue of self-acceptance is key to a distinctly Christian, theocentric understanding of what it is to be human. Virtue is an ancient name for human rightness, and when we

---

[50] Quoted in "The Gift of Failure," by Steve Baskin, *Psychology Today*, 31 Dec. 2012: https://www.psychologytoday.com/blog/smores-and-more/201112/the-gift-failure.

[51] Ibid.

apprehend virtue, we are beholding the true nature of human existence. Where the tradition of modern psychology has focused on understanding psychopathology, it is the prerogative of Christian psychology to illuminate human wholeness, the redeemed and perfected image of God in men and women. The language of virtue helps us in this creative task. The virtue of acceptance of the self, or patience with the self, opens the door to human maturity.[52]

The virtue of self-acceptance begins in humility and faith but it also involves personal struggle, love, and encouragement from others (especially one's father), along with the rich experience of God's love. Accepting ourselves as we are, being patient with our limitations and weaknesses, liberates us to find emotional well-being, deliverance from self-hatred, and freedom from the opinions and judgments of others. No longer envying those we deem superior, no longer hating ourselves and putting others in hierarchies, those who have achieved the virtue of self-acceptance have, in a deep sense, come into a state of emotional and spiritual rest. Understanding we are accepted and loved by God, not for any effort or accomplishment of our own, we are at peace with ourselves and with others.

How do we create an environment that promotes this virtue? First of all, struggle, opposition, and failure need to be re-contextualized. These are not indicators of weakness or a means for self-condemnation. Failure at a task is not a judgment of the self, but a challenge to it, an opportunity. A distorted value of performance has made everyone think student effort is all about achievement and getting the blue ribbon. Instead, we are teaching a method, a stance or attitude, a way of approaching difficult problems or obstacles which is not connected to a student's worth or self-concept. Performance does not equal value. While modern public education seeks to remove difficulties and make the way easy, wrapping every student in the soft, cotton balls of self-esteem, we want to add obstacles and problems and encourage students to struggle so that we build overcomers. Our schools need to reflect this attitude and practice.

Traditional, classical, and University-Model® schools should

---

[52] Sarah Groen-Colyn, "The Virtue of Self-Acceptance." Society for Christian Psychology, May 4, 2014: http://www.christianpsych.org/wp_scp/the-virtue-of-self-acceptance/.

always be promoting the virtues, but especially this foundational virtue of self-acceptance which has been missing from our understanding of spiritual development far too long. Coaches, counselors, and teachers need to understand that the **virtue** of self-acceptance is not at all the same thing as the **feeling** of self-esteem, and that patience with the self is something that can be taught and caught through a process that takes time, a lot of encouragement, the consistent application of faith, and ongoing experiences of God's love.

LEARNING SELF-ACCEPTANCE IN HIGH SCHOOL

The great enemies of self-acceptance in high school are perfectionism, the illusion in the **mind** that the student can do all things equally well; passivity, the paralysis of the **will** that prevents students from ever becoming anything at all; and despair, the sickness in the **emotions** that says since nothing matters anyway, nothing is worthwhile to achieve. If we give room for any of these diseases of the soul we shall never become what God created us to be. We will never be satisfied or happy, and we will never feel free.

Self-acceptance begins with surrender. We give up all our own efforts to obtain the right stuff we think we need to be accepted—high grades, great athletic skills, confident leadership, and special artistic and social gifts—in exchange for God's grace and power, which transform us and call us to our true selves. In Christ we cease competing with others, comparing ourselves to others, and trying to possess the talents we admire in others. We stop being envious and jealous of those who seem to be superior. We stop listening to the lies that tell us we are inferior in some area and therefore bad, unworthy, or unacceptable in some way, and we learn to fill our souls with truth from God's word and with experiences of the Father's love. When that happens, we go free. We feel good deep down inside. We feel at home in the world for the first time, like we actually belong here with a purpose and destiny of our own.

Encouraging students toward self-acceptance involves three

objectives. The first is to help students understand their special calling and design in God's image. Each student is genuinely unique with a certain ratio of gifts and talents. Discovering this as early as possible will go a long way toward helping a student achieve meaning, purpose, and well-being. The second objective is for parents and teachers to build confidence in students by encouraging them to choose activities (classes, summer camps, special training, internships, and part-time jobs) that will enhance and flesh-out their God-given design. Since their design already disposes them in some way toward success in that activity, students will readily excel in it, which will build their confidence, and spur more desire. Examples include the engineering student who takes a class on building robots, the artistic student who takes up photography, the political-minded student who goes to Boys' State. The third objective is for school leaders and parents to frequently remind students that we are always **becoming** persons. Self-acceptance is a process of discovery; we never stop growing, and talents, personality, and aptitude are not fixed quantities unless we believe them to be.

Students can discover their design and grow in self-acceptance in many ways. The love and affirmation of other adults is powerful. Understanding their several roles in Christ (son/daughter, priest, artist, and so on) is also helpful. Realistic parents and teachers can help students develop a true view of themselves without illusions and without career fantasies that often lead to costly mistakes and many wasted years. In addition, standardized aptitude and personality tests administered in junior high and high school and combined with discussion and prayer can also help students toward developing this virtue.

Even the simplest assessment of students' gifts can be beneficial. Identifying the ratios of giftedness in four common areas of student activities—academics, leadership, athletics, and the arts—will give them a basic view of their specialness as God's workmanship, freeing them from self-doubt, competition with others, and the fear of failure. On a scale of one to ten, a parent and a teacher assign a numerical value to the student's level of giftedness in each of the four areas. The student also completes the assessment herself and then all three discuss and pray about their findings. Rather than a means for condemnation and shame, an opportunity for wish fulfillment, or an excuse for students to grow in a single area and not in any others, a simple assessment like this should be understood as a conversation starter to help students discover a realistic sense of self and stimulate a desire for personal growth and change. Input from parents and teachers will probably challenge the student's view of herself and motivate her to focus on improving her weaker areas. And it will help her understand a little bit more "the way she should go," the special and unique calling God has for her.

Informal or formal assessments can produce much good counsel and many good discussions. A highly gifted student in academics, for example, might be encouraged to strengthen weak skills in leadership, so that his knowledge might bring about effective change. The strong athlete might recognize that athletics and the arts are not incompatible and be encouraged to take up the electric guitar. The highly creative person must accept that he or she also has a physical body in need of training just as his or her artistic skills need perfecting. Strong leadership will gain little if one's academic performance is substandard and so on.

Finally, assessments of this kind can help students focus their vocational choices and career goals. A student weak in the musical arts should not be encouraged to think he or she will play for the Boston Philharmonic, even though the desire to do so is strong. Strength in athletics does not automatically mean one should pursue a career in professional football. High academics will not necessarily produce a scholarship to medical school. Of course, we know that in each of these cases God can work miracles. Generally speaking, however, helping students grasp their particular ratios of talent in different areas will correct the identity and career illusions that often come from a lack of self-knowledge or a low self-concept and encourage them to make wiser, more realistic college and career choices.

FIVE PRAYERS TO LIVE BY

Prayer #1: Lord, show me something new about you. God is infinite and unfathomable, but because He is a good Father, He is always speaking to us. And Jesus said, "My sheep listen to my voice; I know them and they follow me" (John 10:27). God is not static, subject to our control, or predictable. We will never be able to say, "I know Him completely." Pray that He will reveal something new about Himself, something you will discover in your relationship with Him you have not seen or known before. You will marvel at the revelation and love Him all the more. This keeps life really exciting because it keeps us growing and gives us hope!

Prayer #2: Let me really encounter you and experience your love. A relationship with Christ is about an encounter, what C.S. Lewis called a "meeting."[53] We cannot control encounters; they happen to us as we present ourselves to Him, as we open our hearts to Him and allow Him to know us (Galatians 4:9). God uses all sorts of ways to help us discover and encounter Him—nature, worship, music, beauty, art, other believers, and most of all, His Word. However, it is not an encounter for an encounter's sake—nor is it merely an emotional or subjective experience. What we seek and desperately need is to know and experience His real presence among us and His great love.

---

[53] See Chapter 23, "'Real Life is Meeting'" in C. S Lewis' *That Hideous Strength* (New York: Scribner Paperback Fiction, 1986).

Prayer #3: Keep me free from the burden of criticizing others. It is a great step forward in the Lord when we discover we are free from the burden of needing to criticize other people. We then can simply let others be themselves and love them anyway, in spite of their limitations, which we had thought made us superior, or their strengths, which had made us feel inferior. We can also just acknowledge the truth that we too are imperfect, which is why we see faults in others in the first place, but which does not diminish at all God's love for us or our value to other people. What freedom comes with this revelation!

Prayer #4: Show me how my hunger for significance motivates my speech and actions. This one cuts very deep. We all have deep down inside us a desperate hunger to be significant, to be important, to matter. We have no idea how utterly it motivates our speech and actions and drives us to promote ourselves and put down others. Solomon captured the idea when he wrote: "And I saw that all toil and all achievement spring from one person's envy of another" (Ecclesiastes. 4:4a). It is this hunger for significance that drives us to compete, perform, out-perform, over-achieve, criticize, judge, and dominate others. And it is satisfied when we experience God's fabulous love, which sets us free.

Prayer #5: Help me to love others and sincerely celebrate their success. This is the surest antidote to the hunger for significance—to get into the habit of honestly desiring and celebrating someone else's success, the very opposite of envy or jealousy. Great joy comes on the day we can honor another without thinking something is wrong with ourselves. Great joy also comes when we can regard those lesser and greater with the same love and respect and without placing them or ourselves in some sort of hierarchy from least to greatest. Loving others is the whole point, the mark of maturity in Christ, and it begins when we insist on looking for the best in others and willingly honor it. We should remember here what Paul said: "The only thing that counts is faith expressing itself through love" (Galatians 5:6b).

PARENT CULTURE

THE MEASURE OF A MOM'S INFLUENCE

"For the hand that rocks the cradle is the hand that rules the world."

This famous line, from a poem written in 1865 by William Ross Wallace, captures the power and authority God has given to wives and mothers. Moms nurture the future leaders of the world. Because they are at home, they have the freedom and the power to shape local culture in a community. They have power to speak the words of life their husbands need in order to do the work that produces the means of living for the entire family.

We all acknowledge and celebrate the blessings that come from women making a difference in our world through their actions in the workplace. In law, government, business, economics, education, media and communications, and in so many other spheres women have significantly impacted our culture.

But sometimes a woman's power to shape our world is even greater through her more indirect influence: training her children to follow the Lord, teaching them how to become good parents and wise leaders themselves, and supporting her husband who ventures into the workplace every day to support the family. Some moms might be tempted to minimize their influence and see their work as small and mundane. But we have to remember that the mundane, the day-in and day-out routines of life, are sometimes how great heroes are made.

Commenting on this very idea, former U.S. Senator Dan Coats once said: "The only testing ground for the heroic is the mundane. The only preparation for that one profound decision which can change a life or even a nation is those hundreds and thousands of half-conscious, self-defining, seemingly insignificant decisions made in private."[54] What a mom thinks and chooses for herself and her children every day really matters. She is shaping the destiny of her children. As uneventful as her work might seem, it is anything but insignificant.

The book of Proverbs underscores the powerful influence of a wife and mother, *provided that she is full of wisdom*. The "Wife of Noble Character" passage in Proverbs 31 is a portrait of what a mom filled with wisdom looks like. She brings her husband good, not harm; she works hard and provides food to her family. She buys a field, plants a vineyard, helps the poor, makes clothing for her children, and sells homemade products in the marketplace. She speaks with wisdom, faithfully teaches her children, and watches over all the affairs of her household. The hymn of praise to her in this passage ends with the words "but a woman who fears the Lord is to be praised. Honor her for all that her hands have done, and let her works bring her praise at the city gate" (Proverbs 31:30b-31).

And so, when a wife and mother gets to heaven and the sum total of her influence is weighed, how will she have made her greatest impact on the world? Can any amount of successful work in the workplace compensate for, let's say, the raising up of a Billy Graham? Or a great president? Or a scientist who will find a cure for cancer? Or someone who will reach the Supreme Court and overturn Roe v. Wade at last? Or perhaps what is even greater, simply a spiritually mature adult who is a good husband or wife and a wise parent?

Moms—do you understand how important those small, everyday moments at home with your children really are? Do you recognize the authority and power God has placed in your two hands, those hands that work so hard and do so many things well, those hands that rock the cradle *and rule the world?*

---

[54] Dan Coats, "America's Youth: A Crisis in Character," *Imprimis*, Sept. 1991.

THREE KINDS OF MEN

According to the Proverbs, the secret to a man's success is the orientation of his will, whether it is informed by folly or guided by wisdom. Three kinds of men exist in the Proverbs and the other Wisdom books of the Bible—the sluggard, the tyrant, and the sage. The sluggard suffers from a lack of will, the tyrant suffers from too much will, while the sage is the one whose will has been tempered, balanced. Characteristics of all three types show up in every man, of course, but regardless of which type he is, the goal is to seek wisdom and eliminate folly in order to become a sage. Dads will tremendously benefit in their marriages and in their parenting from knowing how to conquer the tyrant and the sluggard in themselves.

The Sluggard. Sluggards love sleep (Proverbs 26:14) and tend to sleep during harvest (10:5), which, if continued, will make them poor (10:4). They do not roast their game (12:27), meaning they are impatient, lazy, and careless, defects which explain the condition of the sluggard's field (full of weeds, walls broken down, 24:30-31), and the condition of the man's home, which leaks because the rafters sag. These conditions exist because the man is lazy (Ecclesiastes 10:18), fearful (Proverbs 22:13), wise in his own eyes (3:7), and therefore not teachable or able to take correction. Because of these defects, the sluggard is an unreliable man (10:26) who never prospers.

The Tyrant. This type of man generally oppresses and crushes everyone he meets—his wife, his children, his co-workers, and especially the poor (14:31)—because he lords it over others (Proverbs 28:15; Ecclesiastes 8:9), often to "his own hurt." He is described as a roaring lion, a charging bear (Proverbs 28:15), and a driving rain that destroys all the crops (28:3). As a result, the people go into hiding when the tyrant rises to power, and they groan under his rule (28:12, 29:2). A tyrant's leadership, wherever it may be, suffers because tyrants lack judgment and seek dishonest gain (28:16) sometimes through exorbitant interest. They lack self-control and care nothing for justice (25:28, 28:5). This naturally makes sense because, unfortunately, power is often on their side (Ecclesiastes 4:1).

Interestingly, both the sluggard and the tyrant suffer from variations of the same problem and are corrected through the same solution. Both suffer from a **lack of judgment** (Proverbs 24:30; 28:16), which is a defect in **wisdom**. When personified Wisdom speaks about her virtues in Proverbs 8, she says: "Counsel and sound judgment are mine; I have insight, I have power. By me kings reign and rulers issue decrees that are just" (8:14-15). A man filled with wisdom is a man whose passivity and aggression have been tempered, which is the chief characteristic of the third kind of man, the sage.

The Sage. One of the definitive marks of a wise man is his life-giving effect on others including his wife, children, and co-workers. His teaching is a fountain of life (Proverbs 13:14); he brings joy to his father (10:1) and healing to others (12:18) because he spreads knowledge (15:7), and so his lips promote instruction (16:23) wherever he goes. Those who walk with him become wise themselves (13:20). Being wise benefits the sage as well. He gives thought to his ways (14:8); he shuns evil (14:16) and has great wealth (14:24), such as stores of choice food and olive oil (21:20). He stores up knowledge (10:14) and is praised for his wisdom (12:8), which gives him great power and strength (24:5) and which allows him to attack the "city of the mighty, and pull down the stronghold in which they trust" (21:22b).

A child who lives under the roof of the sluggard will never see anything get done and will himself not receive the attention he needs. He will learn that laziness and irresponsibility are the norm and will likely lack self-control and good judgment because he has never seen them and was never challenged to develop them. The child who lives under a tyrant will be oppressed and beaten down to the point that he will not develop into his full potential. His interests and desires will be stymied, and he will very likely become rebellious because he has grown up in an unjust home based on power and control. But he who has a sage for a father is certain to be blessed. He will enjoy freedom and prosperity and grow in knowledge and power. He will know fairness and justice. He will be filled with life and become wise himself. He will know who he is and what he is born to do.

When a man becomes a sage, all those under his leadership will prosper. Wives, children, and employees will be productive and happy. Their domain will be ordered, and they will never lack for food and resources because there will always be an abundance. Peace and safety will exist on all sides, leading to freedom, innovation, and creativity. Their realm will expand and they will receive great honor (1 Kings 3-5).

Is there a father anywhere who would not want this for his children?

FOUR TRUTHS ABOUT EVERY MAN

Dads can accelerate their growth in the Lord by understanding a few simple truths not found in our culture and rarely discussed even in our churches. And yet, such truths are gateways to incredible freedom. This freedom will absolutely change a man's view of himself and therefore, the way he treats his wife and children.

First, every man has a natural **limitation** of some kind. Most men will never play for the Boston Red Sox, hold a political office, or command an atomic submarine, and even those who do still have limitations with respect to others. We have limitations in physical and mental ability, education and training, as well as emotional, social, and psychological limitations that come from different family backgrounds. Accepting one's limitations, whatever they are, is essential if a man is to mature.

Second, every man has some form of **brokenness**. A wound from a father, abuse and shame from the past, problems with trusting others, or inabilities in forming relationships are some of the more common ways a man is broken. Of course, brokenness, which is natural to the human condition, is not a cause for shame, condemnation, or embarrassment nor is it a surprise or hindrance to God. We are fallen creatures, but our God is a healer. Brokenness can be mended.

Third, every man has a **weakness or bent in some sin area**. Maybe it is overeating or an addiction or problems with anger. Maybe a man is over-controlling or dominating. Maybe he is a sluggard—he just can't seem to do what he is supposed to do when he is supposed to do it, like the son in the Proverbs who sleeps during harvest time.

Acknowledging our sin without making excuses and then agreeing with God about it—actions which are difficult because our culture does not consider them masculine—takes great humility, another virtue also rejected by our culture because it is considered weakness. This humility includes accepting the responsibility for the damage our sins have done to others and then taking the steps necessary to restore our relationships with them.

Finally, every man has some kind of **blind spot**, but this one is harder to describe. The reason is blind spots can take the form of one of the other three problems. We don't see the whole picture and our point of view is often completely wrong. We form unwarranted assumptions and make unsubstantiated accusations and judgments. We also tend to have a high view of ourselves which is not corroborated by those closest to us or those with whom we work.

A man with a limitation, a form of brokenness, a weakness, and a blind spot can achieve wholeness, well-being, and meaningful relationships but only through an honest, man-to-man relationship with the greatest man who ever lived: the man John called "the one and only," Jesus Christ, who is "full of grace and truth" (John 1:14b). Not religion or religious actions, but a real relationship with a real Jesus and obedience to a sovereign Lord—that is what transforms us!

A relationship with the Lord is completely redemptive: His **grace** covers our limitations, His **healing** corrects our brokenness, His **forgiveness** cancels out our sin, and His **wisdom** compensates for our blind spots. A relationship with the "Son of Man" enables us to have true and fulfilling relationships with others and a meaningful life. There is no man He cannot fix, no problem or sin His blood cannot cover. That is because nothing is impossible with God. He will heal and restore us as long as we continue to follow Him and do what He says.

Dads, we need to consider how we are doing right now in this most important of all relationships. When we get our walk with the Lord right, everything else comes into alignment. Two questions might serve as starting points: How much freedom do we desire? And what specific changes can we make today—in prayer, worship, community, service, or in the study of God's word—that will strengthen our relationship with the Lord?

WHAT HAPPENS TO THE SON WHEN THE FATHER IS ABSENT?

The ancient Greeks knew well what happens to a young boy when he is not nurtured and encouraged by his father.

In Homer's *Odyssey*, Telemachus has grown up without a father, who was twenty years away at sea, ten years at Troy and ten more years just trying to get home. The very first time we meet Telemachus, he is being visited by the Goddess Athena (Wisdom), and this first depiction of the young man is quite revealing for what it says about the impact of a father's absence on a teenager: "Long before anyone else, the prince, Telemachus now caught sight of Athena—for he, too, was sitting there unhappy among the suitors, a boy, daydreaming."[55]

In this marvelous passage, we see four profound effects of the father's absence on the son. The son was **sitting**, the son was **unhappy**, the son was **daydreaming**, and this twenty-year-old son was...**still a boy**!

Telemachus' sitting shows us that his will was inactive. His sadness reveals his dominant emotion, and his daydreaming shows the principal occupation of his mind. Here is a most amazing truth: Homer is saying that the father's absence has shut down the son's entire soul. And that is why Telemachus is still a boy. Because of an absent father, he is stuck in adolescence!

A twenty-year-old should be active and moving, engaging his will,

---

[55] Homer, *The Odyssey*. Trans. Robert Fitzgerald (Garden City: Anchor Books, 1963), 5.

challenging himself and exploring his world—not sitting around. He should be optimistic, confident, curious, and adventuresome, not mired in sadness, dejection, boredom, or apathy. Most of all, he should be rooted in reality, in the real world of real people and real experiences—not daydreaming or idling away his time, as so many young men are doing today.

At the end of the book, when father and son finally meet, a one-sentence line by his father Odysseus sums up the whole sad story: "I am that father whom your boyhood lacked, and suffered pain for lack of. I am he."[56]

Let us not be fooled by a culture that tells us the father is an unimportant, somewhat comical imbecile. A father's absence affects the son's mind, will, and emotions, stunting his growth and robbing him of his purpose and calling while causing him great emotional pain. However, the opposite is also true: a father's steady presence injects life and energy into the son's heart and soul. An active, present father encourages the son to grow and motivates him to conduct his own quest to know and understand the world and to find what he was born to do. A true father calls down blessings on his son, conferring upon him happiness, peace, and emotional well-being.

---

[56] Ibid., 295.

WHAT REALLY MAKES A MAN GREAT?

All he wanted to do was go home.

He was a man's man. A brilliant strategist, a skillful warrior, and a man of cleverness and wisdom, Odysseus had seen and done it all. He fought and survived a ten-year battle and siege at Troy, then he spent another ten years struggling against the gods to get back to his beloved island of Ithaca. He had been tempted by goddesses and shipwrecked; he had fought hideous monsters like the giant one-eyed Cyclops (a symbol of the stupid and foolish man) and watched all his men die from disasters at sea. In terms of manhood, he was one of the greatest men ever conceived in literature.

But the great Odysseus had been humbled by these experiences, which of course was intended by the gods in the first place, and now he only wanted to go home and be with his wife and son, Telemachus, whom he has never seen.

It is amazing that one of the greatest epic poems in history—Homer's *Odyssey*—is essentially about a man who longs to go home. Or to put it another way, it is the story of what it takes for a man **to be able** to go home and simply be what he is supposed to be—a father, a husband, and a king. Homer seems to be suggesting that to be the hero takes an extraordinary man of skill and courage but to be the man at home takes even more. It requires not skill but virtue, especially the virtue of humility—man's right relationship to the gods and to others.

Being a husband and father are difficult roles for men. We must remember that when Adam was created, he was in the presence of only God and the created world. He was put to work naming the animals, to take dominion over the created realm by ordering his world. Only after he named the animals did Adam meet Eve. Eve's initial orientation was different; soon after she was created she was in the presence of another human being—Adam. In other words, Eve was initially and fundamentally **relational**, while Adam was initially and fundamentally **vocational.**

For men, work may have come first, but it is not primary. Men and women were created to rule creation *together.* Therefore their partnership—their marriage—is primary. Therefore men must **become** relational for that partnership to work. Ultimately, a man's greatest joy and peace will come from the relationships he creates at home, first with his wife and second with his children, working with his wife to raise noble sons and daughters.

Some men may disagree and try to persuade themselves that work is really more important, and they will rationalize their viewpoint with the economic argument that someone must be the provider if the family is to succeed at all. So many men hide behind this argument which essentially justifies their continued non-involvement with their families. But the argument is only partially true. They forget they are "one flesh" with their wives and vital to their children's academic, emotional, social, and spiritual wellbeing. Men are never to be providers alone; they must be in unity with their wives and involved with their children, both of which require men to be relational.

A righteous man knows that the well-being of his marriage and his family is impossible without God. In Psalm 144, David asks God to part the heavens and come down into David's world. Then, David describes the effects of God's presence on his children: "Then our sons in their youth will be like well-nurtured plants, and our daughters will be like pillars carved to adorn a palace" (144:12). In other words, with God's help, a man's sons will have abundant life (well-nurtured plants) and his daughters will possess incredible strength and beauty (pillars, works of art).

The noblest men excel in two arenas, not just one. They excel in work and career but also in the realm of home and family, where, contrary to the messages our culture is sending, men do have a special place and a vital role to fulfill. Being a father is one of the most fulfilling roles a man can ever have. The greatest men are good and Godly husbands and fathers—men who encourage and bless all those under their authority.

PRAYER POINTS FOR DADS

Anyone married knows that marriage is the one relationship relentlessly assaulted by the world and the Accuser of our souls. If the enemy can tear apart a husband and wife, he can damage even their children's children. A ruined marriage can produce a devastating chain reaction of destruction in innocent, vulnerable human beings literally for generations.

Obviously, a primary target in marriage is the husband and father. Created to wield authority as a life-giver, an encourager, a man of unconditional love, and a man of wisdom mandated to provide proper boundaries for his family, the father is tremendously powerful. He is a power for good if he abides in the Lord and walks in grace and humility, but a power for evil if he denies his brokenness and chooses to follow his own desires, making the kind of choices that benefit only himself, usually at his family's expense.

Two prayers by husbands and fathers will powerfully move God's heart and bring wisdom and revelation for any issue they might face.

Lord, show me my pride. Our own unresolved brokenness, consistent sin, natural human weaknesses, and ignorance of the truth give the enemy permission to launch deadly missiles at those we love. The root of all these is pride, or the illusion that we are sufficient in ourselves to carry out our duties. We do not realize the extent of our pride, how thoroughly it shapes our perspectives, attitudes, beliefs, and actions, and how blind we have become because of it. Therefore, asking God to show us our pride is one of the most fundamental prayers a man can ever pray. It is a prayer God loves to answer for the simple reason that pride's replacement—humility—is the doorway to revelation and the catalyst for growing in all the virtues.[57]

When we pray for humility, for God to show us our pride and eradicate it, God will quickly reveal pride we never dreamed we had. This will be almost too much to bear—we had no idea. Then He will show us all the conflict it has caused in our most important relationships. And we will discover, though we can still hardly believe it, that the son, daughter, wife, teacher, or boss we thought was the problem, was not the problem at all. We were the problem. Our pride was the problem. We have been blind in some area. And now, if we have the courage and the humility, we will do everything we can to set our relationships right.

What unresolved issues from my past are keeping me ineffective as a husband and a father? Most men do not want to face their past. The issues are too shameful or scary, the emotions are too strong, and the pain is too real. A single scripture from Genesis will help unlock the problem. Before the fall, Adam and Eve were naked but they felt no shame. After Adam and Eve sinned God called for them in the garden, but they were hiding. Adam's response is a classic archetype for any man caught in sin. Adam said, "I was afraid because I was naked, so I hid" (Genesis 3:10b). Every man born since Adam can say the same thing about his own life.

An initial shaming incident produced fear of being shamed again, which motivated Adam to hide. Every man can relate to this. Some incident occurred in a man's past, usually through treatment by a father or another adult, and it brought great shame, embarrassment, or humiliation. Because it was so painful, fear set in as a sort of protective mechanism ensuring that the experience would never occur again. Out of that fear came various forms of hiding, masking, withdrawal, or escape from reality in some form—drugs, alcohol, sex, recreation, or work. Instead of courageously exercising his authority to rule over some aspect of creation, the broken man is false to himself and disconnected from the real world because he is full of fear.

Thankfully, there is good news. The Lord can reveal the whole

---

[57] Andrew Murray's simple book, *Humility*, is unsurpassed on this topic. See Andrew Murray, *Humility and Absolute Surrender* (Peabody, MA: Hendrickson Publishers, 2005).

ugly root system behind the most painful moments of our past. If we let Him, He will reveal the core incidents, put us in touch with the tremendous fear behind those events, and then start to show us all the ways we men have chosen to hide from ourselves and from others. As we continue to obey, He will continue to heal. This is a difficult and painful process, but God is faithful to do His part and there is much grace. We must go through with it. The result will be a more loving husband, a stronger father, and a freer and happier man.

YOUR MOST VALUABLE PLAYER?

When we get to heaven we will probably want to remind God of all the good things we did while we lived on earth. We will want Him to know how active we were at church, and we might list for Him all the markers of our success in our jobs and careers. Maybe we will recite all the Bible verses we memorized or boast that, in our humble opinion, we are returning His investment thirty-, sixty-, or a hundred-fold.

However, when we get to heaven, the first thing on the Lord's mind will not be anything about our work or our accomplishments, as important as these are to us. He will ask us questions about our relationships, about how we treated the people He placed in our lives while we were doing all that work for Him. And the first question He might ask will be: "In all your years together, how did you treat your husband?" or, "In all the years I gave to you, how did you treat your wife?" He will say, "Did you choose your wife or husband first each day after you have demonstrated your commitment to me?"

Parents often find themselves having to "tag-team" in the years they are raising their children because there is so much that needs to get done. School, homework, extra-curricular activities, duties at church, and so much more have to be done while one or both parents handle the responsibilities of jobs, changing jobs, moving, caring for grandparents, and so on.

During this time it is easy for married couples to pull apart from one another and function more as a partnership (you do your part, I do mine) than two people in a sacred covenant and committed to serving, honoring, and laying down their lives for one another. Couples might take one another for granted, perhaps the passion in the relationship starts to dull a little, and in all kinds of small ways each person settles into beliefs that may not be true or actions that fall short of God's standard.

A wife might believe her husband will always be lazy, irresponsible, or generally inactive with the kids. That is just the way he is, and he will never change. Or a husband might lower his expectations little by little and settle for an irritable, joyless, and unresponsive wife, assuming that she will be that way until death do us part. So he might as well get used to it.

Parents raising children sometimes fall into the **parent abdication cycle**. For some reason or another, dad abdicates his position and authority as leader of the household. Maybe he travels too much. Perhaps he has decided to spend all his time on his computer or do things with friends, but for whatever reason, he abandons his leadership role. Perhaps he has the absurd notion that education is solely mom's responsibility![58] As a result, mom has to step up and take on the responsibilities he has neglected. This increased burden causes her to become resentful (she already has enough work to do!), then angry (this is wrong!), and then disrespectful. She subtly and not so subtly begins to tear down her husband, the kids pick up the now toxic atmosphere in the home, and gradually God's order and design for the family breaks down. The parents have lost sight of God's plan. It is a very simple one: **wives respect, husbands love, children honor** (Ephesians 5:33; 6:1-2).

We forget that growing in a relationship with the Lord is a dynamic process of ongoing transformation, which means husband and wife should always be growing, changing, and becoming more like Christ. We must remember that nothing is impossible with God and that He can fix the most broken of married relationships. We must remember and really believe that there is no sin or amount of sin, no condition or situation that remains outside of His grace and mercy. Remembering these things, we can walk in hope that our prayers for our spouses will not only change them but will also change us.

Each day after fulfilling your commitment to the Lord, choose to honor, respect, love, and serve the most important person God has

---

[58] See, for example, Deuteronomy 6:6-7 or Chapters 1-10 in the Proverbs where the Father is the primary teacher.

given to you on this earth—that person is your spouse. That person is your most valuable player. Your child's education, personal well-being, walk with the Lord—indeed, *your child's entire future*—depends upon it!

CHANGING MINDSETS: WHO NEEDS EDUCATION?

The students, the parents, the teachers, or the administrators?

The answer is, all of the above!

Leaders of Christian schools, whether they come from classical, traditional, or a blend of both in the University-Model®, are becoming more convinced of the necessity of training and encouraging parents as partners in the academic, moral, and spiritual education of their children.

Having been brought up in widespread cultural confusion and profoundly wrong Supreme Court decisions, a time when the family is rapidly disintegrating and where Facebook offers more than fifty-six gender possibilities for its users, today's parents, especially our younger ones, have a lot of "un-learning" to do. So, who is going to un-learn them?

School leaders have probably already experienced, for example, the mom who posts her issues with the school all over her Facebook page, slandering school leaders and stirring up the entire community as she does so. Or the mom who consistently appears on campus dressed immodestly. Or the dad who loses all self-control at football games. Or parents who simply do not understand their roles as those primarily responsible for their children's education.

Since our culture no longer supports our values, schools must begin to focus more on strengthening parents—reminding them of their God-given roles, encouraging them to persevere when it gets difficult, and correcting so much disinformation they have already unconsciously and uncritically accepted and integrated into their family culture and habits.

At the Summer 2015 "Repairing the Ruins" conference of the Association of Classical and Christian Schools, along with workshops focused on redeeming sports in our culture and protecting our schools from gender identity lawsuits, educators could attend a session entitled "90 Days, 90 Dads: Finding Meaningful Connections and Insights from Parents in a Growing School."[59]

Not surprisingly, the workshop addressed how one school tried to strengthen its community through a concentrated ninety-day campaign to get to know every one of its dads and by encouraging moms to become more engaged through in-home coffees, classes, and grade-level meetings. This is a school that understands the rich resources that exist in a diverse Christian community. However, bringing parents and school together is only a beginning!

Other schools are meeting the need for parent education in equally creative ways. Some schools have formed dad groups which provide opportunities for dads and their kids to enjoy fun activities together (games, sports, campouts), to sharpen one another in small, special interest groups (topical studies like how to raise boys), and to tackle school building projects or hold fundraisers to provide scholarships for colleges or mission trips.[60] Other schools have developed week-long parent education seminars that offer a blend of pastoral counsel (marriage, family), practical co-teacher instruction (research papers, reading programs, or college entrance exams), and general tips on parenting (resolving conflict, parenting children with different dispositions, or protecting kids from social media).[61]

We should not forget, however, that in this highly distracted age, administrators and teachers also have some serious catching up to do. Social media is not going away. Leaders need to reflect on how this new environment challenges everything we know in traditional

---

[59] Davies Owens, "90 Days, 90 Dads: Finding Meaningful Connection and Insights from Parents in a Growing School." ACCS Annual Conference, *Repairing the Ruins*. Dallas, TX. 18 June 2015. Workshop.

[60] As, for example, in the Patriot Dads group at Wylie Preparatory Academy in Wylie, Texas.

[61] Veritas Academy in Austin, Texas runs an excellent week-long parent training program.

education: curricula, homework, and teaching itself. Social media prevents students from developing habits of discipline, concentration, and critical thinking. It is compromising the value of the teacher, destroying relationships, and threatening true community. We must learn how to work with it so that it does not work against us.

Who needs education? We all do because the world we have known is changing more rapidly than we can possibly imagine.

CHANGING MINDSETS: WHO IS THE AUTHORITY?

With creative forms of Christian education sprouting all over the country, such as the University-Model® and the various hybrids of classical Christian schools, Christian parents are realizing they need to revise their thinking in several areas in order to be effective co-teachers to their children. Taking on a new mindset involves confronting some of the more erroneous educational myths parents have unconsciously accepted about home and school. Chief among them is the myth that the school is the "authority."

In fact, the parents are the authority, the ones ultimately responsible for the education of their children. They may choose to partner with the school to fulfill that responsibility but in doing so they do not surrender their authority. The school does not usurp it but comes alongside to support parents in their God-given, Biblically mandated roles (Deuteronomy 6:6-7).

Several other truths stem from this idea. Parents do not simply drop off their children at school each day and then remain uninvolved in their child's education during the week. That is because a Christian home and a Christian school are naturally in a **partnership**. They are tag-teaming, on the same side, pursuing the same goals as different but equal **co-partners**. Parents are still teaching and training their children academically, morally, and spiritually, even as their children attend a school. Although they may delegate to other agents some portion of their children's education, parents never surrender their ultimate authority as the primary teachers of their children.

The second truth to flow from this involves the need for ongoing parent education. In order to remain effective teachers and co-partners, parents and school must grow together and continue to learn from one another. They need to meet periodically to strengthen parenting and co-teaching skills and to receive encouragement and help when social, academic, moral, or spiritual problems arise, as they most surely will.

Almost all professionals have to re-certify to maintain their credentials in their respective fields and parents and teachers are no exception. There is so much to learn, especially in our day as information is exploding, as families and schools face challenges from social media, as local communities are disintegrating, and as home, church, and school confront a culture that for a long time now has not only not supported their values but is now actually undermining them. More than ever before, parents and schools need to learn from one another and the best way to do that is to meet regularly during the school year for training and instruction. If we want Christian education to succeed in our day, then parents, teachers, and administrators are obliged to periodically "go to school" together from now on.

It is not that we **have** to meet together but that we **get** to meet together. God has invited us to collaborate with Him on a project very important to Him—to encourage and train young people for their future roles in the Kingdom. We are partnering with each other and pooling our intellectual, professional, Biblical, and financial resources to help our children understand their design and calling and to train them to rule excellently over whatever aspect of creation is in need of their leadership. It is indeed a privilege, not an extra thing on our "to do" list and definitely not a distraction or a low priority. It is the main thing. It is a duty we undertake with sacrifice, humility, and thanksgiving.

So, in our day, we parents (teachers too!) have to make many adjustments to our thinking in order to be successful in whatever form of Christian education we undertake. We have to unlearn some things, relearn others, and learn still others for the first time. We must develop different priorities, adopt different values, and, as always, continue to die to self, to sacrifice, so that our children receive the very best education we can give them in the very short time we have left.

FIVE TIPS FOR PARENTS IN CHRISTIAN SCHOOLS

First, don't forget Deuteronomy 6:6-7! "These commandments are to be upon your hearts. Impress them on your children. Talk about them when you sit at home and when you walk along the road, when you lie down and when you get up." Two important principles come from these verses. First, parents, not the state, have the primary responsibility for the academic, moral, and spiritual education of their children. Parents can delegate that responsibility to different entities to help them get the job done, but the ultimate responsibility for the children's education belongs to the parents. Second, educating our children should naturally arise out of the normal ebb and flow of a day: when we sit at home, when we lie down, when we get up, and so on. It is not formal; it is natural. Parents, in a sense, are always teaching, always modeling, always explaining things while their children are with them at home.[62]

Second, the school community can help! Our school communities offer resources to help parents become informed and successful. Those resources include other parents who have already been through the process, as well as teachers, counselors, and

---

[62] For these insights on Deuteronomy 6:6-7 I am indebted to John William Turner, Jr. and his book, *Character Driven College Preparation: Parents and Teachers in Partnership Through University-Model® Schooling* (Fort Worth: Magnolia Media Group and GPA Ministries Inc., 2001).

administrators who understand the importance of home and school having a strong relationship built on trust. Whether students attend a classical, traditional, or University-Model® school, that school by definition functions as a Christian community. This community is rich in collective resources for families searching for wisdom, counsel, mentoring, or practical advice.

Third, remember the 70/30 rule. One way for parents to think about the partnering process is the 70/30 rule. The school partners with parents for roughly 70% of the student's academic training while the parents, according to Deuteronomy 6:6-7, oversee the remaining 30%.[63] When it comes to moral and spiritual instruction, however, this ratio reverses: parents take on 70% of the moral/spiritual training while the school supports the home with the remaining 30%. Parents lean on the school for academics, and the school leans on the parents for moral instruction, and each supports the other in both.

Fourth, true parenting flows out of intimacy with Christ. He is the Vine, we are the branches. As Jesus said, "apart from me you can do nothing" (John 15:5b). The parents who are most successful in loving and preparing their children for adulthood are those who continue to pursue a personal, passionate relationship with Jesus. Vitally connected to the Lord through their obedience, they move in rest and peace and parent by grace instead of by striving in their own strength. No matter how busy parents can get, protecting this one vital relationship should always be priority #1.

Fifth, it is never too late to begin a sincere relationship with your children. Do not listen to the lie that you may have already lost your children. There is no relationship that cannot be mended by humility, forgiveness, and reconciliation, and by learning to speak the truth in love. The older our children get, the more they need our guidance. It is never too late to have a genuine, sincere relationship with your children!

---

[63] Many thanks to Scott Reuthinger for this insight!

THE WASTING DISEASE OF AFFLUENCE

In his final semester of high school, a naturally intelligent and very gifted young man "from a good home" appears in danger of failing two of his easiest classes. He is eighteen. Almost a man.

His teachers are very concerned. Not all that interested in finding the cause, they feel it is their responsibility to enable him to pass. They let him retake quizzes and tests. They allow him extra time on project deadlines. They spend hours of their free time tutoring him. They think this is helping him. But he still does not turn in assignments and he is still failing the quizzes even after the re-takes, even after he has already been told all the answers.

His mother, fearing the shame she will feel when her son is not allowed to "walk" at graduation and becoming more furious with the school because of it, commits to checking his homework every day and challenging him to finish strong. She is concerned and the boy's father is concerned too, but that concern does not move beyond a command to just "work harder" or the lame parental decree that the boy is simply lazy. The dad returns to his main preoccupation, which is making more money, and that, no one seems to notice, is exactly the problem.

Everyone is concerned, except the child. Why does he not care? Why is he not passing? Why is he not passing after he has been given so many chances? Why does his mother have to follow him around wiping his nose? The child is eighteen. Why is his father not involved? What in the world has gone wrong here?

It is the soul-wasting disease of affluence.

Affluence becomes a disease when it entangles the student in the deadly sin of sloth. An abundance of wealth and material possessions create a selfish dependency on others and a sense of entitlement which kill desire and destroy initiative, effort, and personal responsibility. The result is a weakening of the soul and a dullness of the spirit that will become deadly if the parents and teachers do not aggressively confront it.

When a child grows up never having to learn personal responsibility, never having to expend effort or struggle for something worthwhile and good, because his parents have already provided him with everything he needs, he will form an untrue picture of himself, of others, and of life itself. He will think others exist to serve him and give him whatever he wants. That is, he will form a mindset that is essentially self-centered. He also will mistakenly believe that happiness comes from having things, from an abundance of possessions. As a result, he learns early on that personal effort is unnecessary because struggle and self-sacrifice are for others on his behalf, not for him. If he does not need to work, why should he? Emotionally, he becomes easily discouraged and frequently dejected—first, because he cannot always have what he wants and second, because the desire for things creates a desire for more things which in the end cannot satisfy his soul.

The pernicious effects of this disease are not unlike the effects of the lotus flower described in Homer's great epic, the *Odyssey*. When islanders gave this flower to Odysseus' men, they "never cared to report, nor to return: they longed to stay forever, browsing on that native bloom, forgetful of their homeland." Odysseus' solution was severe discipline: "I drove them, all three wailing, to the ships, tied them down under their rowing benches, and called the rest: 'All hands aboard; come, clear the beach, and no one taste the Lotus or you lose your hope of home.'"[64] The lotus flower sapped desire, deadened the will, induced forgetfulness, and killed all hope. The disease of affluence has exactly the same effects.

Because they have made idols of their possessions, students afflicted with the disease of affluence become dull and uninteresting, spiritually lukewarm and blind, much like the people of the Laodicean church in Revelation 3:14. God rebuked the people of this church,

---

[64] Homer, 148.

saying, "I know your deeds, that you are neither cold nor hot. I wish you were either one or the other! So, because you are lukewarm— neither hot nor cold—I am about to spit you out of my mouth" (Revelation 3:15-16).

The next lines describe the effects of affluence in no uncertain terms: "You say, 'I am rich; I have acquired wealth and do not need a thing.' But you do not realize that you are wretched, pitiful, poor, blind and naked" (3:17). Jesus' solution is refinement, purity, and the healing of their vision: "I counsel you to buy from me gold refined in the fire, so you can become rich; and white clothes to wear, so you can cover your shameful nakedness; and salve to put on your eyes so you can see" (3:18).

The disease of affluence appears in many guises. In the classroom, a student with the disease does not turn in homework, expends little effort on assignments—just enough to pass—and therefore performs far below his God-given ability. In the school, he does not respect authority because teachers and leaders make him work, nor does he think school policies apply to him because he has been taught to do whatever he wants. This mindset easily morphs into unethical behavior. He may lie about how he spends his time or why he has not turned in his work. He will at first put off and then eventually not even do assignments that require work over a period time. As a result of his inactivity and procrastination, he will learn to cut corners and do as little as possible, or he might resort to manipulating others, copying another student's work, or cheating because it saves effort and allows him to do what he wants.

The antidote is tough love on the part of every adult who has been enabling him: moms need to toughen up and let their baby fail; dads need to be more involved with the child and then create more challenging home conditions that reverse the effects of affluence on his children; and all the merciful teachers who have been sweet-talked or manipulated to serve this child, unwittingly playing into his hand and making the problem infinitely worse, need to toughen up, keep firm boundaries, act like adults, and cut no deals. The child needs to suffer the consequences of his choices to such an extent that he will come to his senses, recognize the misery he has caused himself and others, and grow up.

THE SCHOOL ASSIGNS TOO MUCH HOMEWORK

Now and then school administrators hear the accusation that the school assigns too much homework. And that is a serious problem, the argument goes, because the homework is placing an undue amount of stress, which is bad, on the students. The implied judgment of the school here is most unfortunate. From that premise, it is easy to draw the conclusion that the school—rather than the family—needs to make some changes.

Before that premise is accepted, parents (and school leaders) need to be sure they have ruled out other possibilities.

1. Is the student under the deception that he or she "can do it all"? Is the student believing he can take full course load, play on the worship team, and expect to make the Honor Roll, while also working a part-time job? So many parents unconsciously buy into the hyper-narcissistic "superhero myth" of our culture—that their children can be MVP's in everything—never realizing that they (parents) really do possess the power of "no" and need to exercise it often to help students make good choices to steward their time well.

2. Does the student have any learning issues that may require him to take more time on school work than his peers? Students with disabilities like dyslexia might need more time. Slow or poor readers will naturally spend more time on homework than

would average students. A student with an attention deficit will need more time if he cannot control his distractions. If any of these conditions exist, the issue is not that the school requires too much homework, but whether the school and the family are a fit. There may be another school that can better support that particular student.

3. Does the student have unrestricted and unsupervised access to social media? It is becoming more common for students to stay up late texting, snap-chatting, or roaming the Internet to such an extent that the habit is affecting school performance. Actually, such activity creates two problems: because the students are unsupervised, they are using social media when they should be doing their homework, and because many of them lack discipline and self-control, they stay up too late and are losing sleep, which ruins their effectiveness for the next day.

4. Does the student have a problem prioritizing activities or managing time? This is a problem of sound judgment. Not being able to place the right values on activities will lead to errors in the use of time. All activities are not equal. Some are priorities, some necessities, some luxuries. Students must learn to allocate the right amount of time and energy to each activity if they are to manage time well. Choosing to spend a lot of time on a fun activity, like texting, while spending less time on a necessity, such as studying for an exam, is not wise. Some activities, such as working consistently on a class project or writing a research paper in stages, require the student to do certain things first and early before he can work on other things. So managing time involves not only the ability to prioritize activities but also the ability to recognize the right timing—which time slots are best for the various levels and kinds of work the student must do.

5. Could managing homework and priorities be an opportunity to develop an overcomer's mindset? We need to be sure we don't remove problems to such an extent that students never have opportunities to build resiliency and overcome them. Making priorities and managing conflicting values are life

skills—adults have to do this all the time. This means students may not be able to give 100% to everything all the time—something perfectionists have trouble accepting. In some cases, not being able to devote oneself fully to a task must simply be okay once in a while. Sometimes we can only resolve to do the best we can with the responsibilities we face, trusting that all things will work out in the end. Allowing students to resolve homework and time issues on their own may be good for them. It might drive them to exercise grit, determination, and resourcefulness—excellent virtues in and of themselves and vital to their success beyond high school.

6. Has the family given its "times" over to the Lord? David prayed, "My times are in your hands," suggesting he understood that his life's direction—his times—were not his responsibility but God's (Psalm 31:15a). Therefore, he did not need to worry about his current circumstances or future direction. Very closely related to this is the blessing of the Sabbath rest. Does the family honor the Sabbath, which is graciously given to us by God for our health, restoration, and well-being, or do the parents consider that day just another work day? "Then God blessed the seventh day and made it holy" (Genesis 2:3a). This is not a redemptive ordinance nor did it originate in Israel's law, although it later became enshrined in it. This is a creation ordinance, meaning the Sabbath principle is embedded in the very structure of creation itself. At **creation** this day was blessed and made holy for man's benefit, so we are to always honor this day, not in a legalistic sense, but out of our freedom. Like so many other practical applications of our faith, when we faithfully honor this day, we find that God actually economizes our times and gives us much grace for all we are to do.

7. How badly do we want to build overcomers? Seven times in the book of Revelation Jesus emphasized overcoming or conquering as a means of future blessing, and frequently in the scriptures believers are challenged to struggle against sin, stand firm in spiritual battles, or tenaciously hold on to the faith, especially in the last days when disorder, sin, and confusion will be rampant. We need to remember that our students are in

training. We are always teaching them how to grow up and confront challenges without complaining, grumbling, blaming others, or quitting. Instead of removing our students from difficult situations, we might challenge them to summon the inner strength along with the wisdom God gives to rise up, meet their challenges, and find solutions on their own.

8. Do the parents understand grace? Grace is that wonderful ability God gives to help us do what He has called us to do. The opposite of grace is striving. Parents and students walking in faith will walk in rest and grace even in the midst of challenges to their time. They will experience an ease, a peace, a calmness as they meet each challenge and overcome it. On the other hand, a student ignorant of grace will believe he is to do all the work himself. That is why bodies and minds break down, why students get sick or develop migraines, why we develop long-term illnesses—it is because we have made choices apart from the Lord's counsel and without God's grace. We are to never trust in ourselves or do anything on our own but with the grace God gives through His Spirit.

So before accusing the school of assigning too much homework, parents must be sure they have considered other possibilities. Christian parents especially need to be aware of the extent to which cultural ideas and pressures are at work here. A grossly narcissistic culture like our own encourages a sense of entitlement, which, combined with an over-emphasis on individual rights and a distorted idea of personal freedom, undermines the virtues that in every generation have made noble men and women: hard work, perseverance, self-sacrifice, courage, initiative, resourcefulness, optimism, and great faith.

BEWARE OF TIME MANAGEMENT!

There is a time for everything, and a season for every activity under heavens. (Ecclesiastes 3:1)

And the wise heart will know the proper time and procedure. For there is a proper time and procedure for every matter. (Ecclesiastes 8:5b-6a)

The scriptures from Ecclesiastes make the point that everything has a "time" which only the wise in heart are able to discern. In our way of speaking, wise people know when to do things and when not to. And the inverse is true too: those who fail to do what they should be doing when they should be doing it are not wise—they are foolish.

However, if we listen to the wisdom of the world about matters of time, we get a very different story. The problem is not lack of wisdom or even simply foolishness, let alone an issue of sin, but a problem with "time management." In other words, instead of suffering from a deficiency of virtue, which is a serious matter of the heart, or even a sin problem, the person merely lacks a "skill" which can be remedied by practicing it enough times until one "gets" it.

It is one thing to say a baseball player cannot hit fastballs. It is another thing to say that the baseball player has no desire to hit anything at all or even to play, even though he is very good at hitting fastballs. The one is simply a skill problem—we can improve the skill of hitting fastballs by a lot more practice. The other, however, is a heart problem. **No amount of practice will correct a lack of desire.** That is because the problem is much deeper and more fundamental—it goes to the very core of who the baseball player is; it goes to his will and heart, to his moral character.

If we continue to call heart problems "skill problems," we will continue to invite confusion and bring on much trouble. Not only will we fail to correct the real problem, but we will probably make it much worse.

The person suffering from "time management" issues is described rather harshly in the book of Proverbs. He is one who is, in fact, lazy because he lacks sound judgment (24:30, 12:11). As a result of bad judgment, he ignores and hates correction (10:17, 12:1) and stops listening to instruction (19:27) because he actually despises himself (15:32) and is contemptuous of his own ways (19:16). He finds pleasure in evil conduct (10:23), is trapped by his own evil desires (11:6) in the form of cravings (13:4) and the love of pleasure (21:17), including especially, sleep (26:14), but he also chases fantasies (28:19) because he is deceived (14:8), which makes his course of action seem right (16:25) and which he prefers because it delights him (10:23). He scorns instruction and ignores discipline (13:13, 13:18), especially his father's discipline, and talks all the time instead of actually working (14:23), and **so he does not do the things he should be doing at the right time** (20:4). In fact, he keeps going down the wrong path until he suffers for it (22:3). He lacks self-control and he repeats his folly over and over because he actually thinks he is wiser than everyone else (26:16), which is yet another deception and essentially puts all his trust in himself, making him a true fool (28:26).

As a result, he is full of irrational fears (22:13); his way is blocked with thorns (15:19), which means he never makes progress, and he gets nothing (13:4) except punishment (16:22), trouble (13:21), poverty (21:5), shame (13:18), and slave labor (12:24). He is brother to one who destroys (18:9), and because of his persistent folly, he will, in fact, die (21:25).

Solomon's counsel is very severe because Solomon knows that if one lets this character issue continue, he will die. This is most assuredly NOT a time-management problem; it is a very serious deadly sin. And we get free of it not by practicing time-management skills but by repenting of our sin—our selfishness, our foolish behavior, our indulgence in the flesh and flat-out rejection of God's grace. Then we overcome the problem by trusting in the sanctifying work of the Holy

Spirit: "For if you live according to the flesh, you will die; but if by the Spirit you put to death the misdeeds of the body, you will live. For those who are led by the Spirit of God are the children of God" (Romans 8:13-14).

We should no longer agree with the wisdom of the world here. Time mismanagement is at root a form of selfishness and foolish behavior which is corrected by repentance, receiving God's grace, and growing in God's wisdom. When this happens one will become wise. He will finally be able to "know the proper time and procedure" for all that he does.[65]

---

[65] Of course, not every situation where a student fails to manage time is a sin issue, and developing good habits to manage time can also be helpful.

MOMS WITH SCISSORS: CARING FOR HELICOPTERS

A fall 2010 publication of Christian Schools International contained a good definition of what is now a well-known phenomenon—the helicopter parent: "These are parents who 'hover' over their children and monitor their every activity. Helicopter parents feel that it is their responsibility to watch over their children in order to make sure they receive good grades, visit with the right people, and make wise choices. These children are expected to report to their parents daily, via text message, email, or cell phone—sometimes even after they've left home for college or university."[66]

The author goes on to explain the kind of damage helicopter parents do to their children. They inhibit children from developing responsibility and prevent them from learning the wisdom that naturally comes from mistakes and failures. They rob their children of the freedom to try new experiences and develop new skills. As a result, children controlled by helicopter parents never grow up. They never have to because the parent does all the work for them. The parent talks to each of the child's teachers incessantly, instead of training the child to approach adults on his own; she hyper-vigilantly monitors his grades and assignment sheets, teaching the student to care less, and she never stops interrogating her child, which will most surely encourage him to rebel as soon as he can get away with it.

Think of helicopter moms as moms running with scissors. Then

---

[66] Christian Schools International, *Home and School Magazine*, Fall, 2010, 17-19.

think of their children as butterflies in cocoons struggling to get out. Butterflies need to work their wings against the walls of the cocoon to break free, but also to strengthen their wings for future flight. They need to exercise their wings, even though they cannot yet fly. But here comes the helicopter mom, rushing in with her scissors, wanting to "help" her children by cutting the cocoon for them, so they can be sure of getting out on time with no complications. They will get out all right but at a terrible **future** cost. Such an action would kill real butterflies because their opportunity to struggle and grow strong has been taken away.

So the damage to the children is very real. However, such parents, very often pathologically fearful moms, can do great damage to a school community as well. Since they all too easily take their child's side in everything, helicopter parents are easily deceived by the fiction that their child can do no wrong, making it very easy to blame the school for the child's problems. And since helicopter parents are hyper-protective, they are often contentious and combative in conversations with teachers and very skilled at enlisting other parents to their cause. This happens because such parents have developed a blindness when it comes to their own children. They cannot "hear" other parents and teachers who have a different point of view. Their child is always right and always, therefore, the victim. This is why helicopter parents continue to bring up issues everyone else assumed had already been settled. They just cannot let the issues go. The helicopters still believe their child continues to be wronged by a conspiracy of the school's leaders so they continue to bring up the issues again and again, wearing out a great number of teachers and administrators in the process. Helicopter parents, in their blindness and confusion can, therefore, cause great damage to a school.

Help for moms with scissors requires that we see the false beliefs that motivate their behavior. Three beliefs, in particular, are worth noting.

My child's performance is a direct reflection of my parenting and my worth. Parents do have responsibilities to raise, teach, and discipline their children, and their efforts certainly will show up in their children. For example, "a child left undisciplined disgraces its mother" (Proverbs 29:15b). If a mother abandons her responsibilities to train up her child in the way he should go, the child will turn out badly and bring shame to the mother. Helicopter moms know this and will do all that they can to ensure that neither eventuality happens. In another sense, however, a child's performance should not be seen as a reflection of the parent. Children have sin natures. They like to rebel. Sometimes they deceive. They make their own choices in opposition to their parents. Such children are not necessarily a reflection of the parents.

If I don't keep on him, my child will fail. Notice the implied belief in that statement. The belief is that failure is bad, and it most certainly is if the parent thinks her child's performance is a reflection of her worth. But what is so wrong with failure? Failure is good if it motivates a child to work harder and challenges him to be resourceful to overcome obstacles. In fact, obstacles and failures can be very powerful motivators if the parent does not incessantly hover around her child and rescue him before he can experience these opportunities.

The school is to blame for my child's behavior and performance. A helicopter parent's excuses can be amusing and highly imaginative. My son has not turned in assignments because the teacher's directions were not clear. My son's test grades are low because the teacher did not explain what will be on the test. My son misbehaves in class because the teacher is dull and uninteresting. My child was sent home because the school's dress code is too rigid and unfair. And on and on and on. By the way, children are very good at recognizing mom's hyper-involvement and they are more than willing to let her do all the work. At some point, however, if her child is to survive at all, that mom needs to step back and let consequences be consequences. Then she remains uninvolved until the child summons the inner strength to find his own way to overcome that obstacle.

Helicopter parents need to see that much of their efforts are motivated by fear. Once they can acknowledge the power they have given to fear, they may very well get better. They will release their children into more independence. The result will be a happier, more responsible child, and an army of teachers and school leaders who can breathe a sigh of relief now that the onslaught from this unbalanced parent is finally over.

WE CAN CHANGE OUR MINDS!

Some kind of circumstance is troubling you. Maybe it is an ongoing conflict or tension with a parent or teacher. Or there is talk at work of layoffs which means your children might have to change schools again. Perhaps one of your children is going through a phase which has been difficult for the family. Maybe your daughter does not talk to you or is no longer following the Lord. Perhaps your son, who is very athletic, just blew out his knee in football practice.

When difficult and challenging circumstances occur, some of us begin to feel all kinds of negative feelings like discouragement, dejection, grief, or despair. And every time we think about those circumstances we feel more weighed down, more powerless, hopeless, or trapped. We think those feelings are caused by the actual event or circumstance, but they are not. They are caused by our *thinking* about the problem, the mental framework we have for understanding it.

Talk of layoffs creates the thought that we might lose our job, followed by the thought that we might not get another one or might have to uproot our families to get another one, or that we will go bankrupt, and it is these thoughts that produce the negative feelings of fear, dejection, discouragement, and despair. In other words, the negative feelings don't come from the circumstance; they come from *the way we are choosing to think about* the circumstance.

Other people can hear talk of layoffs and think positive thoughts like "A change will be exciting" or "This will open new opportunities" or "This has not caught God off guard" or "God has always watched out for me and for my children and He will continue to do so, which means I have everything to look forward to!" We can think that when it comes to our children's education, since God knows where He wants them to be, He will provide the means for them to get there. Such thoughts produce the opposite feelings of excitement, hope, encouragement, happiness, and joy. Remember: *the feelings come from our thinking, not from our circumstances.* If we think the right thoughts, we will enjoy the right feelings and remain in a place of faith rather than fear.

The good news, the news we often forget, is that in any circumstance—your son doing poorly at school, your spouse not in alignment with you, the closing of a cherished Christian school—we have the freedom and power **to choose** how we wish to think about it. We really do have a choice here. We can choose to see the situation through the framework of God's sovereignty and God's love for us and trust in His ability to work out everything for our good. Or we can choose the other.

Thoughts are like dominoes. That first thought will produce a chain reaction of thoughts and feelings just like it if we do not take it captive. If, by effort and self-control, we reject the negative and choose the positive, the faith position, we will produce further thoughts and feelings in that direction. We will see that circumstance from the right perspective, freeing us from fear, worry, or confusion.

What power we have when we finally realize that in *any situation* we will always have the freedom to actually change our minds!

CURRICULUM AND CULTURE

MARVELS OF DIVINE WISDOM: AN OVERVIEW

Leaders in classical and University-Model® Christian schools and many home-school parents as well are sincerely committed to training students in wisdom. For instance, the Circe Institute, which serves the classical school community, states on its website that "The purpose of Classical Education is to cultivate wisdom and virtue." And a popular book in Classical Christian circles has been, *Wisdom and Eloquence: A Christian Paradigm for Classical Learning.*[67]

Biblical wisdom is mysterious, multi-faceted, and complex—"manifold" as Paul writes in Ephesians (3:10). Christian school parents, students, teachers, and leaders can pursue any of several fascinating avenues for study and contemplation:

Wisdom is a She. Throughout the Wisdom literature wisdom is personified as a woman. What should this personification mean to us? How is wisdom like a woman? What is "feminine" about her? At the very least, this is telling us to pursue her. But she is also pursuing us. She is calling out from the busy streets of the city. What does she want to tell us? Why the urgency? What happens when we capture and "embrace" her? (Proverbs 8). Is this woman calling out in the streets a prophetic image of the Church?

---

[67] See the Circe Institute's website at: www.circeinstitute.org. See Robert Littlejohn and Charles T. Evans, *Wisdom and Eloquence* (Wheaton: Crossway, 2006).

Wisdom is a Set of Virtues. Proverbs 8 and James 3:17 each list seven virtues associated with wisdom. In Proverbs 8 they are: prudence, knowledge, discretion, counsel, sound judgment, understanding, and power. In James 3:17, "the wisdom that comes down from heaven is first of all pure; then peace-loving, considerate, submissive, full of mercy and good fruit, impartial, and sincere." It will take serious reflection and study to discern the differences between the two lists!

Wisdom is a Divine Template. In Proverbs 8:27-30, wisdom uses building and construction language to describe her activities. She assisted God in laying down forms, outlines, boundaries, and foundations at creation. When she repeats five times that God brought her forth "before" He created a single thing (8:22-26), it is clear she represents the blueprint or template for anything we are to do or build—a company, a school community, a department, and a life.

Wisdom is a Craftsman. Proverbs 8:22-31 and Psalm 104:24 show wisdom in the role of the creative artist assisting God when He created the universe. Knowing that God made everything in wisdom and then observing what and how He made it in Genesis 1 reveals more clues about wisdom's creative activity: she was involved in making the "forms" (templates) of the created world—land, sea, and sky—but also the "filling" of those realms with uniquely created animals, fish, and birds. She is therefore both the Design and Substance of every created thing.[68]

Wisdom is a Tree of Life. Eve ate from the forbidden tree because she saw it was desirable for gaining wisdom (Gen. 3:6) even though she was free to eat from the Tree of Life also. In Proverbs 3:18 we find that the tree of life is wisdom, and in the Book of Revelation this tree, which will once again be freely available to all after Jesus returns, is used for the healing of the nations (Revelations 22:2). Will wisdom be the means for healing the nations? Much to ponder here!

Wisdom is a Name for the Holy Spirit. In both the Old and

---

[68] A beautiful example of wisdom's association with form and substance is the creation of man himself. Adam, the "form" and Eve, taken from his rib or insides, the "substance."

New Testaments wisdom goes by the same name. Isaiah 11:2 refers to the Spirit of the Lord as the Spirit of Wisdom, and in Ephesians 1:17 Paul asks for the Spirit of Wisdom and Revelation. What is the connection between the Spirit and wisdom, the Spirit and the Tree of Life, the Spirit and creativity? Everyone, but especially our artists, needs to explore these great questions!

Wisdom is an attribute of each member of the Godhead. The Father's expression of wisdom consists of the forms of creation and the plan of redemption through the form of the perfect Man—Jesus. Jesus, the Power of God and the Wisdom of God (1 Corinthians. 1:24), expresses His wisdom in the form of the perfect government, the Kingdom of God. And the Holy Spirit, the Spirit of Wisdom and Revelation, is even now building the form of the perfect community, the Church, the Body of Christ, the Bride of Christ, who is, interestingly enough, also a **woman**!

Surely these great and exciting mysteries are crying out for serious investigation!

ALL THE TREASURES

My goal is that they may be encouraged in heart and united in love, so that they may have the full riches of complete understanding, in order that they may know the mystery of God, namely, Christ, in whom are hidden all the treasures of wisdom and knowledge. (Colossians 2:2-3)

We straddle two realms, the earthly and the spiritual, but they are not separate and neither should be favored or neglected. We are obliged to pay our bills, perfect our talents, and manage our property as well as follow God, love our neighbor, and develop virtues like purity, peace, sincerity, and mercy. God deeply cares about our happiness in both realms, and that is why He has given us His wisdom. In Christ we have God's marvelous gift of wisdom for everything we do on this earth.

For prosperity in the kingdom of man—the realm of home, work, and city—God gives the practical virtues of wisdom in Proverbs 8: prudence, knowledge, discretion, counsel, sound judgment, understanding, and power. Symbolized by a woman calling out to men at the city gates, wisdom has counsel for all human activities: insight for those who govern, counsel for relationships with parents, friends, and neighbors; knowledge for conducting business, caring for the poor, avoiding unethical behavior, managing property, guarding one's speech, and making a fortune.

In Proverbs 31, wisdom is "made flesh" through an example of a wise woman who embodies the same practical virtues found in

Proverbs 8. She prudently buys wool and flax, artfully turning it into clothing for her family. She shows discipline when she gets up early and goes to work and sound judgment when she buys a field and plants a vineyard. She displays knowledge as she trades in the market places and power when she blesses the poor and instructs her children. In the beginning of the book of Proverbs Wisdom, personified, calls out at the city gates; at the end of the book, wisdom, more actualized, receives praise at the city gates.

For success in the Kingdom of God, God has given us the virtues of wisdom in James 3:17: purity, peacefulness, consideration of others, submission, mercy, impartiality, and sincerity. Emphasizing spiritual goodness or maturity, these virtues are also symbolized in a woman—the Bride of Christ, the Church.

Each virtue in James exists in a context describing the Body of Christ, the People of God, or the Church. In Ephesians, Paul describes the Bride as being without stain or wrinkle (5:27). In Colossians he says, "as members of one body you were called to peace" (3:15b). He reminds Titus' church to be peaceable and considerate (3:1-2) and asks the Ephesians to "submit to one another out of reverence for Christ" (5:21). Peter, defining other attributes of God's people, reminds the church they have received mercy (1 Peter 2:10), while James exhorts his community to not show favoritism (James 2:1).

All the treasures of wisdom and knowledge—virtues for practical success and moral goodness—are found in Jesus, the amazing gate for the sheep (John 10:7) and the one sure door to happiness and success. In Him alone does man become wise: whole, fruitful, morally good, and holy.

CHRIST, THE WISDOM AND POWER OF GOD

Jews demand signs and Greeks look for wisdom, but we preach Christ crucified: a stumbling block to Jews and foolishness to Gentiles, but to those whom God has called, both Jews and Greeks, Christ the power of God and the wisdom of God. (1 Corinthians 1:22-24)

In a poem describing the awesome sovereignty of God, Job said: "To God belong wisdom and power; counsel and understanding are his" (Job 12:13). In a poem praising God's marvelous revelation of King Nebuchadnezzar's dream, Daniel said, "Praise be to the name of God for ever and ever; wisdom and power are his" (Daniel 2:20). Then Daniel thanked God for giving him that same gift: "I thank and praise you, God of my ancestors: **you have given me** wisdom and power" (Daniel 2:23a).

Only two others in the Scriptures are specifically described as having the same gifts, and one of those is Jesus Christ. In a prophecy, Isaiah cited Jesus' wisdom and power when he described the coming Christ in words identical to wisdom's virtues in Proverbs 8: through the Spirit, Jesus will have wisdom, understanding, counsel, power, and knowledge (Isaiah 11:1-2). In 1 Corinthians 1:24b, Paul refuted both Jews and Greeks when he described Christ as "the power of God and the wisdom of God."

The second person mentioned in the Scriptures as having these same gifts was Stephen, the first martyr. Selected by the Church because he was full of the Spirit and wisdom, Stephen was also described as a man full of faith and the Holy Spirit, and as a man full of God's grace and power (Acts 6:3, 5, 8). His wisdom and power were most formidable; Stephen's opponents could not argue against him because they could not stand up against his **wisdom** or the **Spirit** by whom he spoke (6:10).

Daniel is the exemplary prototype, Jesus is the marvelous incarnation, and Stephen is the first fruit. They are evidence and encouragement that our destiny is to share in this same wisdom and power of God. Daniel and Stephen are models of the righteous believers we are expected to be. Wisdom and power were the essence of their witness and the reason for their success. Since Daniel's wisdom was greater than the wisdom of the other wise men because it was given to him by God, Daniel could resolve mysteries in dreams and visions (Daniel 1:17). Because Stephen was "full" of God's wisdom and power, he did great wonders and miraculous signs among the people (Acts 6:8) and was powerfully effective in evangelizing unbelieving Jews. The witness of Daniel and Stephen is our hope that we are to have exactly the same authority of God through the Holy Spirit.

Isaiah 11 and 1 Corinthians reveal that the wisdom and power of Jesus come from the Holy Spirit. This Spirit of Wisdom and Revelation (Ephesians 1:17) is God's presence with us today, graciously given to us so that we "may understand what God has freely given us" in Jesus Christ (1 Corinthians 2:12b). Poured out at Pentecost after Jesus had commissioned His disciples to go in His authority and power (Matthew 28:18-20, Luke 24:49), the Holy Spirit will indwell every believer through a simple request from the Father (Luke 11:13).

Confident in Jesus (the source) and the Holy Spirit (the means), and encouraged by the exemplary witnesses of Daniel and Stephen, school leaders should help believing students to be *just like them*: authoritative and powerful witnesses for Christ, civic and cultural leaders whose arguments none can refute because our students have been filled with the wisdom and power of God.

WISDOM FROM GOD: JESUS

I was there when he set the heavens in place, when he marked out the horizon on the face of the deep. (Proverbs 8:27)

Christ Jesus, who has become for us wisdom from God— that is, our righteousness, holiness and redemption. (1 Corinthians 1:30b)

As members of the Church and as leaders in Christian schools, we have not yet begun to fathom the depth of the riches and mysteries of the wisdom of God. Wisdom is the supreme virtue our students must understand, desire, and possess for themselves. Every Christian school in the country should, therefore, be a cutting-edge research center for studies in divine wisdom.

Wisdom is the genetic code for all creation. Identified in the Proverbs as the craftsman at God's side and associated with forms, outlines, boundaries, and foundations, wisdom was the blueprint or plan for the construction of every created thing (Proverbs 8:22-31). This fact alone has profound implications for all our work here on earth.

In 1 Corinthians, Paul calls Jesus "wisdom from God" and then qualifies that statement with the phrase, "that is, our righteousness, holiness and redemption" (1:30b). Viewing the two texts together, we discover a striking syllogism: Jesus is wisdom, wisdom is a plan, and therefore, Jesus is a plan. Jesus is a plan or blueprint for the complete salvation of man, literally a second Adam (Romans 5:14; John 1:1).

God's perfect "template" for this salvation, Jesus is the genetic code for a new humanity.

This plan for a new humanity unfolds in three stages. As our righteousness, Jesus puts us back into the right relationship with God. Right standing with God then serves as the foundation for our becoming holy like God, for, "without holiness no one will see the Lord" (Hebrews 12:14b). As we develop, deepen, and maintain a relationship with Jesus over time, we grow in holiness, which is the essence of our redemption. We were saved, we are being saved, and we will be saved—the wise plan of salvation is all of this and all of this is in Jesus Christ. As Paul described it, this marvelous plan in Jesus is "God's wisdom, a mystery that has been hidden and that God destined for our glory before time began" (1 Corinthians 2:7b). Surely, our schools can encourage our students to eagerly pursue these fabulous mysteries!

"His [God's] intent was that now, through the church, the manifold wisdom of God should be made known to the rulers and authorities in the heavenly realms," (Ephesians 3:10). This means an irresistible and wonderfully mysterious relationship exists between Jesus, wisdom, and the Church.

Correspondences abound between the woman Wisdom and the man Jesus. In Proverbs 8:22a, Wisdom says, "The LORD brought me forth as the first of his works"; in Colossians 1:15b Jesus is "the firstborn over all creation." Wisdom was appointed "at the very beginning, when the world came to be" (Proverbs 8:23b); "He [Jesus] is before all things" (Colossians 1:17a). Wisdom is the craftsman at God's side during creation (Proverbs 8:30), but "all things were created through him [Jesus] and for him" (Colossians 1:16b). Psalm 104:24a says, "How many are your works, LORD! In wisdom you made them all." In Hebrews 1:2b Jesus is "heir of all things, and through whom also he made the universe." Wisdom is personified as a woman in the Old Testament, on her way to becoming real (the Church) in the New. Jesus is pre-incarnate in the Old Testament, on His way to becoming the Word made flesh in the New. Perhaps the best analogy is a matrimonial one: very closely related, yet distinctly different, Wisdom and Jesus are "one flesh," like marriage partners.

Should not a growing wisdom tradition be one of the chief marks of a Christian school? And should not our students be the seekers, guardians, practitioners, and champions of the wisdom of God so that others, as they did in Solomon's day, will come from miles around simply to hear their wisdom? Is not wisdom the rightful heritage of those who follow the Lord?

WORLDVIEW MADE SIMPLE: AN OVERVIEW

In recent years, discussions about "worldviews" have become prominent in Christian educational circles and today many high schools and colleges now offer some form of worldview instruction. The work of Francis Schaeffer (*Trilogy*), Harry Blamires (*The Christian Mind*), and Focus on the Family (*The Truth Project*) have been a few of the more important contributions to this discussion. More recent works include James K. A. Smith's *Desiring the Kingdom* and *Imagining the Kingdom*.

On an intellectual level, a worldview is *a way of thinking or perceiving the world*. It has variously been defined as a lens, a framework, or a set of presuppositions about basic questions of reality—Is there a God? What is the nature of the universe? Who is man?—and so on. Worldviews can be personal (the unconscious heart assumptions that guide our daily choices and actions) or formal (theistic, humanistic, naturalistic, and so on). They permeate every sphere of public and private life: art, music, media and entertainment, government, business, the family, our educational institutions, and even the church.

As Western civilization has abandoned its theistic foundations in reason and revelation, a host of humanistic worldviews have filled the void, and the results have been catastrophic. When man sins and separates himself from God, he loses the good of reason—his thinking becomes "futile," his heart is "darkened," and his mind becomes "depraved" (Romans 1). With his heart and mind no longer valuing or beholding Truth, his way of seeing and understanding the fundamental issues of life—his worldview—becomes distorted, no longer providing him with an accurate picture of reality. As a result, many people today cannot even recognize, much less solve, the serious social, political, and cultural problems that confront the nation and the world.

In the United States, the need for a Christian worldview emerged from the cultural changes caused by the fracturing of the Christian cultural/religious consensus of the 1950s, the radical leftist social revolution of the 1960s, and the Roe v. Wade Supreme Court decision of 1973, which had the effect of rallying Christians of different traditions to a common cause. The entrance of large numbers of Christians into the public square naturally brought the concept of "worldviews" into the national debate, which very quickly broke down into a series of polarizing "Culture Wars" between the orthodox and the progressives, the liberals and the conservatives on issues like abortion, feminism, the First Amendment, and gay rights.[69] And, as several recent presidential elections have shown, these culture wars of competing worldviews continue to exist in our day; they are simply the latest skirmishes in the great cosmic battle for Truth that began in the Garden of Eden.[70]

A Christian worldview, however, is much more than an intellectual stance, a perspective on the world, a body of knowledge or ideas; it involves the whole person—body, soul, and spirit. With it, thinking is wedded to being, information is connected to action, and worldview instruction addresses not only what one **knows** but also what one **loves or ought to love**.[71] A Christian worldview, then, requires not just new information, but a complete transformation of the mind and heart—a new person.

Crucial to the transformation of thought and action is simply what the Bible has always called the wisdom of God. Biblical wisdom addresses both thought and action; it is God's way of seeing (His "worldview"), as well as God's way of being (His virtues or character) (Proverbs 8:12-14; James 3:17-18). As believers grow in the wisdom and knowledge of God, their minds get renewed and they begin to see

---

[69] This is the thesis of James Davison Hunter's *Culture Wars: the Struggle to Define America* (New York: Basic Books, 1991).

[70] The "Cosmic Battle" is a term coined by Del Tackett in Focus on the Family's *Truth Project*, Lesson 1 "Veritology: What is Truth?" See www.thetruthproject.org.

[71] Smith, *Desiring the Kingdom*, 18.

themselves, others, and their world from God's perspective. Incarnate with the Truth, they begin to think from a Kingdom perspective, but they also begin to act righteously according to Kingdom virtues produced by the Holy Spirit, the Spirit of Wisdom and Revelation.

Biblical wisdom ultimately comes to fullness in a Person, Jesus Christ, "in whom are hidden all the treasures of wisdom and knowledge" (Colossians 2:3), and in whom all knowledge is rightly ordered and meaningfully integrated. That is, God's wisdom flows from Jesus to His followers through their **union with Him.**

As individuals come to know Christ, they become aligned with the truth and the exciting process of the renewing of their hearts and minds begins. Followers of Christ no longer take their views of the world from those who frame it falsely. They refuse to "walk in step with the wicked" (Psalm 1:1b) or be taken "captive through hollow and deceptive philosophy which depends on human traditions and the elemental spiritual forces of this world rather than on Christ" (Colossians 2:8b). Instead, they are to put on the mind of Christ (1 Corinthians 2:16), recognizing that a Biblical worldview is not only a comprehensive truth system that speaks to every area of life but also one which involves an ongoing heart transformation that leads to righteous behavior and Kingdom actions, the "good works, which God prepared in advance for us to do" (Ephesians 2:10b).

With the survival of our families and way of life at stake, students in traditional, classical, and University-Model® schools must recover and then learn how to think from a Biblical worldview framework anchored in the person and work of Jesus Christ, the Spirit of Truth, and God's Word. Students must not only discern the faulty worldviews in contemporary culture but also be able to courageously defend and boldly champion Kingdom ways of "thinking" and "being" in the competitive and often combative secular marketplace of ideas.

WORLDVIEW MADE SIMPLE: A FORMAL WORLDVIEW IN ACTION

A passage from Acts 28 illustrates what a formal worldview looks like. When Paul and his companions were shipwrecked on the island of Malta, they were greeted by islanders who built a fire for them since it was rainy and cold. As Paul was gathering wood for the fire, a viper hiding in the brushwood bit him in the hand. The islanders' reaction revealed a lot about their understanding of the universe: "When the islanders saw the snake hanging from his hand, they said to each other, 'This man must be a murderer; for though he escaped from the sea, the goddess Justice has not allowed him to live'" (Acts 28:4).

We can deduce a lot about the islanders' formal worldview here. First, they believed in right and wrong. Murder was wrong. Second, the islanders saw the universe as a place governed by universal Justice where, third, human beings are paid back for their wrongs. Since Paul had survived the sea but had been bitten by a poisonous snake, they reasoned, Paul was getting paid back for his crimes.

What is fascinating is how accurate this view is on one level. Paul had been a murderer of Christians before he encountered the Lord. There is a universal Justice in the universe in the form of God's rule and reign. And men do reap what they sow in this world. Not bad for a pagan island culture's view of reality.[72]

---

[72] The islanders' worldview also reminds us that pagan worldviews do contain various shades of truth, which can serve as access points for delivering the gospel. Paul relied on that fact when he spoke to the Athenians in Acts 17:22-31.

However, in another sense, the islanders' view of reality, was inaccurate. The snakebite was not payback for a crime because Paul had not committed any crimes. "But Paul shook the snake off into the fire and suffered no ill effects. The people expected him to swell up or suddenly fall dead; but after waiting a long time and seeing nothing unusual happen to him, they changed their minds and said he was a god" (Acts 28:5-6).

Even more of the islanders' understanding of the world appears here. They expected that when a certain kind of snake, a viper, bit a human being, that person would display certain symptoms and die. That was how things worked in their world. When Paul did not die, the people changed their minds and concluded that he had to be a god.[73]

The islanders' formal worldview, then, consisted of the following main ideas: Universal Justice rules the universe. Right and wrong exist. Men are paid back for their crimes. Cause and effect are aspects of this world. Gods exist and sometimes appear on earth in the form of men. Also, these gods have special powers and are not subject to natural laws.

Notice how this way of seeing reality helped the islanders interpret and explain a situation they experienced in their world. Likewise, our worldviews help to explain our experiences. The question is, are there aspects of our formal worldview that are not accurate and therefore give us a false picture of reality in some area? Do our formal beliefs line up with the universe as God made it, as it really is?

Does our worldview, for example, allow for the existence of miracles? Does our worldview include the notion that God speaks to His children or that angels are His messengers? Do we believe we can hear God Himself speak to us through other people, our experiences, or through Scripture? Do we believe God longs to reveal His plans for us here on earth regarding anything we are to do or build, such as a marriage, a home, a family, or a Christian school?

Is it possible our worldview is actually a mixed bag of true and untrue assumptions, with many aspects of our thinking still in need of correction by the Spirit of Truth and the truth of God's Word?

---

[73] For insights on Acts 28 I am indebted to John Wimber's teachings on the Kingdom of God and worldviews. See *Signs and Wonders and Church Growth*, "The Kingdom of God," Vineyard Ministries International, Placentia CA, 1984. See also, *Signs and Wonders* Conference, Lecture 4, Part I, "Worldviews," 1985.

WORLDVIEW MADE SIMPLE: OUR SACRAMENTAL WORLD

We say a lot about worldviews and Biblical thinking, but do students know the Christian "worldview" of their own physical world? What should be a student's proper understanding of the created world in which we live? Calling our universe "open" does not capture it. It is not just open, it is wide open, shot through with holes. And God can break in and reveal Himself through His creation at any time.

A worldview of our world reminds us that our world is full of **wonders**. So many wonders! Spiders who tip-toe to the top of high places and release silken parachutes that can sail them to mountaintops. Flowers that trap and capture insects. Weaver ants that bend and sew tree leaves together. Crane flies that have little gyroscopes on their backs. Grasses that break into tumbleweeds and roll, replanting themselves. The coordinated functions of the human eye and brain. The intricacies of the immune system. Blood clotting. Stupendous whirlpool galaxies with billions of stars. Black holes, supernovas, light, the quantum world. Do we marvel at these wonders? Do they thrill us and urge us toward contemplation?

The created world beckons us to know and to understand. Embracing God's creation brings out the very best in the human soul. With the splendors of God everywhere, we live in a kind of paradise where we can be thrilled and fascinated by what we encounter. Wonders make us wonder, and wonder drives us toward exploration and discovery. Discovery surprises and delights us, compelling us to know more. Should not a Christian education account for this? Should not a Christian education *foster* this? To what extent are we teaching our students to encounter this magnificent world where "earth's crammed with heaven and every common bush [is] afire with God?"[74]

A Christian worldview of our world celebrates a world radiating with **beauty**. We are thrilled, enchanted, and lifted up and out of ourselves when we engage with it. Every artist who has ever tried to capture a landscape, an interesting animal, light sparkling on water, wildflowers, a grove of trees, anything in nature, is implicitly saying to the viewer: "This is the enchanting world in which you live. See your world for what it is!" Art is nature revealed; it tries to get us to realize that we do in fact live in the world the artist has tried to depict, however much he falls short in capturing it.

Classrooms abstract real-world experiences, removing students from them and robbing them of their power. Returning our students to the natural world, man's true home, and training them to attend to it, to engage with it, to embrace it, puts them in touch with wonder, delight, enchantment, and mystery. The beauty of our world points to a beautiful, wise, and good Creator who demonstrates His love by placing us in a home which is very good for our souls.

This worldview celebrates that ours is a **sacramental world**.[75] Created by God, sustained by God, and contained in God, this world is filled with the living presence of its Creator. He does not enter it only one way, from above so to speak; since it exists in Him, He is always in, through, and behind every created thing, always revealing Himself to us because His signature and fingerprints are on everything. Any object in nature can become an icon or window into His presence; any created thing can be a means of grace leading straight to Him.

We might rethink our Christian school curricula so that it is informed by a true worldview of the world. Perhaps we can now understand, for example, mathematics from the perspective of precision, order, and intelligibility, the hallmarks of a wise Creator? Should a sacramental worldview bring truth, order, goodness, and even

---

[74] Lines from *Aurora Leigh* by Elizabeth Barrett Browning.

[75] This was the topic of First Prize speech in the Chrysostom Oratory Contest in 2015. See Cooley, Rachel. ACCS Annual Conference, *Repairing the Ruins*. Dallas, Texas. 19 June 2015. For a video of the speech see http://www.accsedu.org/school-resources/chrysostom_oratory_competition/.

beauty into our scientific discussions?[76] Will such a worldview encourage superior choices in literature, such as Flannery O'Connor, Richard Wilbur, Sarah Orne Jewett, George Herbert, and others? Could not a true worldview of our world enhance students' spiritual lives—worship prompted by the book of nature, contemplative personal devotions derived from keen investigations into the natural world, and long, meditative retreats deep inside the heart of the iconic wilderness?

---

[76] A point Thomas Dubay makes in his book, *The Evidential Power of Beauty: Science and Theology Meet* (San Francisco: Ignatius Press, 1999).

WORLDVIEW MADE SIMPLE: YOUR SIDE, MY SIDE, ANOTHER SIDE?

Studies in worldviews show how different presuppositions and perspectives create frameworks that explain the great questions of life. The stories of Joshua and the angel (Joshua 5:13-15) and Abram and Lot (Genesis 13:8-15) provide excellent but contrasting examples of thinking from man's perspective as compared to God's.

On the eve of the invasion of Jericho, Joshua saw a man standing in front of him with a drawn sword in his hand (Joshua 5:13). Joshua approached him and said from a classically human point of view, "Are you for us or for our enemies?"(5:13b).

Down here on earth, it is easy to assume only two perspectives exist, our "side" and the other "side," with our side naturally being the right one and the side God is on too. It is amazing that even Joshua, who had been at Moses' side for years and had most recently seen God punish Israel for forty years, was captured by this way of thinking.

The angel's reply clearly stunned him. "'Neither,' he replied, 'but as commander of the army of the LORD I have now come'" (5:14a). Joshua's next move is a beautiful example of the kind of humility that willingly yields up the human point of view: "Then Joshua fell facedown to the ground in reverence and asked him, 'What message does my LORD have for his servant?'" (5:14b).

Joshua discovered that a third side existed, above and beyond his own. He realized the question was not whether the man with the drawn sword was on his side, but whether he and all Israel intended to be on

God's side.

The Abram and Lot story in Genesis provides a different slant on the same idea. Lot's men and Abraham's men were quarreling because "…the land could not support them…for their possessions were so great that they were not able to stay together" (13:6). To keep the peace Abram said to Lot: "'Is not the whole land before you? Let's part company. If you go to the left, I'll go to the right; if you go to the right, I'll go to the left'" (13:9).

Abram gave Lot the first choice, and from the perspective of human reason (there is good land and bad land), Lot chose the plain of the Jordan because he rationally concluded it was well-watered and therefore the best. Abram then went west, toward the land of Canaan, not seeming to care where he landed because he was not thinking from a human point of view. Unlike Joshua, Abram knew there were three sides—Lot's, his, and God's—and rather than choose from his own perspective, or fear that he would get the short end of the deal by letting Lot choose first, Abram was content to trust God and let Him decide. After all, God had already revealed to him that He would make him into a great nation; surely God could direct Abram to where He wanted him to be.

At the very least, our worldview students must learn to grasp the divine perspective and then practice yielding up their point of view in favor of it. If they do not, they will not understand the Kingdom. Jesus, who pointed out that His Kingdom is not of this world, said that His purpose in coming into the world was to "testify to the truth." Then He concluded: "Everyone on the side of truth listens to me" (John 18:37b).[77]

In this world, with respect to Truth, there are only two "sides." Right and wrong, truth and lies do exist and those on the side of Truth are on the Lord's side. However, in terms of perspectives, as Abraham and Joshua teach us, we must always be aware that sometimes our perspective, our side, is not God's side and so we must yield up our point of view in favor of the only perspective that matters, the best perspective of all, the only perfect one: God's.

---

[77] Del Tackett, *The Truth Project*, Lesson 1, "Veritology".

WORLDVIEW MADE SIMPLE: LEARNING TO THINK FROM A KINGDOM WORLDVIEW

In order to live in a foreign country, we must learn its language, customs, and laws if we wish to live well. Living in God's Kingdom requires the same thing. We must reject what we have learned and renew our minds in order to be effective and responsible citizens in that Kingdom.

We were born into the kingdom of darkness under the authority of the devil, who is called a ruler and a prince and who has a territory or realm in which he exercises his tyrannical rule. That realm is the earth and all its institutions. Since, as John said, "the whole world is under the control of the evil one" (1 John 5:19a), all the institutions of the earth, all the governments, laws, cultures, and economies have come under Satanic control. Since we have been shaped by these institutions all our lives, our thinking is naturally "bent" toward darkness and evil.

When Jesus came announcing that a new Kingdom was at hand, He was offering a way of escape from the kingdom of darkness. And when He said, "Repent and believe the good news!" (Mark 1:15b), He was saying we all need to change our minds, our ways of thinking and acting which have conformed to this kingdom of darkness, in order to live new lives in God's Kingdom. Paul reminded the Galatians that Jesus came to rescue us from the present evil age (Galatians 1:4) and all that goes with it, in order to be Kingdom citizens.

Transformation into Kingdom ways of thinking is marvelously expressed in God's call to Abram in Genesis 12:1b. God said, "Go from your country, your people and your father's household to the land I will show you."

Notice that God was asking Abram to leave the three most powerful "worldview" influences on his life: his country with its laws and customs; his people group or tribe with its history, traditions, and special ways of thinking; and his father's household, with its habits, beliefs, rules, customs, and unique family dynamics. Then, Abram was asked to "go" to another country and start over.

Abram's journey is archetypal, a template for our own. We too must leave our country, people, and father's household, what Peter called the empty way of life handed down to us by our ancestors (1 Peter 1:18), in order to live in the Kingdom of God. But while Abram's journey was literal and physical, involving a real change of land and country, our journey is symbolic, inner, and spiritual, involving a transformation of our minds and the taking on of a new identity. We do this by allowing the Lord to show us all the ways we have been structured for death from growing up in the darkness of our country, our people, and our father's household.

Leaving our country means leaving the destructive and untrue ideas and traditions of our national public culture that has taught us what it means to be an "American." The cult of self-reliance does not work too well with the message of grace, and racial hatred is incompatible with God's call to love our neighbor. Leaving our people group means leaving the destructive influences of our ethnic or kinship group, or the influences of church and school that existed in our local culture growing up. Worshipping Mary, if we were raised Catholic, or thinking the gifts of the Spirit are of the devil, if we were raised in a Fundamentalist home, are examples. Finally, leaving our father's household means leaving and being healed of all the ways our home life under our father's authority kept us from our true identity and calling. Growing up in poverty, with an abundance of material possessions, or with alcoholic, fearful, distant, absent, or abusive parents can do great damage to the heart and soul.

To "leave" these influences means that we recognize how they have wrongly shaped us into the people that we have become. It means recognizing the lies, beliefs, habits, customs, and traditions that have shaped us in ways contrary to the Kingdom. It means recognizing their origin and effects on us, and then taking that first step toward the Kingdom of God, which is separation from all that is unholy, untrue, contaminated, destructive or impure. We must break all the ties that have given us the "empty way of life handed down to us by our ancestors" (1 Peter 1:18).

A wonderful passage in Ephesians is the New Testament counterpart to the call of Abram. Discussing our oneness in Christ, Paul concludes: "Consequently, you are no longer foreigners and strangers, but fellow citizens with God's people and also members of his household, built on the foundation of the apostles and prophets, with Christ Jesus himself as the chief cornerstone" (Ephesians 2:19-20). In other words, leaving the country, people, and father's household of our past means we become citizens of a new country (the Kingdom), and part of a new people group (God's people), and members of a new household (God's household) with God Himself as our Father.

As we do this, as we allow the Lord to renew our thinking, we will gradually learn to think from a totally new perspective, that is, from a Kingdom worldview, and ultimately possess a completely new identity as a child of God.

WORLDVIEW MADE SIMPLE: FOUNDATIONAL TEXTS

Foundational Biblical texts for worldview studies come from Romans 1, Ephesians 4, Colossians 2, and Psalm 1.

Romans 1 describes the progressive deterioration of the fallen mind and by extension, the corruption of culture. Although "God's invisible qualities…have been clearly seen" because they are self-evident from "what has been made," fallen men in their sinfulness have suppressed this truth. They knew God but failed to thank and glorify Him. As a result, "their thinking became futile and their foolish hearts were darkened." So God gave them over to their own sin. Sexual impurity and "the degrading of their bodies with one another" followed, even as they "exchanged the truth about God for a lie," and continued to worship created things instead of God. Their sin led to more sin (unnatural and perverted relations with each other) and their minds and deeds became even more depraved. However, they continued in their sin and even approved of those who did likewise (Romans 1:18-32).

A similar description of the fallen mind appears in Ephesians 4:17-19, which serves as a succinct summary of the ideas in Romans 1:

So I tell you this, and insist on it in the Lord, that you must no longer live as the Gentiles do, in the futility of their thinking. They are darkened in their understanding and separated from the life of God because of the ignorance that is in them due to the hardening of their hearts. Having lost all sensitivity, they have given themselves over to sensuality so as to indulge in every kind of impurity, and they are full of greed.

Fallen men's thinking has become futile, darkened, and ignorant due to their hard hearts. As a result, their choices drive them to indulge in ever-increasing impurity. This reality has great implications for Christians living under the leadership of those whose thinking has been similarly darkened. This means it really does matter who gets elected to public offices. It matters a great deal what kind of principals, teachers, leaders, and board members govern the public schools (or any schools for that matter), what kind of judges sit in the state and federal courts, and what kind of people run the entertainment industries. Citizens need civic and cultural leaders who can see reality, people who will stop evil instead of celebrating it and encouraging those who do it.

The goal for all of us, Jew and Gentile, is a renewed mind, which comes from accepting Christ and submitting to His lordship. Romans 12:2 reminds us that transformation of our hearts is the important thing because it will actually change our thinking, which will then cause our choices and actions to change: "Do not conform to the pattern of this world, but be transformed by the renewing of your mind. Then you will be able to test and approve what God's will is—His good, pleasing, and perfect will." Not conforming to the world requires vigilance. Even Christians can be taken captive by ideas not founded in Christ. In Colossians 2:8 Paul writes: "See to it that no one takes you captive through hollow and deceptive philosophy, which depends on human tradition and the elemental spiritual forces of this world rather than on Christ." Rejecting deceptive ideas from the world requires not only a renewed heart and mind but also training in scripture and systematic thinking from a Biblical worldview perspective. The best context for that is a Christian community centered on Christ (Colossians 2:2).

Psalm 1 has a similar exhortation. We should never take our thinking from the wicked. We do not take our ideas, points of view, habits, or actions from those who frame reality falsely: "Blessed is the one who does not walk in step with the wicked or stand in the way that sinners take or sit in the company of mockers" (Psalm 1:1).

The counsel of the wicked does not control the believer's "walk" (how he patterns his life and actions); sinners will not determine his "way" (his direction or path); and mockers will not control where he "sits" (where he does his work). Instead his delight "is in the law of the Lord" for it alone will show the righteous person where to sit, walk, and stand.

Because these foundational texts contain both personal (Psalm 1 and Colossians) and social/political applications (Romans and Ephesians), instructors in almost any subject-area will find them useful. The texts can not only help teachers to generate interesting cultural and worldview discussions, but they can also train students how to frame and understand issues in almost any discipline from a basic Christian worldview perspective.

EXPANDING WORLDVIEW STUDIES

For a long time, worldview studies have been generally one-dimensional, knowledge-based approaches designed to help Christian students think Biblically about their world. The goal has been to help students recognize and then challenge the presuppositions and premises of the secular worldviews which currently control public and private culture. These approaches have been useful and necessary but they are limited, perhaps even somewhat flawed.[78]

The premises, content, and scope of worldview studies are in need of an overhaul and an upgrade. We might call it a worldview reclamation project. The objective would be for worldview studies to reflect more comprehensively the great Christian truth system that we possess; it is far wider, deeper, and richer than mere apologetics! We should include not only what should be taught but *how we should then live* on the basis of what is taught. Instead of focusing on the supremacy of our arguments, we should focus on the supremacy of our lifestyle.

Worldview instruction should have as its foundational premise the glorious Kingdom of God message with all its ramifications for thought and action. Jesus said the Kingdom is here but not yet here; it has come and yet will come in fullness at the end of the age (Romans 14:17, 2 Peter 1:11). To enter that Kingdom we must be born again by the Spirit who radically transforms the heart, the seat of thought and action, and out of which comes all the issues of life (John 3:3, Mark 7:20-23). Before that point, things of the Spirit are foolishness to us;

---

[78] This is James K. A. Smith's view. See Smith, *Desiring the Kingdom*, 32.

after that point, we see everything—ourselves, others, our world, and God—from a true perspective (1 Corinthians 2:14). This ought to be the very first goal of worldview studies—to experience this radical conversion, this complete transformation, this dynamic "incarnational reality," in order to finally and simply see.[79] Without it, students will never own a Biblical worldview because they will never see the Kingdom; they might be able to give right answers to worldview and Bible questions, but they will not live and think from a radical new center on their own. Not understanding incarnational reality, they will have no witness of lifestyle.

Worldview studies begin with the proclamation of the Kingdom message with authority and with power. To be born again, Jesus said we must repent and believe the good news. We must change our minds to accommodate a completely new reality: there is a new King who has come to save His people, to make war against the prince of this world, and to set right all creation. Believing from the heart this incredibly good news sparks this change of thinking in us. When this happens, our thinking and our actions change by the work of the free gift of the Holy Spirit, who joins us to Christ and forms the mind of Christ in us (1 Corinthians 2:10-16, Romans 12:2). "You, however, are not in the realm of the flesh but are in the realm of the Spirit, if indeed the Spirit of God lives in you. And if anyone does not have the Spirit of Christ, they do not belong to Christ" (Romans 8:9). Thus, the ministry of the Holy Spirit is indispensable to our restoration but also vital to our understanding anything from God.[80]

The Holy Spirit's role in mediating to us the wisdom of God opens up a second rich vista of worldview study. In both the Old and New Testaments, the Spirit is called the Spirit of Wisdom (Isaiah 11:2, Ephesians 1:17). Understanding wisdom in all its facets is vital to anyone in the Church, which collectively is to reflect the manifold wisdom of God to the rulers in the heavenly realms (Ephesians 3:10). Wisdom, then, is a chief mark of the Church and the goal of every believer: "Teach us to number our days, that we may gain a heart of wisdom" (Psalm 90:12). Wisdom's link with right living and virtue, with creativity and divine templates, and with understanding the

---

[79] Leanne Payne's term. See Leanne Payne, *Real Presence: The Holy Spirit in the Works of C.S. Lewis* (Westchester: Cornerstone Books, 1979), 10.

[80] Ibid., 84. Payne writes: "Christ in man resurrects the whole of man: his intellectual, his sensory, his emotional, as well as his intuitive being."

scriptures, especially the prophetic scriptures, absolutely demands its inclusion in any serious study of worldviews.

With the Kingdom of God as the foundational message and the wisdom of God as the basis for knowing how to live rightly on this earth, we can then introduce students to four broad categories of instruction and training—a proper Biblical worldview of the Self, of Creation, of the World, and of the Future of the World.

Study of a true view of the Self begins with an understanding of incarnational reality and of the variety of expressions of our one identity in Christ. The most basic of these is, first of all, our identity as natural artists, since we have been created in God's image. Second, is our identity as co-rulers with God, since we have been called by God to rule over some portion of creation. Third, is our immutable gender identity which uniquely expresses the nature and personality of our Creator, since God made us male and female. In addition to these three fundamental expressions of our identity as human beings, we have several public and private social identities in Christ (son, daughter, priest, soldier, citizen, and so on), all of which need to be explored and understood in any worldview study of the Self.[81]

A Worldview of Creation (our physical world), shows students the true nature of the marvelous home our good Father made just for us. First, although it has been subjected to frustration (Romans 8:20), it is still worthy of our study and reflection. It is a source of beauty, enjoyment, and wonder. It surprises and delights us; when we are connected to it, we are blessed. Created, sustained, and contained in God, our world is sacramental, a manifold source of blessings. We live in a place where "earth is crammed with heaven," meaning any aspect or object in creation can become a means of experiencing God and perhaps learning something about His personality (Genesis 2).

A Worldview of the World brings students more clearly into the practices and products of contemporary life by showing them the worldview narratives which have set themselves up against the knowledge of the Kingdom of God. This is indeed the place for apologetics. Here students should explore the progression of worldviews which have shaped life today: deism to naturalism and its expression in the horrendous political philosophies of the 19th and 20th centuries—nihilism, existentialism, and post-modernism, all

---

[81] For a theology of the Self, C.S. Lewis is excellent. See his *Till We Have Faces: A Myth Retold* (Orlando: Harcourt Brace and Co., 1956).

humanistic and all without real hope. Students should explore these worldviews with a clear rubric in mind: What do these worldviews say is wrong with the world? What solutions do these worldviews propose? What is their source of hope? Students will quickly discover that hope, if there is any hope at all, is being placed in some aspect of man himself: his mind (Freud and B.F. Skinner), his will (Hemingway), his feelings (Camus), or in his body/machine, found in the current ubiquitous proposals for droids and mechanical humans, all of which show the bankruptcy of modern thought even more, being hopelessly syncretistic hybrids of humanism and mechanism.

Finally, a Worldview of the Future will introduce students to the reality of their times because it will show them the vital end of the story—the last days and end times and the consummation of the Kingdom at the end of the age. A new King is coming. He will enter the world miraculously when it is about to destroy itself through war. This is not Christian fairy tale; this is reality and it is coming fast. Jesus is coming as King to rule and reign from Jerusalem in a resurrected body with His saints ruling with Him over a world that contains no evil. Before that occurs, however, the greatest battle of worldviews in history will take place—the consummate evil of all the kingdoms of the world, prophesied in Daniel and in the book of Revelation, will manifest itself in a single political ruler leading a confederation of nations and their armies against the Jews and the Holy City of Jerusalem. That Islam has a central role in this final drama is without question.[82] Unfortunately, our students today have little knowledge of eschatology, and even less knowledge of Islamic eschatology or the religious and political worldviews that are even now paving the moral, intellectual, cultural, and spiritual highways for the events soon to follow.

Until now, worldview instruction has taken on mainly an apologetics approach emphasizing knowledge and information, the logical defense of the faith. Methods have been textual and/or media curriculums via classroom instruction, special speakers, and intensive conferences.[83] Are these really the best ways to teach and impart an entirely new way of thinking and living?

A worldview reclamation project requires that we emphasize

---

[82] See Joel Richardson, *The Islamic Anti-Christ* (Washington D.C: WND Books, 2015), as well as Richardson, *Mideast Beast* (Washington D.C.: WND Books, 2012).

[83] Ministries such as Axis (https://axis.org/) and the *Truth Project* are examples.

formation with a **limited apologetics** approach based on four integrated components: private devotions; sequenced courses of classroom instruction; a master/disciple relationship to the students; and participation in the symbols, ceremonies, and rituals of Christian community devoted to the apostles' teaching, the fellowship in worship, the breaking of bread, and prayer (Acts 2:42).[84]

Whether a high-school or college curriculum or both, the foundation for worldview thinking might begin with a four-year personal devotional study thematically centered on the Kingdom of God and carefully integrated with four years of discipleship and classroom instruction. Such a devotional brings personal formation, experiencing God, and transformation to the forefront. It might consist of four broad divisions corresponding to coursework: overview of the grand story in year one, proclamation and demonstrations of the Kingdom in year two, the apologetics of the Kingdom in year three, and the coming Kingdom in year four. It would cover the prophetic announcement of the Kingdom by the prophets, the inauguration and demonstration of the Kingdom by Jesus, and the consummation of the Kingdom at the end of the age—all of the grand story.

A matching four-year sequence of courses could take a variety of forms, depending on resources, teachers, and time. The first two years might be literature-based, the last two years, history-based.[85] The first semester would focus on the grand story, the overview from announcement to consummation. The Bible and George Eldon Ladd's *The Gospel of the Kingdom* are necessary texts here. The second semester would focus on the works of C. S. Lewis, who has imaginatively expressed a Kingdom worldview of the Self, Creation, the World, and the World of the Future better than anyone else. Focus would be his *Narnia* books and science trilogy. The second year might consist of biographies of great Christian practitioners (Lincoln, Wilberforce, Solzhenitsyn), fiction by Homer, Shakespeare, the Russian Christian novelists and selected writers upholding incarnational reality and a sacramental view of the world (O'Connor, Wilbur, Lewis, Herbert, Herrick, and others).

Year three shifts into historical studies; the first semester might focus on selected works from the Greeks to the Reformation and the

---

[84] Smith, *Desiring the Kingdom*, 25.

[85] Thus compatible, or at least adaptable to the various classical curriculums.

second semester on representative selections through the modern period, including an overview of modern philosophies and worldviews. This and the final year of study would have an apologetics emphasis, but not exclusively. The final year would investigate more deeply the premises of naturalistic, existential, and post-modern worldviews in semester one, followed by studies in Islam, the Middle East, and the End Times in the final semester. All are suggested approaches: any number of sequences, combinations, and courses are possible within this conceptual framework.

Creating a master/disciple relationship with students to complement and reinforce private devotions, classroom instruction, and individual moral behavior is an exciting prospect to contemplate. We need to *disciple* students into correct worldview thinking and Kingdom living. Perhaps this component would take the form of weekly meetings with each student or small groups of students. Is this not how Jesus passed on the Kingdom to His friends? Time would be structured to include discussion about the student's commitment to the Lord, as well as teaching, training, and evaluating each student's grasp of Kingdom concepts or ideas in the coursework—call it a worldview studies lab. Always the goal would be to produce students who own the knowledge, spiritual disciplines, and spiritual habits for themselves in order to pass them on to others. Much good personal ministry could happen in a calculated relationship like this. We have only to try it.

Expecting students to participate in revised rituals and practices of Christian community, that is, to worship the right things, is an equally exciting prospect for developing comprehensive worldview thinking, behavior, and practice. Students may be able to explain all the modern "isms" and show how a Biblical worldview surpasses them, but still remain untouched in their hearts and unchanged in their daily actions. "...I think there remain legitimate concerns with even the best rendition of worldview approaches," writes James K. A. Smith in *Imagining the Kingdom,* "insofar as these approaches tend to still conceive the task of Christian education as the dissemination of a *perspective*, a way to *see* the world.[86] Having spent "a generation thinking about thinking," Smith points out that in fact, "we don't think our way through to action; much of our action is not the outcome of rational

---

[86] Smith, *Imagining the Kingdom*, 8.

deliberation and conscious choice."[87] Instead, he argues, we act from the gut and heart on the basis of what we love. And what we love is shaped by the practices and rituals of our culture, which Smith calls liturgies, which implicitly contain various visions of the good life, that is, various worldviews.

Students are shaped more by these unconscious liturgies than by ideas.[88] Therefore, Smith argues for student participation in the counter-rituals of the worshipping Christian community—prayer, the Eucharist, worship, song—that challenge the worldviews embedded in the liturgies of our culture. Tuning students' hearts to the Kingdom, so that they become Kingdom citizens, requires appealing to their imaginations—"their hearts through their bodies"—via habits and practices of a Christian community whose collective rituals point them toward that end. Thus it is not information, but formation that students need, and our educational practices should help prepare them to be a "certain kind of people."[89]

Immersing students into the kind of communities formed by the early Christians (Acts 2:42) parallels or complements Smith's proposals. The first Christians held four practices in tension: They were devoted to the apostles' teaching, communion, worship, and individual and corporate prayer. These practices should tell us something. In a different way, each one nourished the **real presence of God** among them. The apostles' teaching put them in touch with Truth. Communion promoted union with Christ as they remembered what He did on the cross and as they anticipated His Second Coming and the consummation of the Kingdom. Worship, which evidently included the practice of the spiritual gifts (1 Corinthians 14:22-25), acknowledged the presence of God among them, while prayer vitally connected them with God's will and the fulfillment of their mission. Together, head and heart, imagination and intellect were nourished in the real presence of God. Bringing students into the powerful ways the presence of God is mediated to us profoundly shapes the imagination of the heart, orienting us to a complete "worldview" of the Kingdom.

As leaders and cultural architects in traditional, classical, and University-Model® schools, we have before us exciting opportunities

---

[87] Ibid., 6.

[88] Smith, *Desiring the Kingdom*, 25.

[89] Ibid., 25-26.

to upgrade the "truth" component of our common mission. New premises, new content, and new methods—a reconfiguration and expansion of traditional worldview studies and approaches—are not only necessary but vital to the education of the present generation of young people. More than ever, our students must capture and hold truth in their imaginations and intellects if they are going to live the lifestyle that proclaims a powerful Christ and proves them to be loyal citizens of His Kingdom.

NATURE STUDY IN CHRISTIAN SCHOOLS

As students move through the higher grades, their education becomes more cerebral and abstract, thus removing them from experiences and encounters with reality that could profoundly change their lives. Students are losing the sacramental dimension of learning. This also happens to their faith; abstract presentations of the gospel leave students with an increasingly unreal Jesus until God Himself becomes merely a concept. All this is happening as they become more absorbed with social media. The solution to all three problems may be surprising: we need a revolution in nature studies that returns young people to the environment for which they were designed: the natural world.

We need to get our students outdoors—a lot. Not only when they are young, but all the way through high school, especially in the junior and senior years, and place demands on them to know their world. Nature is their true home. Education without direct experience is dead; encounters with the natural world are encounters with reality. Students need to be outdoors studying weather, soils, forests, and wetlands and all the life within them—wildflowers, insects, birds, and fish. This is their beautiful and fascinating world.

Who will write the scope and sequence for this? Who will set the objectives, the standards of knowledge and experience for each grade level?[90] Of all the people on the planet, Christians should be the most conscientious stewards of creation, the most fervent environmentalists, and the champion ecologists. Is it not strange, then, that we have not added this dimension of study to our curriculums? A few isolated units devoted to nature studies in an occasional science course won't do it. What we need are coherent and systematic approaches that honor the magnificent benefits and wonders of our true home.

Because it is our home, the natural world is a place of **peace**. We relax when we are outdoors. We slow down and start to notice things. The air wakes us up and we become more alive. The beauty we see and the sensations we feel prompt us toward observation, wonder, reflection, and meditation. Jesus loved to be in the world His Father made. Mark's gospel seems to emphasize this. Jesus walked by the Sea of Galilee (1:16) and sought out a solitary place outdoors to pray (1:35). We find Him walking through a grain field (2:23) and then withdrawing to the lake again (3:7). He goes up a mountainside (3:13), then comes back down to teach by a lake (4:1) and then He takes a boat to the other side (4:35). We see Him at the caverns in the region of the Gerasenes (5:1). He visits the lake again (5:21) and withdraws again to a solitary place so that His disciples could rest (6:32). Jesus liked being outdoors. He liked resting outdoors, praying outdoors, and going to solitary places. So should we. So should our students.

The created world is a source of **enrichment**. Our first and most rightful home was a garden. In that garden, God made trees that were pleasing to the eye and good for food (Genesis 2:9). The Lord Himself enjoyed walking with man in the garden in the cool of day. Aromas, colors, sensations, and textures richly fill our souls. All types of living creatures evoke curiosity, wonder, excitement, and even laughter as we come to know them. We are most enriched, however, in the presence of **mystery**. Outdoors, we are surrounded by marvels and mysteries we cannot explain. God's great discourse to Job makes this very point. "'What is the way to the abode of light and where does darkness reside?...Do you know the laws of the heavens? Can you set up God's dominion over the earth?'" (Job 38:19, 33) We are thrilled, enchanted, and humbled as we live and play in the world God has made for us.

---

[90] In Texas, alliances with the Texas Master Naturalist Programs could easily provide this dimension of learning. See http://txmn.org/about/become-a-master-naturalist/.

The natural world is a source of **wisdom**. All creation is suffused with the wisdom of God. Wisdom was the great craftsman at God's side before He created a single thing (Proverbs 8). The Psalmist declared, "How many are your works, LORD! In wisdom you made them all" (Psalm 104:24a). And Proverbs reminds us that, "By wisdom the LORD laid the earth's foundations, by understanding he set the heavens in place; by his knowledge the watery depths were divided, and the clouds let drop the dew" (3:19-20). So it is easy to see why the scriptures urge us to find wisdom in the natural world. "Go to the ant, you sluggard, consider its ways and be wise!" (6:6). In the Sermon on the Mount Jesus asks us to look at the birds, to consider how the flowers of the field grow (Matthew 6:26-28) and to think about His Kingdom through imagery taken from the natural world (Matthew 13).

The earth is our **home**. God designed it and gave it to us for our peace and well-being, for our enrichment and enjoyment. Christian school students are missing a vital dimension of their faith and a crucial element in their education when they are estranged from it, with few opportunities to experience it firsthand in the years they are young, at the time they are most alive.

PUSHING THE FRONTIERS

What would happen if a few of the most dynamic educators and leaders in traditional, classical, and University-Model® schools convened a yearly summit devoted exclusively to prayer and unity, research and development, and the sharing of new ideas? We are called to be the head, not the tail; Christian education should not only be radically different from public education but clearly superior to it. And for this to happen, we must have unity—we must come together. At such a summit, leaders might think of pushing the frontiers in several areas.

A Yearly Schedule. It is time to explore the merits of a yearly academic schedule. It would obviously add more time for instruction, either in the form of remediation as in our traditional "summer schools," or in the form of supplementary or advanced instruction in other areas. It would give schools the opportunity to expand the range of its offerings to include courses in practical life skills, personal enrichment, and advanced spiritual formation. We need to think about how we are stewarding our time. A school schedule with roots in our agrarian past calls for a review because reasons justifying it no longer make sense and an increasing number of educators are seeing valid reasons for abandoning it.[91]

---

[91] See "Agrarian roots: Think again. Debunking the myth of summer's vacation origins" at: http://www.pbs.org/newshour/updates/debunking-myth-summer-vacation/. Also, "The History of School and Summer Vacation." James Pederson, *Journal of Inquiry and Action in Education*, 5 (1) 2012, 54. Also at:

Advanced Teacher Training Programs. Substantive, effective, and truly holistic teacher training and certification programs are crying out to be developed. A teacher is more than the sum of "skills." A teacher is a soul, and the quality of one's teaching depends on the condition of that soul. External skills like managing classrooms or constructing lesson plans are important, but not central as they are in our minimalistic public schools. Souls need healing, pastoral care, and restoration; a teacher's self-concept, degree of self-acceptance, and emotional and spiritual maturity are most surely matters of teacher training because they directly affect teacher performance. A Christian teacher-training center should exist in every major city and the local churches in each city should care about establishing it. Sunday school teachers, public school teachers who are Christians, and Christian school teachers would all benefit. Curriculum should include preparing teachers for work in classical schools or in University-Model® settings because the classical curriculum and the University-Model® are clearly the future of Christian education. It would certainly also include training in social media, educational technology, and online education. With so many church buildings sitting empty during the week or in the evenings, surely church leaders or entrepreneurs could find a way to create the first training center prototype for their city. Yes?

Upgrades and Additions: The Four Curriculums. Christian schools should base instruction on four areas with clear goals and objectives in each: academic, spiritual, moral, and practical. **Academic**. We might consider a new organizing principle for our academic curricula—the Kingdom of God as the grand "map" of all that is important in Christ and the ground of all study in history, science, mathematics, the arts, and literature. Jesus proclaimed the Kingdom, the Kingdom has been steadily advancing, and the Kingdom is the great message the Church has been called to proclaim. It is the one concept that rightly frames all history and all human endeavor. A Kingdom focus would also place worldview studies in their proper context. The "worldview" we want our students to have is a Kingdom worldview and all it entails.

Spiritual. Instruction here should stress formation and

http://digitalcommons.buffalostate.edu/cgi/viewcontent.cgi?article=1050&context=jiae.

275

instruction about the message of the Kingdom of God, a much wider concept than the salvation message. Traditional book-by-book or verse-by-verse approaches need to yield to instruction in the whole narrative, to make it less about the Bible itself, and more about Christ and His message: living in the Kingdom, learning the secrets of the Kingdom, and being ambassadors for the Kingdom. And whether or not we are in the "last days," instruction in basic eschatology, an emphasis that would correct our imbalance toward apologetics, should be a feature of every contemporary Christian spiritual education program.

Moral. Since it is true that we become what we love, what we worship, we must teach our students to love and worship the right things. Becoming like Christ and leading a life of holiness and virtue would be a good place to start. In the coming days, students will need the strong virtues essential for overcomers: courage, boldness, initiative, hope, perseverance, long-suffering, and self-sacrifice. And here is where ignorance of the ministry of the Holy Spirit is so worrisome. Students acquire these virtues not so much by practicing character traits, but through the ministry of the Holy Spirit, by being mentored in them by great men and women, by experiencing them in worship, and by engaging in the practices and rituals of the community.

Practical. What do students really know, intellectually and experientially, of their world? Can our graduating seniors name and find the constellations? How many students can name even five trees native to their region? Do they know which wild plants are edible? Do they know how to survive outside in harsh conditions? Can they cook a wholesome meal for themselves, fix household appliances, or change the oil in their cars? Do they know how to adapt to conditions of scarcity or wisely stock a pantry? This "fourth curriculum" of practical instruction in life is waiting to be developed in the many existing unused spaces of the school year. The University-Model® school is in a prime position to take the lead in this area.[92]

---

[92] With three days of teaching at school and two satellite days at home under the supervision of a parent co-teacher, the University-Model® has tremendous flexibility and time for students to pursue not only a practical education, but also instruction and training in each student's own individual bent—art, music, athletics, and so on. For more on the University-Model® see www.umsi.org.

KEEPING CHRISTIAN SCHOOLS COMPETITIVE: A CHECKLIST OF QUESTIONS

A checklist of fundamental questions on a school's vision, mission, and practices will keep leaders attentive to how their community measures up in crucial areas. How would you and other stakeholders in your school answer the following questions?

Are you protecting the vital relationships in your school community? The goal is to not only guard but actively nurture the five vital relationships in every Christian school: board and administrator, administrator and leadership team, leadership team and teachers, teachers and parents, and teachers and students. Regularly evaluating your school's commitment to protecting these relationships and giving the Lord space and time to reveal any issues will prevent areas of vulnerability from developing. Vigilance will show you where you need to direct time, energy, and resources to keep relationships healthy and communication flowing. Since it is true that *relationship comes before revelation and revelation before resources,* investing in the relational integrity of your school is guaranteed to bring God's favor, protection, and blessing.

Do you have an annual school-wide prayer plan? (See page 83.) Independent Systemic Prayer Cells (ISPC) are an excellent way to engage the entire school community in consistent, focused prayer but in a way that is flexible for all. Each sphere—students, staff, teachers, parents, coaches, and board members—divides into smaller prayer cells of five to seven people. Each **cell** then makes up its own prayer schedule for the school—that is the **independent** part. Then members pray for the school from their unique vantage point (grade level parents, leadership team, board, etc.). Since the cells make up the spheres and the spheres collectively represent the entire school community, the entire community will be covered in prayer. This is the **systemic** part. Leaders can decide for themselves how much time to allow for this season of prayer, generally from one to three months.

How do you know that effective moral training occurs in your school? Many leaders seem to believe that "character" comes by osmosis simply because the school defines itself as Christian, teaches the Bible, and runs a sports program. Christian school leaders talk a lot about character, but few are intentional in bringing it about. If you do not intend to teach something, you will not teach it. Our mission demands that we produce effective, measurable programs in moral instruction in order to build a **culture of virtue** in our communities. This culture will involve special training to encourage teachers and coaches to develop core values for themselves and their programs. It might also require the formation of a new "third curriculum" like what scouting used to be, which teaches moral virtues through outdoor activities, life-skills, and leadership training. We must submit to a radical change in mindsets here: a Christian school is obliged to do much more than stuff the mind with information. "We need to retrace our steps," writes Stratford Caldecott, "to find the 'wisdom we have lost in knowledge,' the 'knowledge we have lost in information.'"[93]

How successful have you been in recruiting men? Young people need the wisdom, guidance, correction, encouragement, and perspective of men. Besides the usual natural benefits of having a male presence on campus, men can become effective surrogate fathers and influential mentors to young people lacking that influence. Have you prayed men in or have you lost all confidence that strong men and mature fathers can be a part of your program? "If you believe, you will receive whatever you ask for in prayer" (Matthew 21:22).

---

[93] Stratford Caldecott, *Beauty for Truth's Sake: On the Re-enchantment of Education* (Grand Rapids: Brazos Press, 2009), 12. Caldecott is quoting T. S. Eliot here.

Do you regularly conduct a sober evaluation of your "product"? What does that evaluation contain? When you graduate another class of young people, how do you know what they really know? Can they summarize the great message of the Kingdom of God? If you were to pull a random number of graduating seniors aside and ask them to give a basic overview of the end times could they do so? Do they understand their design and calling? Do they demonstrate a commitment to obey the Lord? Do they exhibit a desire for holiness or show perseverance in loving their neighbor? Do they understand how events in the Middle East might relate to the return of Jesus?

Asking questions of ourselves is challenging and usually sobering. This is good for us. Consistent self-evaluation keeps us lean, hungry, and always growing.

ADDITIONAL ACKNOWLEDGEMENTS

Portions of the following essays appeared in documents, workshops, and presentations for University-Model® Schools International (UMSI) and are used with permission: "Introducing the Christian School Community"; "What is a Kingdom Education?"; "Conditions for Blessing"; "Small Groups, Prayer Meetings, and Great Awakenings"; "How Personal Brokenness Affects Teaching"; "Changing Mindsets: Who Needs Education?"; "Changing Mindsets: Who is the Authority?"; "Worldview Made Simple: An Overview"; "A Virtue for our Times"; "Encouraging a Growth Mindset"; "Sleep, Diet, Exercise: Are they Spiritual?"; "What Happens to the Son when the Father is Absent?"; "Fallout of Social Media"; "God's Strategy for Discipline: Dealing with Cain"; "Have Fun, Do Your Best, Be a Blessing"; "The Cry of the Adolescent Girl"; "The School Assigns too Much Homework"; "Beware of Time Management"; "Marvels of Divine Wisdom."

Portions of the following essays appeared in publications from Wylie Preparatory Academy and are used with permission: Cornerstones of Truth, Virtue, Family, and Purpose; "Independent, Systemic Prayer Cells"; "Praying from a Center of Offense"; "The Culture We are Trying to Build"; "What is a Student?"; "Self-Esteem Versus the Virtue of Self-Acceptance"; "How Do We Want our Children to View the Bible?"; "What Kind of Christian Culture?"; "Five Tips for Parents in Christian Schools"; "The Measure of a

Mom's Influence"; "A Kingdom Approach to Athletics"; "What is the Message?"; "God's Strategy for Discipline"; "Changing Mindsets: Who is the Authority?"; "Changing Mindsets: More than a School"; "Your Most Valuable Player"; "Have Fun, Do Your Best, Be a Blessing"; "A Culture of Encouragement"; "Resolving Conflicts Between Home and School: Overview"; "Have You Become a Judge?"; "The Bad Report"; "How Personal Brokenness Affects Teaching"; "Another Way to Understand Laziness"; "Helping Families Conquer Perfectionism"; "Beware of Time Management"; "The Wasting Disease of Affluence"; "The Cry of the Adolescent Girl."

Portions of the following essays appeared in publications from Lucas Christian Academy and are used with permission: "What is a Student?"; "Opportunities to Affirm Uniqueness and Design"; "Self-esteem Versus the Virtue of Self-Acceptance"; "Training in Character or Virtue?"; "Beware of Time Management"; "Helping Families Conquer Perfectionism"; "A Growth Mindset"; "How Personal Brokenness Affects Teaching"; "The Power of a Bad Teacher"; "A Teacher's Intimacy with Jesus and Self-Awareness"; "The Power of a Great Teacher"; "Teachers and Core Values"; "Teaching Tips"; "What is Teaching?"; "Thoughts on Athletics"; "What is a Kingdom Education?"; "Exercising Authority, Being Authoritarian, and Truth"; "Shaping Class Identity"; "God's Strategy for Discipline—Dealing with Cain"; "God's Strategy for Discipline: Questioning Cain"; "Another Way to Understand Laziness"; "Attitudes Toward the Bible."

ABOUT THE AUTHOR

Michael Chrasta (MA English, MA Public Policy, PhD Humanities-History of Ideas) has taught in public and private schools, colleges, and universities in Virginia, Massachusetts, and Texas. He has served as Dean of Family Ministry for private Christian schools in the Dallas area and as the Director of Ministry for University-Model® Schools International (UMSI).

64880657R00164

Made in the USA
Lexington, KY
22 June 2017